# The Holy Spirit as Person and Power

By the same author

*The Return of Jesus: Earthing the Christian Hope*

*The Discovery of the Beginning: How the Greatest Scientific Discovery of Our Time Points to the Creator*

*Fences of Freedom: The Ten Commandments for Today*

*A Terrifying Grace: Sexuality, Romance and Marriage in Christian History*

*Restoring the Fortunes of Zion: Essays on Israel, Jerusalem and Jewish-Christian Relations on the Fiftieth Anniversary of the Six-Day War*

# The Holy Spirit as Person and Power

*Charismatic Renewal and
Its Implications for Theology*

ROB YULE

*Foreword by Murray Talbot*

WIPF & STOCK · Eugene, Oregon

THE HOLY SPIRIT AS PERSON AND POWER
Charismatic Renewal and Its Implications for Theology

Copyright © 2019 Robert M. Yule. All rights reserved. Except for brief quotations in critical publications or reviews, no part of this book may be reproduced in any manner without prior written permission from the publisher. Write: Permissions, Wipf and Stock Publishers, 199 W. 8th Ave., Suite 3, Eugene, OR 97401.

Wipf & Stock
An Imprint of Wipf and Stock Publishers
199 W. 8th Ave., Suite 3
Eugene, OR 97401

www.wipfandstock.com

PAPERBACK ISBN: 978-1-7252-5158-8
HARDCOVER ISBN: 978-1-7252-5159-5
EBOOK ISBN: 978-1-7252-5160-1

Manufactured in the U.S.A.             DECEMBER 20, 2019

Unless otherwise indicated, all biblical quotations are from the New International Version®, NIV® Copyright © 1973, 1978, 1984, 2011 by Biblica, Inc.® Used by permission. All rights reserved worldwide.

The cover symbol is from the backlit glass altar frieze of the Cathedral of the Holy Spirit, Palmerston North, New Zealand. Photo © Paul Gummer, 2019. Used by permission.

The epigraph is from James D. G. Dunn, *The Acts of the Apostles* (Grand Rapids: Eerdmans, 1996), 12. Used by permission.

To the memory of John Brook (1946–92)

"The Spirit of God transcends human ability
and transforms human inability"
—James D. G. Dunn, *The Acts of the Apostles*

# Contents

*List of Tables and Figures* | viii
*Foreword by Murray Talbot* | ix
*Abbreviations* | xii
*Introduction* | xv

1  The Holy Spirit and the Latter Days | 1
2  The Holy Spirit and Charismatic Renewal | 11
3  The Holy Spirit in the Old Testament | 29
4  Jesus and the Holy Spirit | 44
5  The Spirit in Christ and Christians | 55
6  The Spirit as Presence and Power | 71
7  The Doorway to Life in the Spirit | 86
8  Spiritual Gifts as Charisms of the Trinity | 96
9  From Glory to Glory: The Spirit in Persons | 121
10 The Spirit in the Triune God | 137
11 Persons, Nature, and the Role of the Spirit | 152
12 The Spirit Will Guide You into All Truth | 164

*Appendix 1: New Testament References to (the) Holy Spirit* | 171
*Appendix 2: Charismatic Renewal in New Zealand* | 180
*Appendix 3: Five Prayers to the Holy Spirit* | 186
*Glossary* | 194
*Bibliography* | 205
*Index of Names* | 217
*Index of Subjects* | 223
*Index of Biblical References* | 237

# List of Tables and Figures

Table 1     Jesus' Twofold Work | 62

Table 2     Two Aspects of the Spirit's Activity | 84

Table 3     Two Aspects of the Church | 129

Figure 1    The Parabola of Redemption | 135

Figure 2    The Paradox of Personhood | 155

# Foreword

I RECALL SITTING BETWEEN Rob Yule and John Brook on a flight from Wellington as we were returning from a Presbyterian Renewal Ministries board meeting. I asked them a question. "When Jesus breathed the Holy Spirit on the disciples in the upper room in John 20:22 and said, 'Receive the Holy Spirit,' was that their 'born again' experience?"

This sparked an interesting discussion. The traditional teaching of the day was that this was John's version of Pentecost. But, as John Brook pointed out, that creates historical issues because Pentecost didn't happen until after Jesus ascended.

This led to another question. "Can you separate the empowering work of the Holy Spirit from the work of the Holy Spirit in bringing about new birth?" The teaching of the day said, "You cannot separate the receiving of the person of the Holy Spirit within, from his power." That seemed to make sense, but was quite contrary to my personal experience.

I had received Christ and experienced forgiveness of my sins four years before being "baptized with the Holy Spirit." But with baptism in the Holy Spirit came a whole new faith adventure. I had a new desire to worship and pray, the Scriptures came alive and took on new meaning, I desired to seek fellowship with like-minded believers, and I will never forget opening my check book the first Sunday afterwards and hearing a gentle voice from within say, "Tithe." This was getting really radical for a trained accountant! It was like I was suddenly thrust into an awareness of a whole new realm. Hence my question on the plane flight, as I tried to understand my experience in theological terms.

Rob Yule has produced a book which not only addresses questions like this, but reaches back in time to the early church fathers and across the wide spectrum of Christian theology from Pentecostalism to Eastern Orthodoxy to increase our understanding of this important aspect of Christian living.

Rob brings a depth of understanding and enlightenment seldom found in works on this topic.

When I followed Rob as minister at Hornby (now Hope) Presbyterian Church, Christchurch, one of the first things my wife, Janice, and I did was to read through the minutes of the elders' meetings. We wept as we saw something of the pain and anguish that Rob and Christene had endured. But from the ashes, God began to birth something beautiful. The plowing had been done. It was time for us to water, nurture, multiply, and reap.

Whenever I felt in need of someone to discuss an aspect of theology, I would phone Rob to pick his brains and was never disappointed. I wanted to ensure that I wasn't going out on too much of a limb. I really valued his wisdom and insight at those times.

As you read this book you will understand what I mean. Beginning with an overview of Pentecostalism and the charismatic renewal movement, Rob quotes from Peter Hocken's analysis: "The argument follows that an unplanned and unexpected movement, without any one human founder or place of origin, and whose essential characteristics are the fruit only the Holy Spirit of God can produce (knowledge of Jesus, heartfelt praise of God, love of the Scriptures, greater sensitivity to powers of evil), must represent a sovereign intervention of the Lord."

I particularly enjoyed the chapter on the Holy Spirit in the Old Testament. Moving from chaos to order, Rob focuses on the creativity of the Holy Spirit before giving an insightful analysis of the empowering work of the Spirit, drawing attention to the "rested upon" but not "in" aspect of the terminology. Interesting chapters follow on the Holy Spirit in Jesus, the Holy Spirit in Christians, and the distinction between the Holy Spirit's personhood and power.

Rob presents being baptized in the Holy Spirit as people's "initiation into the realm of the Spirit." He provides a compelling case for reviewing our traditional understanding of initiation into Christ. Finding support from the outstanding British preacher David Pawson, he highlights how the experience of being baptized in the Spirit "is something God intends all Christians to experience" and is "a valid experience for today." He argues for it to be recognized as a foundational experience for all believers, essential for enabling them to live the life Christ has called them to.

A helpful discussion on the gifts of the Spirit follows, showing their Trinitarian nature and availability for all believers. Rob provides a different perspective from those who lump all the gifts together in a single spiritual gifts inventory. Their grace-given character opens up the possibility for all Christians to be used by God in a range of gifts according their availability and situation. He contrasts the dynamic nature of the *charismata* of

1 Corinthians 12 with the more permanent nature of the ascension gifts of Christ in Ephesians and the motivational gifts of the Father in Romans.

Rob's breadth of scholarship is evident as he draws on the church fathers and Eastern Orthodox theologians to discuss the distinctive role of the Holy Spirit. Noting that the Holy Spirit does not become incarnate in our humanity and is not an extension of the incarnation, he supports Vladimir Lossky's view that the Spirit's unique role is to communicate the divine nature to human persons. Here Rob deals with subject matter that was entirely new to me and that I found informative and inspirational. He discusses the disagreement between the Western and Eastern Churches over the "*Filioque*" clause in terms that even I could understand.

Rob draws his argument together in a final chapter which provides both a helpful summary and an appeal. "The time has come for the church's theology and pneumatology to come to terms with the dynamic insights awakened by the surprising and ever-gracious Spirit in the global Pentecostal-charismatic renewal movement."

I can only respond with an "Amen, brother!" The publication of this book is a ground-breaking contribution to this task. I am grateful to Rob Yule for bringing his spiritual experience and scholarly abilities to bear on such an important theme. Most importantly, he does so in a readable and understandable way.

**—Murray Talbot**
Former Senior Minister
Hope Presbyterian Church
Christchurch, New Zealand

# Abbreviations

| | |
|---|---|
| AG | W. F. Arndt and F. W. Gingrich, *Greek–English Lexicon of the New Testament and Other Early Christian Literature* (Chicago: University of Chicago Press, 1957) |
| BDAG | Walter Bauer, *Greek–English Lexicon of the New Testament and Other Early Christian Literature*, 3rd ed., rev. F. W. Danker (Chicago: University of Chicago Press, 2001) |
| CD | Karl Barth, *Church Dogmatics*, ed. Geoffrey W. Bromiley and Thomas F. Torrance, trans. Geoffrey W. Bromiley et al. Vol. I, Part 1—Vol. IV, Part 4 (Edinburgh: T. & T. Clark, 1956–75) |
| CMS | Church Missionary Society |
| DPCM | *Dictionary of Pentecostal and Charismatic Movements*, ed. Stanley M. Burgess and Gary B. McGee (Grand Rapids: Zondervan, 1988) |
| EC | *The Encyclopedia of Christianity*, ed. Erwin Fahlbusch et al., 5 vols. (Grand Rapids: Eerdmans, 1999–2008) |
| EDT | *Evangelical Dictionary of Theology*, ed. Walter A. Elwell (Grand Rapids: Baker, 1984) |
| ELLC | English Language Liturgical Consultation |
| ERT | *Evangelical Review of Theology* |
| IBLP | Institute in Basic Life Principles |
| IBMR | *International Bulletin of Mission(ary) Research* |
| ICEJ | International Christian Embassy, Jerusalem |
| IRC | International Reconciliation Coalition |

# ABBREVIATIONS

| | |
|---|---|
| HIM | Harvest International Ministries |
| KJV | King James or Authorized Version of the Bible (1610) |
| NIDNTTE | *New International Dictionary of New Testament Theology and Exegesis*, ed. Moisés Silva (Grand Rapids: Zondervan, 2014) |
| NIDPCM | *New International Dictionary of Pentecostal and Charismatic Movements*, rev. ed., ed. Stanley M. Burgess and Eduard M. van der Maas (Grand Rapids: Zondervan, 2003) |
| NIV | New International Version of the Bible (2011) |
| NRSV | New Revised Standard Version of the Bible (1989) |
| NZ | New Zealand |
| ODCC2 | *Oxford Dictionary of the Christian Church*, 2nd. ed., ed. F. L. Cross and E. A. Livingstone (London: Oxford University Press, 1974) |
| ODCC3 | *Oxford Dictionary of the Christian Church*, 3rd. ed. revised, ed. F. L. Cross and E. A. Livingstone (Oxford: Oxford University Press, 2005) |
| PGL | *Patristic Greek Lexicon*, ed. G. W. H. Lampe (Oxford: Clarendon, 1968) |
| RSV | Revised Standard Version of the Bible (1952) |
| SJT | *Scottish Journal of Theology* |
| TDNT | *Theological Dictionary of the New Testament*, ed. G. Kittel and G. Friedrich (Grand Rapids: Eerdmans, 1964–76) |
| TDOT | *Theological Dictionary of the Old Testament*, ed. G. J. Botterweck and H. Ringgren (Grand Rapids: Eerdmans, 1974–2018) |
| UK | United Kingdom |
| UPCUSA | United Presbyterian Church in the United States of America |
| YWAM | Youth With a Mission |

# Introduction

I BEGAN MY MINISTRY with six years as ecumenical chaplain at Victoria University of Wellington. I experienced the high-point of the Jesus People Movement, mixed with Christians of every conceivable stripe and affiliation, and worked in a chaplaincy team with the Anglican and Catholic chaplains, from which emerged our celebrated Tertiary Christian Studies Programme.

It was quite a challenge to leave this for my first ministry in a local church, in the working-class suburb of Hornby, west Christchurch, in 1979. There I experienced not one but two church schisms. It was a conservative evangelical church made up of religious refugees from liberal churches in Christchurch, seeking solace in the wake of the Geering controversy. They had formed a gathered church, attracted by the preaching ministry of my predecessor. Lloyd Geering, my Old Testament teacher, had created a storm throughout New Zealand when, during Easter 1966, he publicly denied the bodily resurrection and said that the bones of Jesus would someday be found in Palestine.

A group from Hornby Presbyterian Church encountered Pentecostal worship and speaking in tongues at the Queen Street Assembly of God on a visit to Auckland in January 1979—the same summer that we moved to Hornby. Tensions grew during my first year. I returned from my next summer holiday, in January 1980, with a great sense of foreboding.

On the eve of our elders' retreat in early February, an Irish elder and his wife called round to our home to announce that he was leaving the church. He would be starting an Elim Pentecostal church just around the corner, in the Hornby Power Board theaterette. Later that day, a Lincoln College student visited to tell me that her fiancé had just been killed in an aerial topdressing accident at Mesopotamia sheep station. After our evening meal, the former lay parish assistant rang to say that he and his wife were resigning from the church. At breakfast the next morning—the day of our retreat—another elder with a lovely family came to the manse door to say he wouldn't be coming to the event either. He and his family were joining the new church around the corner.

It was the saddest day of my life. Three other elders also left, as did the leader of the music group—who was the son of the former minister. The remaining elders met in anguish and distress. But ultimately, from our pain came extraordinary gain. They proved a stalwart, faithful, praying group of elders who stuck with the grieving church through the storms of sorrow that followed. I'm grateful to God for these elders, and others in the church, who bore with me, took me on as a prayer project, loved me, and helped me change and grow.

The group who left wanted revival without tarrying for any. When it became evident that I was not about to give up on the Holy Spirit just because his more ardent backers had departed, pressure mounted from the Reformed and conservative evangelical members of the church. They, in turn, began to leave from the other wing of the fellowship. They included notable leaders in the Christchurch evangelical community, including the rector and deputy rector of Middleton Grange School and their wives, and two pews of students involved with the Navigator movement, which was then firmly anti-charismatic.

I associate these months with the Abbotsford landslip in Dunedin, which began not long before. As one household fell into the fracture, another became exposed and tottered on the brink. When that family left, their friends began to consider doing so as well. It never seemed to stop.

In my distress, I began to pray alone—and sometimes with my wife, Christene—before the communion table in the darkened church at night. The table had inscribed on it in beautiful calligraphy the text summarizing the life of the early church: "And they continued stedfastly in the apostles' doctrine and fellowship, and in breaking of bread and in prayers" (Acts 2:42, KJV). I remembered that Graham Pulkingham had done this in the crypt of the Episcopal Church of the Redeemer in downtown Houston, Texas, leading to its amazing transformation from a rundown "mass station" to a vibrant and sacrificial urban renewal community.[1]

I was led to do this not only by Pulkingham's example but also by what the prophecy of Joel says about the conditions that precede the promised outpouring of the Holy Spirit. How would such an outpouring happen? Joel says,

---

1. Described by Michael Harper in *A New Way of Living* and Graham Pulkingham in *Gathered for Power*. My friend John Brook had told the story of "Graham Pulkingham and Charismatic Spirituality" in the course on "Christian Spirituality Today" that I organized for the Victoria University of Wellington combined chaplaincies Tertiary Christian Studies Programme in 1976.

INTRODUCTION  xvii

> Let the priests, who minister before the Lord, weep between the portico and the altar. Let them say, "Spare your people, Lord. Do not make your inheritance an object of scorn, a byword among the nations. Why should they say among the peoples, 'Where is their God?'" (Joel 2:17)

So I prayed, in the darkened church, for God to do just that: to take away the reproach of Hornby Presbyterian Church. I pleaded with God to rend the heavens and come down, to send an outpouring of the Holy Spirit, to create an exemplary Christian community like the early church in the book of Acts, one which would attract people by its worship and witness, by its common life and uncommon service.

I have never seen a church so profoundly changed as Hornby Presbyterian was over those next few years.[2] It was truly a work of the Holy Spirit. God humbled us, broke us, transformed us. Like a vintage car restorer, God took us apart, steam-cleaned us, repainted the metalwork, reassembled us, rebuilt, and restored us.

Since then, I have testified at Hornby (now Hope) Presbyterian Church, saying that God looked down and saw this smug, self-satisfied church and said, "How can I change them?" God looked down and saw this inexperienced little priestling and intellectual and said, "How can I change him?"

"I know," God said. "I'll put them together and see what happens!"

It was like two galaxies colliding! The shockwaves are still reverberating! The results of all the energy that was released are still apparent more than thirty-five years later! God changed me, and he changed the church! There was a remarkable move of the Holy Spirit. What suffering and pain we experienced! What an explosion of joy and creativity resulted!

I certainly do not claim credit for all the changes at Hornby Presbyterian Church. I was an inexperienced pastor and made many mistakes. The difficulties we faced called for decisive leadership, which may have hurt some people, though we did see the establishment of an excellent pastoral team and the growth of home groups for pastoral care.

The consolidation of the renewal was the work of my successor, Murray Talbot, and his wife, Janice. They worked through a long ministry to reestablish trust, to consolidate changes in worship, to build community ministries, and ultimately to develop a multi-staff and multi-site church, the flagship church of the Presbyterian movement in New Zealand. I owe them

---

2. The story has been well told by Michael Reid in his PhD thesis, "But By My Spirit," 183–96, by Nyalle Paris, in his research essay, "Wind of Change," and again by Michael Reid in his history of Hornby Presbyterian Church, *Thus Far*, 184–236.

a profound debt of gratitude. My wife and I couldn't have wished for better successors!

My personal encounter with the Spirit was the catalyst for this turnaround. In the spring of 1981, amid our troubles, I was phoned by Russell James, the pastor of Opawa Methodist Church in eastern Christchurch, a well-known charismatic leader. He had a visiting itinerant American charismatic minister with him, who was available for a midweek meeting. Would I care to have him speak at my church? What topic would I like him to speak about?

I made a quick decision. Yes. The safest and most suitable topic seemed to be "The Holy Spirit in the Church: A Historical Perspective." We hastily arranged a Wednesday evening gathering.

Paul Petersen was a big, bear-like man with a shambling gait. He was a United Methodist minister from Seattle. He had been baptized in the Spirit after being prayed for with the laying on of hands by his Episcopalian colleague, Dennis Bennett, of *Nine O'Clock in the Morning* fame. In the controversy that erupted, he was thrown out of his large and successful church, full of Boeing Company aircraft workers. He now traveled the world by faith, imparting what he had received.

That Wednesday evening Paul Petersen spoke to us about the origins of the Pentecostal movement. I had never heard of this before. It was a surprising move of God: a grace-given revival among the poor and disenfranchised that sparked a worldwide movement in just a few years. God "chose the foolish things of the world to shame the wise; . . . the weak things of the world to shame the strong; . . . the lowly things of this world . . . to nullify the things that are" (1 Cor 1:27–28).[3]

When the meeting finished, I faced a quick decision. Do I invite Paul back to pray for people to be baptized in the Holy Spirit? Would he available for Friday night, two days hence? He was. I announced that he would be with us in the manse lounge.

On Friday night just a handful came. My wife, Christene, and I were joined by a fellow Presbyterian minister who had supported us during our troubles, by a conservative but godly elder, and by the leader of our women's ministry. Paul Petersen clarified what seems obvious but had never been explained to this Calvinist before: if we wish to speak in tongues, we need to speak! He led us in a renunciation of any works of the Evil One. He laid hands on each of us and prayed for us one by one.

Just when I thought I was inventing Hebrew words, I had a flow of speech that I had never spoken before, followed by a profound sense of

---

3. I tell the story of the beginnings of the Pentecostal movement in chapter 1, below.

God's acceptance as his child. My striving and perfectionism ceased. I began to feel a wonderful inner peace and joy, so welcome after the trials of the preceding months.

Meanwhile, Christene came into an experience of the Spirit singing in tongues! Paul Petersen got excited and jumped up and down. "One in a thousand," he exclaimed!

Our encounter with the Holy Spirit took place on 30 October 1981. The present book began, modestly, in teaching that I began to give soon after this decisive event. It originated in an attempt to clarify what had happened to me and to share that understanding with others. I learned a lot from Tom Smail's book *Reflected Glory*, which I used at that time as a devotional study with my remaining Hornby elders. I first shared some of this material in June 1984, at a Presbyterian renewal gathering in the little township of Dunsandel, on the Canterbury Plains of the South Island of New Zealand.

Over the years, my teachings developed. I honed them in new Christians' classes, in preaching series on the Holy Spirit in my churches in Hornby, Christchurch, and St. Alban's, Palmerston North, and on mission trips to other churches. I had no computer in those days. After prayerful and sometimes agonized preparation, I gave my talks extempore from handwritten headings and summaries on scraps of paper. Many times I wanted to take notes from myself! The joke in my family was my writing up my sermons afterward!

Later I was asked to share my teaching on the Holy Spirit at week-long live-in courses at Youth With A Mission (YWAM) Discipleship Training Schools, in Papanui, Christchurch, and at Pukerau, in Eastern Southland.

Many years later, in my retirement in 2013, I was invited to give a lecture series on the Holy Spirit at Emmaus College, Palmerston North. I entitled it "The Presence and the Power: The Spirit in Christ and Christians." I focused on what we can learn for our personal life and service in the Spirit by exploring the role of the Spirit in Jesus' life and ministry.

I have long wanted to publish these lectures. Indeed, I was encouraged to do so by my former Professor of Church History, Ian Breward, who stayed with us on his last visit to New Zealand in April 2014. But the following years have seen invitations to lecture on other subjects and the publishing of three other books. So my cherished teaching and reflection on the Holy Spirit have had to wait. Only now is it seeing the light of day.

In some ways its publication is untimely, for the heyday of charismatic renewal is long past. But the delay has been beneficial, for the material has benefitted from much reflection and refinement. The content is very relevant to the much-needed task of developing a theology of the Spirit that takes into account what has been learned in the spontaneity of charismatic experience. So my book is subtitled "Charismatic Renewal and its Implications for Theology."

*The Holy Spirit as Person and Power* is a biblical and theological exploration of the Holy Spirit in the light of the contemporary renewal movement. The book begins with the eschatological focus and extraordinary grace that the Pentecostal-charismatic movement represents. It reveals overlooked insights from the Bible about the person and activity of the Holy Spirit. It takes what I and others have learned in the variety and dynamism of charismatic experience. It shows how this opens fresh insights into what the Bible says about the Holy Spirit. It challenges the major branches of the Christian church to reexamine their theological understanding of the Spirit in the light of these developments. It interacts with the church's historic teaching about the Spirit, in the Eastern Orthodox, Roman Catholic, Protestant, and evangelical traditions.

Ray Taylor, the founding chairman of the Paraclete Trust, the group serving charismatic renewal in the Presbyterian Church of New Zealand, used to say that "theophany must precede theology." By this, he meant "we must have a first-hand experience of God's manifestation or revelation of himself before we can begin to think about him in any meaningful way."[4]

In the same way, I offer this book in the hope that it may contribute to the necessary and ongoing task of integrating personal experience and theological reflection, to the mutual enrichment of both. It offers many insights about the Spirit, experiential and exegetical, that the more formulaic treatments of pneumatology in the history of theology have overlooked. Like the apostles, I cannot help speaking about what I have seen and heard (Acts 4:20).

Throughout the book I have used small print sections to discuss some issues in greater detail, like the use of this device in Karl Barth's *Church Dogmatics*. These concern matters of biblical exegesis, historical background, theological debate, or philosophical clarification. Some provide illustration from personal experience or the experience of other charismatic Christians.

I thank the following for reading my manuscript and commending it: Rev. Dr. Eldin Villafañe, Distinguished Senior Professor Emeritus of Christian Social Ethics at Gordon-Conwell Theological Seminary in Boston; Murray Talbot, my successor at Hornby (now Hope) Presbyterian Church, Christchurch; Murray Robertson, former pastor of Spreydon (now South-West) Baptist Church, Christchurch; and Nyalle Paris, minister of First Presbyterian Church, Invercargill. My text has also benefitted from the critical observations and helpful suggestions of Fr. Peter Cullinane, the

---

4. Taylor, "Chairman's Letter," 9.

former Catholic bishop of Palmerston North, though I am responsible for its final form. I thank Lynley Trounson of the Hewitson Library, Knox College, Dunedin for help in sourcing books, Liz Ward for help with proofreading and obtaining permissions, my son, Andy, for preparing the two figures, and Paul Gummer for photographing the cover symbol.

I dedicate this book to the memory of my best friend, John Brook, a pioneer of the New Zealand Presbyterian charismatic renewal group the Paraclete Trust (later Presbyterian Renewal Ministries), who died of a brain aneurism in 1992.

This material originated in lived experience and teaching, so preachers and Bible teachers may find stimulation for sermon or lecture preparation. Kindly attribute if you do, just as I have sought to acknowledge those who have influenced me. "Freely you have received; freely give."

**—Rob Yule**
Palmerston North, New Zealand
Advent 2019

# 1

# The Holy Spirit and the Latter Days

*The twentieth century saw a remarkable global reawakening of interest in the Holy Spirit. The only passage in the Bible that foretells such a worldwide outpouring of the Spirit is the prophecy of Joel. Joel prophesies that this phenomenon will be marked by the crossing of intractable social barriers and be associated with the eschatological events of the last days. Reflection on the remarkable movement of the Holy Spirit that has occurred since the beginning of the twentieth century suggests that we are experiencing the fulfillment of this prophecy, that we are living in the latter days, and that God is preparing his people because the times are urgent.*

SINCE THE MID-TWENTIETH CENTURY, after centuries of neglect, Western Christianity has experienced a dramatic resurgence of interest in the Holy Spirit. This has come about through the rise of Pentecostalism, through the impact of the charismatic renewal movement on Protestant and Catholic churches, and through renewed attention in testimony literature and theological scholarship. Pneumatology, not so much as a doctrine as an experience of the Spirit, has been rediscovered as the living heart of Christianity.

## In the Latter Days

In his brief but influential prophecy, the biblical prophet Joel prophesied a global outpouring of the Holy Spirit before the coming day of the Lord (Joel 2:28-32). The apostle Peter identified the initial fulfillment of this prophecy in the events of the day of Pentecost and saw it as inaugurating the "last days" (Acts 2:17). The twentieth-century forerunners of the modern Pentecostal movement described their experience of the outpouring of the Spirit as "the latter rain" of Joel's prophecy, in contrast to "the former rain" experienced by the apostles at Pentecost.

The prophecy of Joel is the only biblical passage that foretells a worldwide outpouring of God's Holy Spirit.[1] The purpose of this chapter is to examine whether the modern Pentecostal outpouring can be regarded as its fulfillment.

Joel's fascinating prophecy contains the following elements:

1. Its context is eschatological: the outpouring precedes, perhaps even sets in motion, the events of the latter days. "I will pour out my Spirit . . . before the coming of the great and dreadful day of the Lord" (2:28, 31).

2. It promises restoration after a period of desolation, suggested by the locust plague and its accompanying devastation of the ecology and economy of the land. "I will repay you for the years the locusts have eaten" (2:25).

3. It hints that the Spirit will be bestowed in two outpourings, an "early rain" and a "latter rain"—corresponding to the autumn and spring rains of the land of Israel. "He sends you abundant showers, both autumn and spring rains, as before" (2:23).

4. It describes an outpouring of the Spirit on "all people," literally on "all flesh" (*kol bāśār*, 2:28). This phrase not only means "all humanity" in its creatureliness, dependence on God, earthly nature, weakness, and transitoriness but in its biblical usage specifically refers to fallen or sinful human beings, humanity in "its ethical inadequacy and inclination to sin."[2] In Paul's thought "flesh" (*sarx*) is the human body

---

1. In Num 11:29, Moses expresses the wish that "all the Lord's people were prophets and that the Lord would put his Spirit on them!" The apocryphal book of Ecclesiasticus refers to "wisdom" as God's "gift" "poured out on . . . all mankind" (Sir 1:9-10). But neither passage prophesies a universal outpouring of God's Spirit.

2. Bratsiotis, "*bāśār*," 2:328-29.

"dominated by sin" and in which sin is present[3] (Rom 7:18, 25; 8:3, 4–9, 12–13; Gal 5:16–24). This suggests that this end-time event will be an ingathering comprised of many unlikely people, with many surprising conversions.

5. It says that this move of the Spirit will be without respect for the divisions of gender, age, and class that commonly divide human beings. "Your sons and daughters will prophesy, your old men will dream dreams, your young men will see visions. Even on my servants, both men and women, I will pour out my Spirit in those days" (2:28–29).

6. It says that the timing of this outpouring will coincide with the regathering of the scattered tribes of Israel, as foretold by the prophets. "In those days and at that time, when I restore the fortunes of Judah and Jerusalem" (3:1).

## Born in a Stable

Over a century ago, in April 1906, revival meetings began in a storefront mission in downtown Los Angeles, in what is now recognized as the beginning of the modern Pentecostal movement.

On 9 April 1906, Edward Lee, a black janitor at the First National Bank, told a black pastor friend named William Joseph Seymour of a vision he had experienced. In the vision, the apostles showed him how to receive the gift of tongues. Both men prayed together, and that night, in a home meeting in downtown Los Angeles, they and some others began praising God in unknown languages. It was something that adherents of the Holiness theology of the day were longing for as a sign of the latter days.

Soon the little wooden house where they were meeting became too small to hold the crowds. They located a vacant two-story wooden frame building at 312 Azusa Street that had been used as a warehouse and a stable. They rented it, cleaned it up, put timber planks on upended nail kegs for seats, and placed a couple of empty boxes on end for a makeshift pulpit. They held their first meeting on 14 April 1906.

Harvey Cox, a historian of the Pentecostal movement, describes what took place:

> The little church on the other side of town used no publicity at all. There was never a printed order of service. There were no handbills or posters. For a while, the worshippers at Azusa Street resisted even putting an identifying sign on the front

---

3. "*Sarx*," BDAG, 915. Cf. "*sarx*," AG, 751.

wall or door. If the Spirit wanted people to come that way, they reasoned, the Spirit would guide their footsteps. . . . The pine planks on the upended shipping boxes were placed in a square, so those who attended sat facing each other. People spoke from anywhere, but for those who felt especially anointed, the shoebox pulpit was generously open to anyone. No collections were taken, but just next to the exit a small receptacle awaited contributions to help pay the rent.[4]

## All Over the World

Word spread rapidly by word of mouth and by articles in the Holiness press. Evangelists and visitors took the revival to other parts of the United States: to the Pacific Northwest, to the South, to Chicago, to New York. Overseas visitors and missionaries spread the message to England, Scandinavia, Latin America, India, South Africa. Critics of the revival meetings said it would blow over quickly. It did. It blew all over the world.

A movement which began, like Christianity itself, in a humble stable, has become the fastest-growing part of the world Christian movement, second only to the Roman Catholic Church in size. From the Azusa Street revival of 1906–1909 has grown a movement which in 2019 now numbers 694 million Pentecostal and charismatic Christians out of a total world Christian population of 2.53 billion. In just over a hundred and ten years the movement now comprises 27.5 percent of all Christians, participating in 5.5 million congregations in almost every nation on earth, including some of the largest churches in the world.[5]

Many of the early Pentecostals grew up in poverty, lacked education, and struggled with personal issues. Yet, for all their faults and limitations, says John Wimber, "the Pentecostal evangelists have done more in this century to evangelise the world than any other group. . . . The church grows fastest where the power of God is in evidence."[6]

> The first serious attempt to count global Pentecostal-charismatic numbers was made by Christian statistician David B. Barrett, editor of the *World Christian Encyclopaedia* and founder of the World Christian Database, for the publication in 1988 of the *Dictionary of Pentecostal and Charismatic Movements*.[7]

---

4. Cox, *Fire from Heaven*, 57.
5. Johnson et al., "Christianity, 2019," 101–2.
6. Wimber, "Some Notable Personalities," 33.
7. Barrett, "Statistics, Global," 810–30.

Drawing on Peter Wagner's concept of a "third wave,"[8] Barrett classified the movement into three consecutive "waves" of renewal in the Holy Spirit, each greater than the one preceding: 1. Pentecostal, comprising members of the classical Pentecostal denominations, 2. Charismatic, representing renewal movements within the historic Christian denominations, including Catholic, and 3. "Third Wave," sometimes called the "Signs and Wonders" movement, referring to more recent nondenominational or post–denominational renewal among evangelicals and independents.[9]

"Alternately called Pentecostal or Charismatic, Renewalist movements grew from just under one million adherents in 1900 to 63 million by 1970 and 628 million by 2013. They are projected to grow to 825 million adherents by 2025. As a percentage of all Christians, they will have grown over the same time period from 0.2 percent (1900) to 5.1 percent (1970) to 26.7 percent (2013) to a projected 30.6 percent (2025). The growth of the movement now stands at 2.43 percent per year, roughly double the 1.32 percent annual rate for all Christians."[10]

By mid-2019, the Pentecostal-charismatic movement had grown to 694 million adherents, comprising nearly 27.5 percent of all Christians. But its rate of growth was slowing, and was now projected to be 795 million by 2025.[11]

In three important respects, the Azusa Street revival exactly fulfills the prophecy of Joel about a great outpouring of the Holy Spirit in the latter days.

## Its Season

First is what Joel says about its timing. Towards the end of the nineteenth century, many evangelical Christians were praying for a new down-pouring of the Holy Spirit, a great "latter rain" revival, based on what the biblical prophet says about the "early" and "latter" rains (Joel 2:23).

In Israel, the winter rainy season usually lasts from mid-October to April or early May. It is preceded by two or three early showers which herald the main rains. In the Bible and in Israel today these first or early rains are called *ha yôre*; the last of the winter rain is called *ha malkôsh* (Deut 11:14). They correspond to the "early" and "latter" rains of Joel's prophecy (2:23). "The rain at the beginning of the season is that on which the farmer depends before he can start to plough and sow his grain, and the slight rains in April are those which he requires just before the harvest if the grain is to swell. If

---

8. Wagner, *Third Wave of the Holy Spirit*.

9. For a fuller elaboration of these terms, see Barrett's statistical update, "Worldwide Holy Spirit Renewal," especially 381–85, 395–97.

10. Johnson and Crossing, "Christianity 2013," 32.

11. Johnson et al., "Christianity 2019," 101–2.

either of these two should fail, his crops will suffer."[12] The early rain germinates the crop; the latter rain prepares the harvest.

The early Pentecostals saw in Joel's prophecy that there would be a "latter rain" outpouring of the Holy Spirit toward the close of the age, preceding a great end-time mission harvest when God will gather many people into his kingdom. As they studied the Bible for signs of the times, they realized that the outpouring of the Holy Spirit at Pentecost (Acts 2) was the "first" or "early" rain to germinate the seed, to get the Christian movement started. They began to pray earnestly for the promised end-time outpouring to swell the crop for harvest at the end of the age.

Joel identifies when this end-time outpouring of the Holy Spirit will occur: "In those days and at that time, when I restore the fortunes of Judah and Jerusalem" (Joel 3:1). There is indeed a remarkable parallelism with the restoration of Israel. The Zionist movement began in the 1880s, Israel became a nation once more in 1948, and the old city of Jerusalem was restored to Jewish control after its unexpected capture in the Six-Day War of 1967. The century in which God has been pouring out his Spirit on an unprecedented, worldwide scale is the time when God has been restoring the Jewish people to their ancient land after nineteen centuries of exile.[13]

## Its Scope

Second is what Joel speaks of the scope of this revival. "I will pour out my Spirit on all people" (Joel 2:28). As already indicated, the Hebrew is "all flesh," meaning not just humanity in general, but "fallen humanity" in particular: humanity as marred by sensuality, selfishness, and sin. In the latter days, Joel prophesies, the Holy Spirit is going to fall on many unlikely people. There will be many surprises of God's grace.

Joel also says this great outpouring of the Holy Spirit in the latter days will be without discrimination of gender, age, or social class. "Your sons and

12. Baly, *Geography of the Bible*, 52. Cf. Smith, *Historical Geography*, 64.

13. Peter Hocken notes that several important prophecies associate the gift of the Spirit with the regathering of the people of Israel to their land (Isa 11:1–2, 11–12; Jer 31:27–34; Ezek 11:17–20; 36:24–30; 37:1–14), suggesting that there is "a link in the divine plan" between these two aspects of restoration (Hocken, *The Glory and the Shame*, chapter 19, especially 140–41). The notable Pentecostal Bible teacher, Derek Prince, also spoke on the parallel restoration of Israel and of the charismatic gifts to the church, and published a booklet, *Israel and the Church: Parallel Restoration*. Christian interest in Israel's regathering is often thought to be a product of J. N. Darby and dispensationalism. In fact, restorationist beliefs predate the rise of dispensationalism and secular Zionism by two and a half centuries. See my book *Restoring the Fortunes of Zion*, 15–16, 105–106, 180–83, and 278–84.

daughters will prophesy, your old men will dream dreams, your young men will see visions. Even on my servants, both men and women, I will pour out my Spirit in those days" (Joel 2:28–29).

The Azusa Street revival took place among the most impoverished and most disenfranchised sectors of American society: cleaners, janitors, occasional workers, odd-jobbers, unemployed, homeless migrants. Its leader, William Seymour, was the poor son of liberated Louisiana slaves. He had lost an eye through smallpox. He had had no formal education and taught himself to read.

Frank Bartleman, a participant from the beginning, gives an eyewitness description of their meetings:

> Brother Seymour generally sat behind two empty shoe boxes, one on top of the other. He usually kept his head inside the top one during the meeting, in prayer. There was no pride there. The services ran almost continuously. Seeking souls could be found under the power almost any hour, night and day. The place was never closed or empty. The people came to meet God. He was always there. Hence a continuous meeting. The meeting did not depend on the human leader. God's presence became more and more wonderful. In that old building, with its low rafters and bare floors, God took strong men and women to pieces and put them together again for his glory. . . . Pride and self-assertion, self-importance and self-esteem could not survive there."[14]

Arthur Osterberg, a young pastor of an independent Full Gospel church, drove his mother to the meetings. Years later, he would recall:

> I was not entirely in favour of the idea, but I saw as soon as I entered Azusa Street that something unusual was going on. . . . I was critical, but I went in and sat down on the rough boards they used for makeshift pews. A club–footed man of Mexican ancestry and his wife sat down next to me. The service began. There was a long prayer. During it I heard someone behind me sobbing. Then there were others.
>
> The sound of their wailing rose like the moan of the wind in the place. This club-footed man beside me became restless and at length made his way to the aisle. He limped up and down. I guess I was the only one watching him. Gradually he ceased to limp. Before my eyes he was cured. He was miraculously cured without anyone praying for him and with no formal "conversion," as we call it, at all. That convinced me there was something

---

14. Bartleman, *Azusa Street*, 65.

different in this meeting from any other that I had ever attended. Somehow those people had gotten back to primitive Christianity when those things were possible. I closed up my own church and joined the movement.[15]

The remarkable thing about the Azusa Street revival was that it was completely interracial. At the height of the influence of racist groups like the Ku Klux Klan and the John Birch Society, the Azusa Street meetings were fully integrated, sixty years before the Civil Rights Movement. Many visitors reported that blacks, whites, Asians, and Mexicans sang and prayed together. The central message was the love of God. Seymour was recognized as the pastor. There were both black and white deacons, and both black and white women were exhorters and healers. Frank Bartleman, the chronicler of the movement, exclaims, "The 'color line' was washed away in the blood."[16]

As historian Peter Hocken notes,

> The inter-racial component at Azusa Street astounded all participants. This was surely an expression of divine wisdom, that such a worldwide explosion of grace should be unleashed at a gathering of the poor and dispossessed of all colors, led by an uneducated black pastor. These origins clearly express the divine gratuitousness, and the difference between God's plans and mere human ideas.[17]

Shamefully, after the First World War, as Hocken also records, many Pentecostal groups reintroduced the color line.[18] Even more shamefully, several Pentecostal histories conceal the evidence that their early meetings had been spontaneously integrated under the leading of the Holy Spirit. The integrated meetings were a sovereign work of God's Spirit and a remarkable fulfillment of the Joel prophecy. The later reversion to racially separate churches is a shocking testimony to how human sinfulness can corrupt a work of God.

---

15. *Los Angeles Times*, 9 September 1956, quoted by Riss, *20th-Century Revival Movements*, 54–55.

16. Bartleman, *Azusa Street*, 61.

17. Hocken, *The Glory and the Shame*, 31, where Hocken quotes 1 Cor 1:27–28, "God chose the foolish things of the world to shame the wise."

18. Hocken, *The Glory and the Shame*, 32.

## Its Sequence

Finally, Joel's prophecy indicates a sequence of events. The latter rain outpouring will take place before the calamities of the last days. "I will show wonders in the heavens and on the earth, blood and fire and billows of smoke" (Joel 2:30). I thought of this prophecy as I watched the dramatic television pictures of the First Gulf War when Saddam Hussein torched the oil wells as he retreated from Kuwait. The immense black plumes of thick, acrid, polluting smoke were like scenes from Dante's *Inferno*.[19]

Joel says the end-time outpouring of the Holy Spirit will precede and herald "the coming of the great and terrible day of the Lord" (Joel 2: 31). During that troubled time, he promises, "Everyone who calls on the name of the Lord will be saved" (Joel 2:32).

The Azusa Street revival began in early April 1906, a few days before the great earthquake that devastated San Francisco. More disturbingly, it preceded the awful global calamity and waste of life of the First World War. Frank Bartleman compared it to the seven years of plenty that preceded the seven years of famine in the biblical story of Joseph in Egypt.[20] Since then, a truly terrible century has witnessed the unprecedented inhumanity of Stalin's Gulag, the Nazi Holocaust, the Second World War—the most widespread and destructive conflict in human history—Mao's famine, the killing fields of Kampuchea, the genocide in Rwanda, and countless regional conflicts.

Paul says that "where sin increased, grace increased all the more" (Rom 5:20). As a favorite Pentecostal text states, "When the enemy shall come in like a flood, the Spirit of the Lord shall lift up a standard against him" (Isa 59:19, KJV). God's purposes are never trumped by evil. God's grace more than anticipates the looming destructiveness of evil. In this great outpouring of the Holy Spirit, God has been offering us a season of grace to prepare for the time of apostasy, distress, conflict, and tribulation that Jesus and the prophets say will characterize the end of the age.[21]

This is why I believe it is vital that each of us search our hearts about our attitude to the Holy Spirit. The Bible warns us not to grieve, quench, or resist God's Holy Spirit (Eph 4:30; 1 Thess 5:19; Acts 7:51). It is all-too-possible to dismiss a work of God's Spirit. We can disqualify ourselves from a place in God's end-time purposes. Like those in Jerusalem who rejected

---

19. See the apocalyptic scenes filmed by Brazilian photographer Sebastião Salgado in the documentary film *Salt of the Earth*, by Wim Wenders and Juliano Ribeiro Salgado.

20. Bartleman, *Azuza Street*, 185.

21. Dan 7:21, 25; Matt 24:4–29; Mark 13:5–25; Luke 12:45; 18:8; 21:10–12; 2 Thess 2:3–4; 1 Tim 4:1; 2 Tim 3:1–5; 2 Pet 3:3; Jude 18.

the Messiah when he came, we may miss the day of visitation and God's time of opportunity (Luke 13:34–35).

# 2

# The Holy Spirit and Charismatic Renewal

*The charismatic renewal movement transformed the lives of many individuals, and the historic Christian churches, in the second half of the twentieth century. But outpourings of divine grace are often marred by all-too-human elements of showmanship and sin. Leaders of manifest integrity and holiness of life are paralleled by religious entrepreneurs of dubious quality, who in some cases exhibit shameful conduct. In keeping with the injunction to "test everything" (1 Thess 5:21, RSV), it is therefore essential to give a theological evaluation of the movement, to discern what elements can be truly said to be from God and represent a genuine work of the Holy Spirit.*

BEGINNING HIS LECTURES ON the Holy Spirit, one of my Edinburgh teachers, Roland Walls, observed, "The Spirit is always a threat to ecclesiastical establishments. Consequently, a great deal of Christian pneumatology exists in the sects, in the sidewalks of Christendom."

In the second half of the twentieth century, however, a new and unexpected development occurred. The Holy Spirit leapt from the sidewalks of Christendom to the main streets. Initially described as neo-Pentecostalism, this diverse and dynamic phenomenon became known as the charismatic renewal movement.

Of all the commentators on this movement, the most godly and perceptive has been Peter Hocken, a British Catholic priest and former secretary of the Society for Pentecostal Studies, who has lived in the United States and Austria. He devoted his life to evaluating the role the foundational gift of baptism in the Holy Spirit has played in the renewal of Christian churches and individuals.

> A power has been let loose: remarkable conversions and healings occur; new patterns of ministry emerge; gifts of the Spirit long regarded as rare or unavailable become regular features of congregational life; new forms of sharing between Catholic and Protestant, unthinkable in past generations, have sprung up. . . . It is important to reflect with open hearts and critical discernment upon this extraordinary phenomenon.[1]

## Remarkable Conversions and Healings

The modern charismatic renewal movement has indeed produced some remarkable conversions and healings. Here are just two examples, each of people who were humanly beyond hope.

Terry Clark is a well-known Christian musician, mainly involved in outreaches to the Spanish-speaking world. In 1971, he was serving with the United States military in eastern Thailand, on the border of Laos and Cambodia. He became so demoralized by the confusions and moral contradictions of the Vietnam War, what he had seen people do to each other and all he had participated in, that he felt he could no longer "justify human existence." He became deranged. He was found naked in no-man's-land, like an animal, out of his mind. He was sent to a psychiatric clinic in Munich, West Germany. His psychosis was so deep that the official diagnosis of his condition gave him "no hope."

There in the mental ward, he had an encounter with Jesus in which he heard the Savior say to him, "You've decided not to be a human being. I decided to become one." He had such an overwhelming sense of Jesus' love that it gave him back his sanity and humanity.[2]

Delores Winder suffered for nineteen years from a painful, disabling bone disease that led to the deterioration of her spine and hips and other chronic bodily malfunctions. Between 1957 and 1972 she had four spinal

---

1. Hocken, *The Glory and the Shame*, 11.
2. See his testimony on the DVD *First Love* (1998).

fusions to fuse broken vertebrae. Her pain was so excruciating that her doctors carried out two percutaneous cordotomies. A cordotomy is a surgical procedure to eliminate pain by burning out the nerve centers at the base of the brain, performed only on terminal patients. This left her with no feeling in half her upper body and all her lower body and legs. Her neck was in a brace and her body was in a body cast. She and her husband Bill had made her funeral arrangements.

In this pathetic state, she was taken on 30 August 1975 to a Methodist meeting in Dallas, Texas at which Kathryn Kuhlman was ministering. She didn't believe in divine healing and was revolted by what she had seen on television. Amid the vast crowd at this gathering, she began to complain to a man who had come and stood beside her about feeling a burning sensation in her legs.

"Excuse me," the man said to her. "Didn't you tell me you'd had a cordotomy? How come you are experiencing feeling?" The man was a doctor on Kathryn Kuhlman's team! He recognized that a miraculous healing was taking place. He got her to take off her neck brace and body cast, then took her forward to be prayed for by Kathryn Kuhlman. With Kuhlman's encouragement, Delores took a few steps. The feeling came back to her hands and arms. By the end of the meeting she had experienced a complete restoration of bodily feeling and function. She went home completely healed.[3]

After a year of reorientating her thinking and overcoming her reluctance, this was the beginning of Delores Winder's own remarkable healing ministry. The sprightly woman's five visits to New Zealand under the auspices of Presbyterian Renewal Ministries have done more to renew the Presbyterian Church in this country than any other single individual.

## A Movement of Surprises

Peter Hocken draws attention to the element of unexpectedness that has characterized the Pentecostal-charismatic movement since its birth in the early twentieth century. "God's works surprise us," he says, "because they do not conform to our expectations and do not fit into our received categories."[4]

---

3. There is a full account by a medical doctor (Casdorph, *The Miracles*, 147–57), and in Winder's two books with Bill Keith (*Jesus Set Me Free* and *Surprised by Healing*). I have heard Delores share her testimony and seen her prime exhibit, the grossly misshapen back portion of her fiberglass body cast.

4. Hocken, *The Glory and the Shame*, 16.

## The Pentecostal Movement

The initial surprise was not just people speaking in other tongues—though after centuries of neglect that was surprise enough. It was, as we have seen in chapter 1, the very circumstances of the movement's appearance: "Nobody would expect a major move of the Spirit to break out at an interracial meeting led by a black pastor in a poor area of Los Angeles in the midst of rather fringe Holiness groups."[5] Like Peter declaring that the Pentecost experience was what had been foretold by the prophet Joel (Acts 2:16), the early Pentecostals claimed to bridge a gap of nineteen centuries and spoke of experiencing "Pentecost" and of being baptized in the Holy Spirit today.

Dale Bruner considers the Full Gospel Business Men's Fellowship International (FGBMFI), founded by Californian rancher Demos Shakarian in 1953, to have been the most effective organization in promoting what came to be called neo–Pentecostalism.[6] It used a simple but effective strategy, hosting breakfast meetings for laymen in hotels and ballrooms, with testimonies following the meal. Many of these testimonies were published in *Voice* magazine, which spread their message about the Holy Spirit throughout the world.

## Charismatic Renewal in the Historic Churches

On 3 April 1960, Dennis Bennett, an American Episcopalian minister, told his affluent congregation in St. Mark's, Van Nuys, California of the spiritual search that had led to his speaking in tongues the previous year. In the kerfuffle that erupted, he tendered his resignation. A sympathetic bishop then appointed him vicar of St. Luke's, Seattle, a tiny church on the verge of closing. Within a year it grew to over three hundred parishioners and became a center of renewal on the Pacific west coast. In the ensuing years, many gifted individuals were baptized in the Holy Spirit and spread the "neo–Pentecostal" experience to other churches and around the world, some pastoring influential churches or founding denominational renewal groups.

Bennett's resignation was publicized in *Newsweek* and *Time* magazines by Jean Stone, a prominent member of the St. Mark's congregation and wife of a Lockheed executive.[7] The *Encyclopedia Britannica* dates the beginning

---

5. Hocken, *The Glory and the Shame*, 17.

6. Bruner, *Theology of the Holy Spirit*, 53.

7. "Rector and a Rumpus," *Newsweek* (4 July 1960) 77; "Speaking in Tongues," *Time* (15 August 1960) 53–55.

of the charismatic renewal movement to this event.[8] In fact, less publicized earlier pioneers of renewal had included the young Lutheran minister Harald Bredesen, baptized in the Holy Spirit in 1946, and the United Methodist pastor Tommy Tyson, baptized in the Spirit in 1951. Richard Winkler, rector of Trinity Episcopal Church, Wheaton, Illinois, and James Brown, minister of Octorara Presbyterian Church, Parkesburg, Pennsylvania, made their churches leading centers of renewal after they were baptized in the Spirit in 1956. Mount Vernon Reformed Church, New York, also became a center of renewal after Bredesen moved there in 1957.[9] Brown went on to found the Charismatic Communion of Presbyterian Ministers to support his beleaguered colleagues in 1966, the earliest denominational renewal group.[10] Larry Christensen, of Trinity Lutheran Church, San Pedro, California, was baptized in the Spirit in 1961 and established Lutheran Charismatic Renewal Services in 1974.

A landmark case took place in the United Presbyterian Church, USA.[11] Robert Whitaker, minister of First Presbyterian Church, Chandler, near Phoenix, Arizona, had been baptized in the Spirit in 1962. In 1967 a group of non-charismatic elders persuaded the presbytery of Phoenix to set up a commission to investigate Whitaker's ministry and the exercise of charismatic gifts in the congregation. The presbytery dismissed him when he refused to promise not to speak in tongues, pray for the sick, or cast out demons.

Whitaker appealed to the synod of Arizona on the grounds that the decision was contrary to Scripture and violated his conscience. Encouraged by Dr. John A. Mackay, president emeritus of Princeton Theological Seminary, and assisted by lawyer George C. ("Brick") Bradford, Whitaker appealed the decision to the General Assembly, the highest court in the United Presbyterian Church. In May 1968, *The Reverend Robert C. Whitaker vs. The Synod of Arizona* was decided in Whitaker's favor. It was a great moral victory for charismatics in the mainline churches. A theological study ordered by the Assembly resulted in a groundbreaking report on *The Work of the Holy Spirit*, which was received in 1970. Comprehensive and biblically based, it served as a model for many other denominational reports. Bradford and Whitaker both made tours of New Zealand in the 1980s under the auspices of the Paraclete Trust.

---

8. Marty, "The Pentecostal Phenomenon," 592. Here I follow the conventional account of charismatic renewal. In appendix 2, I tell the story of charismatic renewal in my own country, New Zealand, which began earlier than this and may have had a more pervasive influence than in any other country.

9. Hocken, "Charismatic Movement," in *DPCM* 131, *NIDPCM* 478. Hocken lists even earlier precursors in *Challenges*, 53–56.

10. Reconstituted as the Presbyterian Charismatic Communion in 1973 and renamed Presbyterian and Reformed Renewal Ministries International in 1984 (Hocken, *Challenges*, 59).

11. Synan, "Presbyterian and Reformed Charismatics," in *DPCM* 725, *NIDPCM* 996.

In Britain, All Souls Church in London, over the road from the BBC, had an opportunity to embrace charismatic renewal, but the well-known evangelical rector, John Stott, took a non-charismatic stance. His assistant, John Collins, from 1963 went on to lead St. Mark's, Gillingham, Kent to become England's first charismatic Anglican church. In 1964, Michael Harper, a curate at All Souls—who had been baptized in the Spirit in 1962—was appointed general secretary of the Fountain Trust, to serve charismatic renewal in Britain. John Collins's curate, David Watson, took over St. Cuthbert's York, a small church destined for closure, in 1965. A Church of Scotland minister, Tom Smail, who had been baptized in the Spirit through the ministry of Dennis Bennett in 1965, succeeded Harper in the leadership of the Fountain Trust in 1975. In West Germany the Lutheran Arnold Bittlinger was influential, founding the European Charismatic Leaders Conference in 1972 and becoming a consultant to the World Council of Churches in 1978.

This move of the Spirit, dubbed "Pentecost outside Pentecost" by Pentecostal ecumenists Donald Gee and David du Plessis, who were instrumental in spreading it, was not at all what most Pentecostals were expecting God to do. They regarded the mainline churches as "dead" and beyond revitalization. Nor did most leaders of Anglican, Lutheran, Reformed, Southern Baptist, or Brethren denominations, holding a cessationist outlook, think they had anything to learn from Pentecostals, whom they regarded as uneducated and uncouth.

## Charismatic Renewal in the Roman Catholic Church

The gulf separating Protestants and Catholics in the early nineteen-sixties was so great that nobody expected a Protestant renewal movement to spread to Catholics. When it did, most Pentecostals assumed that Catholics would leave their tradition-bound church and become Pentecostal.

By the mid-nineteen-sixties, as a result of the Second Vatican Council (1962–65), renewal was high on the Catholic agenda. But attention was mainly on liturgical and structural reform, renewal of biblical studies, and promotion of lay participation. Pope John XXIII had directed Catholics to pray daily throughout the Second Vatican Council for "a new Pentecost." The Council's "Decree on Ecumenism" (1964) had affirmed, "Whatever is wrought by the grace of the Holy Spirit in the hearts of our separated brethren can contribute to our own edification." But few Catholics imagined that a renewal of Catholic life could come from a sectarian source outside the Roman Catholic Church.

The Catholic charismatic renewal began at Duquesne University in Pittsburgh, Pennsylvania in February 1967. Two lay theology faculty members, inspired by David Wilkerson's *The Cross and the Switchblade* and John Sherrill's *They Speak with Other Tongues*, sought baptism in the Spirit. At a retreat, they passed this on to about thirty students, who formed the first Catholic charismatic renewal prayer group. From there the renewal spread to Notre Dame and Michigan State universities, where notable leaders Steve Clark and Ralph Martin were baptized in the Spirit. Publicized by Catholic weeklies and commended by books by Catholic writers Kevin and Dorothy Ranaghan, Edward O'Connor, and Kilian McDonnell, the movement grew rapidly and by mid-seventies numbered three hundred thousand people. In 1973, Cardinal Suenens, primate of Belgium, became Vatican adviser on charismatic renewal, giving it official recognition.[12] The Catholic Church was more welcoming of charismatic renewal than any other of the historic churches. It was the first time that a movement that began outside the Catholic Church had been so received.[13]

A remarkable story from the early Catholic charismatic renewal concerns a charismatic group led by Fr. Rich Thomas in the Catholic parish of El Paso, Texas. They were led by Luke 14:12–14 to share their meal on Christmas Day 1972 with the poor who lived on the rubbish dump at Juarez, Mexico, just across the border. Many more turned up than they had prepared food for. When they got home and took stock, it dawned on them that they had experienced a miracle of the multiplication of food. This joyous realization led to the formation of their celebrated social assistance ministry, "The Lord's Food Bank."[14]

Participants in the charismatic renewal movement at the time remember the joy of Catholics discovering Bible study, Protestants discovering Catholic spirituality, priests and pastors dancing together, and a spring tide that lifted our little boats free from their denominational moorings and prejudices.

## The Jesus People Movement

The late nineteen-sixties and early nineteen-seventies was an era of tumultuous social change in North America, the United Kingdom, Europe,

---

12. Ranaghan and Ranaghan, *Catholic Pentecostals*; O'Connor, *Pentecostal Movement*; McDonnell, *Charismatic Renewal*; Suenens, *A New Pentecost?*

13. Hocken, *Pentecost and Parousia*, 5–6; Hocken, *Azusa, Rome, and Zion*, 87.

14. The story is told by Fr. John Bertolucci on the video *Viva Cristo Rey*, prepared specially for Pope John Paul II (1981).

Australia, and New Zealand. Disillusioned with the materialism and secularity of Western culture, thousands of young people, reversing the journey of the Magi, turned eastward to the Asian religions and inward to psychedelic drugs in search of the meaning of life. Many, as a result, fell into the grip of drug addiction and the demonic.

Their counterculture pilgrimage frequently issued in a stark choice: suicide or salvation. There was a mass turning to Jesus, particularly on the west coast of the United States. An estimated three million hippies and dropouts came to faith between 1967 and 1972 in beach outreaches, coffeehouses, and communes offering deliverance from Satan and drug addiction.[15]

For the established churches, the Jesus People movement came as a complete surprise. One of the few churches to respond to longhaired hippies in bell-bottoms and bare feet was Calvary Chapel, Costa Mesa, California, led by Chuck Smith. They hosted for a while the archetypal Jesus Movement evangelist, Lonnie Frisbee. *Time* magazine (21 June 1971) featured their mass baptisms in the Pacific Ocean at Corona del Mar. Smith later estimated that their church performed over eight thousand baptisms and saw twenty thousand conversions to Christ in this period.[16]

The earliest storefront outreach to hippies was The Living Room in Haight-Ashbury, San Francisco, founded by Ted and Liz Wise during 1967's "Summer of Love." Other well-known outreaches were The Ark, run by Linda Meissner in Seattle, the House of Immanuel, founded by Bud Moegling to reach Vietnam War draft dodgers at Bellingham on the Canadian border, and His Place run by Arthur Blessit, the cross-carrying evangelist, on Sunset Strip, Hollywood. Under its youth pastor, Don Williams, even the wealthy Hollywood Presbyterian Church developed The Salt Company, a coffee bar outreach to street people.[17]

The Vineyard movement, led by John Wimber, emerged out of this youth revival, with connections to Calvary Chapel. It may have even taken its name from the Vine, a coffeehouse outreach in La Habra, Los Angeles, founded by Don Matison. Harvest International Ministries (HIM), the group whose Bible school in the Czech Republic I had the privilege of teaching at in 1992 and 1996, was founded in the Pacific Northwest at this time by Adrian Simila.[18]

---

15. I recall this figure being given by John Wimber, when he was an adjunct faculty member of Fuller Theological Seminary. I have not been able to verify it.

16. Smith and Brooke, *Harvest*, 9.

17. Williams later produced a book on *Bob Dylan: The Man, the Music, the Message* and an important book on *Signs, Wonders, and the Kingdom of God*.

18. This is an earlier and different organization than the larger and better-known Harvest International Ministry, founded in Los Angeles by Ché and Sue Ahn in 1996.

The Jesus People movement gave rise to more than fifty give-away newspapers across the United States. *Maranatha* was produced in Vancouver. *Right On!* was the campus paper of the Christian World Liberation Front at Berkeley. In Los Angeles, Duane Pederson's *Hollywood Free Paper* reached a circulation of more than five hundred thousand copies a month. In San Francisco, the secular newspaper *Oracle* became a Jesus paper with the conversion of its editor in October 1970! In an enterprising outreach in Seattle, Linda Meissner's Jesus People Army rented a small plane and dropped ten thousand copies of the first issue of her paper, *Agape*, on revelers at one of the Pacific Northwest's first pop festivals, at Gold Creek Park. After the airstrike, they sent in the infantry. Jesus people infiltrated the crowd and had a field day witnessing![19]

An even greater outburst of creativity issued in the production of Jesus music. This revolutionized Christian music with its freshness, joy, and power to connect with contemporary culture. Dedicated and creative musicians like Paul Clark, Andraé Crouch, Keith Green, Nancy Honeytree, Phil Keaggy, Larry Norman, Randy Stonehill, and John Michael Talbot, and groups like Love Song, led by Chuck Girard, Resurrection Band, led by Glenn Kaiser, and Second Chapter of Acts, featuring Annie Herring, Nelly Greisen and Matthew Ward, powerfully influenced the direction of contemporary Christian music. Several well-known performers professed faith in Christ, including Johnny Cash, Arlo Guthrie, Paul Stookey of Peter, Paul and Mary, guitarist Eric Clapton, and Bob Dylan, the world's most famous Messianic Jew.[20]

### The Rise of Messianic Judaism

A large number of Jewish young people turned to Jesus during the Jesus People movement, following Israel's dramatic recapture of Jerusalem during the Six-Day War of June 1967. It signified to them that God was back in the camp, and that "the times of the Gentiles" were drawing to a close (Luke 21:24). Rather than assimilating into existing Christian congregations, they began to form fellowships that reflected their Jewish culture and connections.

19. Interview with Joel Staab, Harvest International Ministries worker, Czech Republic, 16 November 1996, in Yule, "More Pages from a Bohemian Diary," 29–31.

20. The most comprehensive resource is Di Sabatino, *The Jesus People Movement*. Chapter 4, "Jesus Music Resources," lists 48 pages and 357 items of discography. Other studies include Graham, *The Jesus Generation*; Plowman, *The Jesus Movement*; Enroth et al., *The Jesus People*; and the Australian "God Squad" leader John Smith, *Significance of the Jesus Movement*.

Joe and Debbie Finklestein began an outreach to countercultural Jewish youth in their Philadelphia home. It became known as "Fink's Zoo." Martin Chernoff established the earliest Messianic congregation in Cincinnati, Ohio, in 1970. Chernoff's son Joel, with Rick Coghill, formed the Messianic rock group, Lamb. The most publicized Messianic outreach was Jews for Jesus, founded by Moishe Rosen, whose confrontational tactics drew widespread coverage in the Christian and secular press.

While many evangelicals and Pentecostals one day expect "all Israel" to be saved (Rom 11:25–26), nobody anticipated the emergence of a genuinely Jewish expression of Christianity. If anything, people only expected more "Hebrew Christians" to join Gentile churches. But since 1967, Jewish believers have been reclaiming *Yeshua* as the Jewish Messiah and affirming their identity as his followers without abandoning their Jewish heritage to join what most Jews perceive to be a persecuting religion. The reappearance of a Jewish form of Christianity for the first time since the first century has come as a complete surprise.[21]

I had a serendipitous meeting with leaders of the movement at the third southwest regional conference of the Messianic Jewish Alliance of America in Anaheim, Los Angeles in February 1988. I met Martin Chernoff's widow, Yohanna, the Golda Meir of the Messianic movement, who explains their motivation:

> They had a desire, born of the *Ruach* of God, to ground themselves in biblical Judaism. They wanted to remain Jewish, not assimilate. . . . To be a Messianic Jew is to be a pioneer. . . . One must be willing to travel down paths that have not been tread by the traditional church. We must be willing to go back to our Jewish roots of 2,000 years ago and to be Jewish regardless of whether this leading of the *Ruach* is understood by everyone, either Jew or Christian.[22]

The reemergence of Messianic Judaism presents a major challenge to the historic churches. "The challenge," says Peter Hocken, "is first to undo all the consequences of replacement thinking that either replaced Israel by the church or subsumed Israel into the church; the challenge is to restore

---

21. See Rausch, *Messianic Judaism*; and Winer, *The Calling*. In 2013, Cohen published "Messianic Jews and the Land of Israel," 107–15. A 2017 research project conducted by the Israel College of the Bible put the number of Messianic Jews in Israel at more than thirty thousand in some three hundred congregations (Israel College, "Findings of New Research").

22. Interview with Robert Winer, in *The Calling*, 60.

the Jewish witness to Yeshua to its rightful and foundational place within the body of Christ-Messiah."[23]

## The Wind in the House of Islam

Perhaps the least remarked but most remarkable move of the Spirit in our time is in the Muslim world.[24] Resistant to the Christian Gospel for the entire fourteen centuries of its existence, the Islamic world since around 1990 has been witnessing a remarkable turning to Christ, including some seventy mass movements of conversion.

Several human factors can be identified in this phenomenon: the screening of the *Jesus* film, the impact of common language Bible translations, the advent of satellite television and the Internet, and focus on global prayer for the "Ten-Forty Window" during the Decade of Evangelism (1990–2000).[25] But by and large, it has not been the result of strategizing by mission agencies. Rather, it has been a sovereign, unexpected, and unprecedented move of God's Spirit, involving spontaneous encounters with *Isa al-Masih*, Jesus the Messiah. These have been accompanied by charismatic experiences such as dreams, visions, answered prayers, healings, miracles of protection, and other signs and wonders, in the face of social ostracism and threats of violence or death.[26]

Just as Messianic Jews seek to keep their Jewish culture and identity, many of these Muslim converts seek to remain in their mosques or retain their Islamic culture. As a group of East African convert leaders said, "We insert Jesus into all of our Muslim practices."[27]

Not one of these movements would have been possible through human initiative or organization. In their sheer gratuitousness, they meet the biblical definition of a surprise: "what no eye has seen, what no hear has

---

23. Hocken, *Azusa, Rome, and Zion*, 134.

24. This phenomenon appeared later than Hocken's list of "surprises." My friend Murray Robertson suggested its inclusion.

25. The term "Ten-Forty Window" was coined by Christian mission strategist Luis Bush in 1989, to refer to the region between 10 and 40 degrees north of the equator, where Islam is the dominant religion, arid desert the predominant landform, and economic deprivation the major societal characteristic.

26. See Goode, *Which None Can Shut*; Trousdale, *Miraculous Movements*; and Garrison, *A Wind in the House of Islam*. Garrison defines a mass movement as comprising at least one thousand baptized believers or one hundred churches (39, 41, 234), and estimates that they number between two million and seven million converts in the Muslim world (42).

27. Quoted by Garrison, *A Wind in the House of Islam*, 75.

heard, and what no human mind has conceived" (1 Cor 2:9). "Each surprise represents a profound challenge to inherited ways of thinking," says Hocken. "But they will challenge the ways our understandings have deviated from the heart of the gospel and the fullness of the mystery of Christ."[28]

## Features of Charismatic Renewal

While there have been some regional variations, the general characteristics of the charismatic renewal movement have been the same throughout the world. Alasdair Heron observes "the rich and deep awareness of God's presence, the sense of the liberating power of his love, the upsurging response of joy and praise, the discovery of a new freshness in the words of the Bible, and the consciousness of communion with the Father through Jesus Christ."[29] Using the biblical test of authenticity ("By their fruit you will recognize them," Matt 7:16, 20), we can identify several features which show that the movement qualifies as an authentic move of God:[30]

### 1. Focus on Jesus

People who have been baptized in the Holy Spirit refer to a transforming encounter with Jesus, fuller experience of Jesus' love, and a deeper yielding to Jesus as Lord. Indeed, the proclamation "Jesus is Lord," in word and song, together with the "one-way Jesus" sign, were the most common slogans of the early charismatic movement. Many people have had life-transforming encounters with the risen Jesus, sometimes from lives of dissolution or despair. This has led to fresh and unexpected insights into Jesus' teaching and new ministry initiatives based on these discoveries.

---

28. Hocken, *The Glory and the Shame*, 21–22.
29. Heron, *The Holy Spirit*, 135.
30. This list is taken from that of Peter Hocken, "Charismatic Movement," in *DPCM* 155–56, *NIDPCM* 514–15, copyright © 1988, 2003, used by permission of Zondervan, to which I have added two further features of my own. Hocken provides a similar list of characteristics in *Pentecost and Parousia*, 21–23, 26–32. The "Charismatic Renewal" is also evaluated in Yves Congar, *I Believe in the Holy Spirit*, 2:143–212. Many of these renewal distinctives were confirmed in "Spirit and Power," a ten-country survey of the beliefs of Pentecostals and charismatics, conducted by the Pew Research Center in October 2006.

## 2. Praise of God

Charismatic experience is universally recognized as evoking spontaneous praise of God the Father and his Son, Jesus Christ. The first result of being baptized in the Holy Spirit is a flow of praise, verifying Jesus' promise that believers will have "rivers of living water" flowing "from within them" (John 7:38). The believer has a new ability to glorify God, evidenced in speaking in tongues in the spontaneity of charismatic praise. There is a move from third-person description to second-person address in speech about God; from the descriptive poetry of traditional hymnody to the personal engagement of charismatic worship. This has brought an explosion of new songs of worship, unparalleled in Christian history.[31]

## 3. Study of the Bible

Despite the widespread view among evangelicals that charismatic emphasis on experience devalues the Scriptures, charismatics have consistently shown a love for the Bible and an enthusiasm for Bible study. Fresh insights have emerged as the Spirit has highlighted neglected parts of Scripture. The publication *Scripture in Song* shows the marked influence of the Bible on charismatic songwriting, and the singing of such choruses, in turn, has enhanced Scripture memorization.

## 4. Intimacy with God

Charismatic renewal is everywhere accompanied by the conviction that God is intimate with people, speaks today, and communicates directly with believers, both in their personal experience and in corporate worship. This claim to direct subjective guidance can perplex or repel other Christians. But it is an expression of knowing God personally as a loving Father who promises to speak through his Spirit and "guide you into all the truth" (John 16:13–15).

---

31. Many New Zealanders were in the forefront of creative songwriting in the early days of charismatic renewal (see appendix 2). In particular, David and Dale Garratt's three-volume compilation, *Scripture in Song*, played a pioneering role and was globally disseminated. For the sheer joy and creativity of this praise, see the previously mentioned DVD set, *First Love*—songs and testimonies of a historic twenty-fifth anniversary gathering of Jesus music pioneers. It includes such notable musicians as Terry Clark, Jamie Owens Collins, Andraé Crouch, Chuck Girard, Melody Green (widow of Keith Green), Annie Herring, Nancy Honeytree, Barry McGuire, Darrell Mansfield, Randy Stonehill, and Matthew Ward.

### 5. Effective Evangelism

Reception of the Spirit invariably leads the believer to a new effectiveness in evangelism. There is a new freedom and capacity to speak to others about the Lord, to share one's testimony of God's forgiveness, and to lead others into an experience of salvation. Many in the Jesus People movement, converted on the street or beach, became gifted open-air evangelists themselves. On the Sunday after I was baptized in the Holy Spirit, a punk girl wandered into our evening service and was converted! I don't know who was more surprised: myself, my congregation, or the new recipient of God's grace!

### 6. Awareness of Evil

Just as Jesus' experience of the Holy Spirit drove him into the desert to engage with Satan (Matt 4:1; Luke 4:1–2), many charismatics, when baptized in the Spirit, become aware of the reality of supernatural evil and engage in confrontation with the powers of darkness. This heightened awareness of evil has brought new relevance to deliverance and exorcism in the context of evangelism and pastoral counseling, and a new emphasis on intercession to confront the principalities and powers that dominate regions and nations.

### 7. Exercise of Spiritual Gifts

One of the most prominent features of charismatic renewal is a rediscovery of the reality and relevance of the nine spiritual gifts (*charismata*) listed in 1 Corinthians 12:7–11. Most common are speaking in tongues (*glossolalia*), prophecy or prophesying (*prophēteia*), and healing (*iama*). In contrast to the widespread cessationist view that the *charismata* were withdrawn at the close of the apostolic age, charismatics boldly show that the gifts of the Spirit are available today as part of God's equipping of his people for effective service.

### 8. Eschatological Expectation

Charismatic experience of the Holy Spirit is often accompanied by an awareness of living in the latter days and a longing for the return of Jesus. This hope was quickened by the unexpected return of Jerusalem to Jewish control in the Six-Day War of 1967, with its implications for God's prophetic program (Luke 21:24). Initially—as in Hal Lindsey's enormously popular

*The Late Great Planet Earth* (1970)—these expectations were cast in the prevailing framework of dispensationalism. But as charismatic renewal matured, a concern emerged for the movement of history towards its climax in the return and earthly reign of Jesus. The rediscovery of the millennial hopes of the biblical prophets, suppressed since Augustine's equation of the kingdom of God with the triumphant church in the fourth century, has been a distinctive feature of charismatic eschatology. This has "earthed" the Christian hope and freed it from dispensational trappings, but challenges the historic church's long-standing claim to be the identified with the kingdom of God.[32]

### 9. Spiritual Power

The power endowment of charismatic experience underlies all the foregoing features since it is the realization of Jesus' promise that believers will have a renewed effectiveness (*dynamis*) for witness and service when the Holy Spirit comes on them (Acts 1:8). In Peter Hocken's words,

> The spiritual power that accompanies baptism in the Holy Spirit is manifest in the capacity to praise, in the capacity to evangelize, in all ministries of deliverance and the overcoming of evil, and in the exercise of the spiritual gifts. This power of the Spirit is experienced as a gift of the risen Lord Jesus, . . . manifested in every form of Christian ministry and service, . . . in ministries within the body of Christ, and in service to those outside.[33]

To these nine signs of the divine character of the charismatic renewal movement listed by Hocken, I would add two further defining characteristics that I have observed: the role of the Spirit in creating community and ministry to the poor.

### 10. Rediscovery of Community

The Holy Spirit's impulse of love leads to a relational revolution. "God's love has been poured out into our hearts through the Holy Spirit, who has been given to us" (Rom 5:5). "We were all baptized [or, incorporated] by one Spirit so as to form one body" (1 Cor 12:13). The move of the Spirit leads to a spontaneous overcoming of individualism and rediscovery of Christian community. This is evident in small groups for prayer and mutual support,

---

32. Pawson, *When Jesus Returns*; Yule, *Return of Jesus*; Hocken, *Challenges*, 129–37.
33. Hocken, "Charismatic Movement," in *DPCM* 156.

in home groups for Bible study or sharing, in team leadership and team ministries, in experiments in new forms of community living, and in the emergence of new initiatives in urban and community ministries, particularly to serve the poor of our cities.[34]

It seems that a key to spiritual power is a lifestyle of availability and sharing. Independence blocks the Spirit's flow and power. Interdependence and community release the Spirit's flow. There is an "interwoven connection between . . . economic liberality and divine power."[35]

In the nineteen seventies many converts of the Jesus People movement rediscovered Christian community. I saw this in experiments in community living by many charismatic students when I was the ecumenical chaplain at Victoria University of Wellington in the early seventies. Harvest International Ministries (HIM), the group I was involved with in two memorable mission trips to Central Europe after the fall of Communism, were living in house buses in the permanent Gypsy circus in Prague when I first met them in 1991. From their bold open-air evangelism, they were seeing the same dramatic conversions on the town squares of Central Europe after the collapse of Communism as they had twenty-five years earlier on the beaches of California.

## 11. Ministry to the Poor

Closely related to the rediscovery of community is the emergence of new ministries of social justice to serve the poor and underprivileged. New Zealanders have been in the forefront of this emphasis. Murray Robertson, long-serving pastor of Spreydon Baptist Church in Christchurch, preached extensively on Jesus' Nazareth declaration of good news to the poor, liberty to the captives, and release for the oppressed (Luke 4:18). This led to a surge of initiatives in community ministries that were commended by Gary Moore, the mayor of Christchurch.[36]

Brian Hathaway of Auckland's charismatic Brethren assembly, Te Atatu Bible Chapel, wrote *Beyond Renewal*, calling for the outworking of

---

34. The pioneering charismatic community was associated with the Episcopal Church of the Redeemer in Houston, Texas. Others were the Word of God Community in Ann Arbor, Michigan, the People of Praise in South Bend, Indiana, the Community of Celebration on the isle of Cumbrae, Scotland, the Emmanuel Community in Brisbane, Australia, and the Lamb of God Community in Christchurch, New Zealand. Some of these developments were influenced by the *kibbutz* movement in Israel (Bettelheim, *Children of the Dream*), others by the Christian monastic tradition (Bessenecker, *The New Friars*), most by the Catholic charismatic renewal (Hocken, *Pentecost and Parousia*, 28–30, 45–48).

35. Foster, *Freedom of Simplicity*, 44.

36. Ward, *Against the Odds*, 54–60, 67–85, 141–48.

Christian compassion in a holistic integration of evangelism, charismatic renewal, and concern for social justice.[37] Student worker Viv Grigg, following his baptism in the Spirit, founded Servants to Asia's Urban Poor, which has mobilized many people to embark on sacrificial lifestyles among the slum-dwellers of Asia's megacities.[38] Youth for Christ worker Justin Duckworth, now Anglican Bishop of Wellington, began Urban Vision, a movement of charismatic Christians living in community houses to serve the poor and underprivileged.

These initiatives have been matched internationally by the extraordinary ministries of Jackie Pullinger in Hong Kong, Heidi and Rolland Baker in Mozambique, and Bob and Gracie Ekblad in Washington state, USA. All are talented and highly educated charismatic Christians who have renounced ease and comfort to serve the poor, the destitute, and those in prison.

## Evaluation of the Charismatic Movement

All these features of charismatic renewal are a consequence and outworking of the central experience of being baptized in the Holy Spirit. The initial experience of the Spirit is the key to unlocking new insight and effectiveness for the believer—which is why charismatic testimony literature lays such stress on its foundational importance.

These features are also central to Christian living and the mission of the Christian church. They concern every aspect of the church's life: a personal relationship with God as followers of Jesus, praise and worship, spiritual formation, pastoral counsel, life in community, evangelism and mission, concern for social justice. This shows that charismatic renewal is not an isolated movement, but as Hocken observes, "a grace for the renewal of the church in all its dimensions."[39]

---

37. Hathaway, *Beyond Renewal*, with a commendatory foreword by Ronald J. Sider. Hathaway's holistic theology of the kingdom of God is paralleled in Villafañe, *The Liberating Spirit*, especially 184–222.

38. Grigg, *Companion to the Poor* (1984); Grigg, *Cry of the Urban Poor* (1992).

39. This and all the following quotations in this chapter are from Hocken's perceptive evaluation, "Charismatic Movement," in *DPCM* 158–59, a section which does not appear in *NIDPCM*. Cf. Hocken, *The Glory and the Shame*, 193. In his "Address to the Renewal" (2015), Pope Francis quoted from the second volume of Cardinal Léon Joseph Suenens's memoirs, describing charismatic renewal as a sovereign work of the Spirit, "not a movement in the common sociological sense." He says, "It does not have founders, it is not homogeneous, and it includes a great variety of realities; it is a current of grace . . . for all members of the church."

Hocken points out that charismatic renewal differs from Christian movements that have a human founder, which reflect their founder's vision and values:

> Its genesis indicates that it had no one human founder, that its arrival was unexpected and unplanned, that it did not come as a set of coherent ideas or with any strategic methodology, and that it was not in its origins the product of any one Christian tradition more than others.

So Hocken concludes,

> The argument follows that an unplanned and unexpected movement, without any one human founder or place of origin, and whose essential characteristics are the fruit only the Holy Spirit of God can produce (knowledge of Jesus, heartfelt praise of God, love of the Scriptures, greater sensitivity to powers of evil), must represent a sovereign intervention of the Lord.

Moreover, unlike other revival movements throughout Christian history, the charismatic movement is restoring elements of Christian life largely unknown since the early days of Christianity. This is particularly so of the exercise of charismatic gifts and the reappearance of a distinctively Jewish expression of Christianity. "All these factors taken together," says Hocken, "suggest that charismatic renewal is not simply a sovereign divine intervention for this age but a grace that is healing and repairing the wounds and the weaknesses of many centuries."

Baptism in the Holy Spirit is, therefore, a personal grace with a wider purpose than an individual's spiritual life. God's agenda is bigger than our personal renewal, though it involves our response and participation. These signs show that the charismatic renewal movement is indeed a large-scale grace of God for renewing and unifying the worldwide church, so that the church may witness God's reality in an age of secularism and growing apostasy and be prepared to welcome her returning Lord.

# 3

# The Holy Spirit in the Old Testament

*The Holy Spirit is mentioned at the very beginning of the Old Testament, overseeing the development of the universe from an unformed to a highly formed state. The Spirit does not dwell within creation but acts upon it as the Creator of form and order. The Old Testament also shows the Holy Spirit to be a God-given source of creative inspiration for selected artists and of divine empowerment for chosen leaders. Unlike the presence of God within believers later described in the New Testament, this empowerment is temporary—given for the accomplishment of a particular task, and then withdrawn. Not until the coming of Jesus as Messiah does the Holy Spirit permanently indwell a human being.*

## Chaos to Cosmos

THE OPENING VERSES OF the Bible reveal the origin of the universe, God's relationship to creation, and our first insight into the activity of God's Spirit (Gen 1:1–5).

## Origin

Genesis 1:1 says that God is the origin of everything that exists. The Hebrew word *bara*, "to create," does not refer to the making or shaping of something that already exists. It denotes the bringing into existence of something that had no previous existence; the origination *de novo* and *ex nihilo*—"brand new" and "out of nothing"—of something that did not exist before. Creation can be defined as "the making or constituting of something for the first time; the bringing into existence of something entirely new or unprecedented that did not previously exist, using no pre-existing material."[1]

Before the beginning, there was only God. The universe did not exist before the beginning. Even time itself, a correlative of creaturely existence, did not exist before the beginning. God's creation is something entirely new. It is not a copy or a rerun of anything else. The words "In the beginning" mark the inauguration of something that never existed before.

Because it indicates complete newness and innovation, the word *bara*, "create," is used sparingly in the Bible. Indeed, even the opening chapter of Genesis uses it only three times: in verse 1, to describe the origin of the physical universe; in verse 21, to describe the origin of life (birds, fish, and animals), and in verse 27 (three times), to describe the creation of human beings in God's image and the origin of human consciousness and creativity.

For two and a half millennia—since the philosopher Aristotle—scholars and thinkers have denied that the universe was created and maintained that it is eternal. But in the last century physicists and astronomers have demonstrated that the opening verse of the Bible is correct: the universe had a beginning. It is not eternal but is finite. There was a time when there was no time, when nothing existed. The universe was created, literally, out of nothing—nothing preexisted it. As the distinguished British astrophysicist, John Barrow says, "the . . . big-bang picture of the universe emerging from a singularity is, strictly speaking, . . . creation out of absolutely nothing. . . . There is no prior time, no prior space, and no prior matter."[2]

## Order

God not only created the universe and brought it into existence. The Bible says that God's Spirit (*rûach*) was "hovering" over the universe, guiding it from its original unformed state to a state of exquisite form and beauty.

---

1. For this definition, see my booklet, *Discovery of the Beginning*, 39.
2. Barrow, *Origin of the Universe*, 113.

"Now the earth was formless and empty, darkness was over the surface of the deep, and the Spirit of God was hovering over the waters" (Gen 1:2).

The Hebrew word used here, *rāchaph*, "to hover," is used in Deuteronomy 32:11 of an eagle fluttering over its young in the nest, to coax them to make their first flight. The image compares the Spirit's oversight of the formation of the universe to an eagle's encouragement its offspring's never-before-attempted venture of flight. As the beating of the eagle's wings pushes the eaglet out of the nest into the abyss, so the Spirit of God impels and oversees the initial development of the universe, launching it forth to guide its journey into the uncharted void.

The universe is not divine. The Spirit of God is not *in* the universe but *over* it. This is no "creation spirituality"—as in the neo-paganism of writers like Matthew Fox. The Spirit of God "hovers over" the universe rather than animating it from within like an Aristotelian entelechy or life force. The Bible does not associate the Spirit with nature, but with God, the Creator of nature.

> Even passages that describe the *rûach* as the "breath," "life," or "spirit" of a human being emphasize the dependence of human beings, along with all other creatures, on God's gift of life and providential care. "All creatures look to you to give them their food at the proper time.... When you take away their breath, they die and return to the dust. When you send your Spirit, they are created, and you renew the face of the ground" (Ps 104:27–30; cf. Gen 2:7). God gives and sustains life by his life-giving Spirit. The Spirit is the source of all life. There is no life without the Spirit as its source. But nature and human beings are not divine. Nature is dependent on the Creator, just as human life is dependent on the animating Spirit.
>
> Alasdair Heron, in his careful discussion of what the Old Testament says about the Holy Spirit, comments on its account of God's *transcendence*, "his utter otherness," and *immanence*, "his universal presence." "On the whole," he says, "it is not some *general* (and abstractly conceived) 'immanence' of God that they set over against his 'transcendence', but his *specific* and *particular* 'making of himself present' *at points of his own choosing*."[3] I would go further and point out that at such times the divine presence is not described in terms of God's *rûach* (Spirit), but rather as a manifestation of God's *kābôd* (his glory), as in the many theophanies or at Solomon's dedication of the temple. Solomon, in his dedicatory prayer, affirms that God's dwelling place is in heaven and that "even the highest heavens" cannot contain him, "much less this temple that I have built!" (2 Chr 6:18). But God's glory so filled the temple that the priests could not enter (2 Chr 7:2).

Today scientists are realizing that the universe is exquisitely customized to develop into a habitat for life. They call this the "Anthropic Principle" (from the Greek *anthropos*, "man"). The universe is finely tuned within very narrow parameters which enable human life to exist. If any of these parameters were changed even by an infinitesimal amount, life would not be

---

3. Heron, *The Holy Spirit*, 9.

possible and we would not be here. The Australian physicist Paul Davies calls this the "Goldilocks enigma" or "Goldilocks effect": like the porridge Goldilocks tasted, the universe is "just right" for human life.[4] These discoveries allow us to see the precision of what the opening of the book of Genesis ascribes to the Spirit of God, superintending the origin of the expanding universe with precisely the right coordinates to form a home for embodied living beings.

According to astrophysicist Alan Guth, the universe's expansion rate, for example, cannot vary by more than 1 part in $10^{55}$ for life to exist.[5] If it expanded fractionally faster, matter would be too diffuse to make galaxies, stars, planets, and a world dense enough to stand on, let alone bodies solid enough to hold together. You and I would be like a vapor. If it expanded more slowly, matter would congeal too much, galaxies, stars, planets, and the earth would shrink to a dense mass, and our bodies would be too compressed to breathe, move, function, or exist.

Reflecting on the staggering pin-point accuracy of the initial highly ordered, low-entropy state of the universe at its beginning, British mathematician Sir Roger Penrose has calculated how precise the fine tuning of the "Creator's aim" had to be in creating our universe. He estimates it has to be just 1 part in $10^{10^{123}}$ to create a universe as special as ours is.[6] What has become known as "the Penrose number" is a mind-boggling figure. One in 10 to the power 10 is 1:10,000,000,000, or 1 in 10 billion. One hundred and twenty-three powers of magnitude beyond that is engineering skill utterly transcending human ability or comprehension. As distinguished New Zealand scientist Jeff Tallon points out, it is "a number so large that it could not be written down in normal notation using the entire breadth of the observable universe."[7]

## Orientation

The Bible attributes this exquisitely skillful arrangement to the Holy Spirit. The Spirit of God "hovered" over the developing universe to ensure that it had precisely the right qualities and orientation to lead to its appointed goal of providing a habitat suitable for the existence and maintenance of human life.

We can sum up this first glimpse of the Spirit's activity in the Bible by saying that the Spirit is the perfecter of creation. There is a teleological orientation of the Spirit's action, leading from concept to consummation, from beginning to end, origin to goal, creation to *eschaton*.

---

4. Davies, *The Goldilocks Enigma*.
5. Guth, "Inflationary Universe," 348.
6. Penrose, *The Emperor's New Mind*, 334; *Road to Reality*, 730, 762–65.
7. Address at New Zealand Parliament, 20 October 2016.

Tom Smail observes, "The perfecting creativity of the Spirit is to be distinguished from the initiating creativity of the Father. Where the action of the Father is characteristically protological [having to do with the beginning or origin], the action of the Spirit is characteristically eschatological [having to do with the end or goal]." He explains, "In other words, what the Father starts, the Spirit perfects. Through the Father's initiating creativity, things that otherwise would not exist come into being; through the Spirit's perfecting creativity, things that already exist become what they were made and meant to be. The Father creates life at the beginning and the Spirit from that beginning sets that life into a dynamic which will lead to its fullness at the end."[8]

Genesis 1:2 provides the cosmic reason why we should be willing to trust the Holy Spirit. The Spirit is God's formative influence, superintending the universe's development from chaos to cosmos, from disorder to order, from an unformed state to a highly tuned state, from a formless emptiness to a superbly beautiful home for human beings.

Thus, to find our life's purpose, it makes sense to trust the One who formed the universe so well, who knows the end from the beginning. "The Spirit searches all things, even the deep things of God. . . . What we have received is not the spirit of the world, but the Spirit who is from God, so that we may understand what God has freely given us" (1 Cor 2:10, 12). It is with confidence that we can allow God's Spirit to lead us from chaos to cosmos, from our present uncertainty or confusion to the peace and harmony that is God's intended design.

## The Holy Spirit and Creativity

The role of the Holy Spirit is to inspire creativity. Creativity begins with the inspiration of a thought or idea and moves to its physical embodiment in a work of art. Just as the Spirit of God is the agent who moves the cosmos from its conception to its consummation, so God's Spirit is depicted in the Bible as the source and inspiration of human creativity. The cosmic role of the Holy Spirit anticipates the Spirit's role as the inspirer of artistic creativity.

### Artistic Creativity

The book of Exodus tells us about the craftsmen who constructed the tabernacle, the portable shrine where God dwelt at the center of the Israelite

---

8. Smail, *Like Father, Like Son*, 186. "To lead the creature to its destiny," says Abraham Kuyper, "to cause it to develop according to its nature, to make it perfect, is the proper work of the Holy Spirit" (Kuyper, *Work of the Holy Spirit*, 21). Clark Pinnock, too, notes the Spirit's role in "bringing God's plans to completion" (Pinnock, *Flame of Love*, 21).

encampment during their wilderness wanderings and where God was worshiped (Exod 31:1–11, 35:30–36:1).

The head craftsman was Bezalel, from the tribe of Judah, and his fellow artisan and helper was Oholiab, from the tribe of Dan. Bezalel was "filled with the Spirit of God" for this creative task. The Spirit gave him "wisdom, understanding, knowledge and all kinds of skills" (Exod 31:3; 35:31). Five different skills or crafts are mentioned: metalwork, jewelry, cabinet making or joinery, cloth weaving and garment making, and the production of perfumes. These craftsmen were also gifted with the ability to train apprentices in these skills. This suggests that the educative abilities that people have are also gifts of God.

Bezalel and Oholiab were commissioned to make the curtains surrounding the tabernacle courtyard, and the supports, curtains, fabrics, and hangings of the tabernacle itself. They were also to make the tabernacle furniture: the gold lampstand or *menorah*, the table and its utensils, the altar of incense and the altar for the burnt offerings, with their utensils, and the laver for washing. Above all, they were to make the gold-plated box known as the ark, with its gold lid or "atonement cover" and overarching winged design of angelic figures or *cherubim*.

The emphasis was not just on the utilitarian aspects of this design—its portability, ability to be dismantled, carried, and reassembled—but on its fitness as a place of beauty for the worship of Israel's God and the Creator of the universe.

> The design of the tabernacle was both functional and pleasing, reflecting technical competence and artistic design of the highest order. It was a place of worship that was transportable and beautiful. One thinks of the special place that the arts have had ever since in the worship of God: the birth of Christian art in the catacombs, the magnificent murals or mosaics of Byzantine churches, the ornate decoration of Baroque churches, or the simplicity and humanity of Protestant worship—exemplified in the paintings of Rembrandt or the music of Bach.

A modern example of the link between the Holy Spirit and artistic creativity is the reconstruction of Coventry Cathedral after the Second World War. Stephen Verney describes how parishes in the Coventry diocese were transformed in the years leading up to and following the consecration of the cathedral in 1962.[9]

The reconstruction took place in the context of the post-war reconciliation between the people of Coventry and Dresden. Sir Basil Spence's new cathedral is entered through the roofless ruins of the old, destroyed by an incendiary bomb during the blitz on the night of 14 November 1940. One's eye is immediately drawn to Graham Sutherland's giant tapestry of Christ in glory, the size of a tennis court, on the wall of the chancel. It depicts the evolution of warfare, with a crossbow at its base and a thermonuclear bomb above it enshrining the exalted Christ.

---

9. Verney, *Fire in Coventry*. The Spirit "is like fire and wind and flowing water.... You cannot trap the Spirit in any form or pattern of ecclesiastical organisation" (67).

Sutherland seems to be suggesting that the next time there is a global war, we will not be entering another cathedral through the ruins of the present one, but the kingdom of Christ itself. Christ the Savior is our only hope from the escalating folly of the increasing sophistication of weapons of mass destruction.

## Creativity as Innovation

We have defined creativity as the bringing into existence of what did not previously exist. God did this supremely in creating the universe. God did this too, in a derivative sense, when he made human beings capable of creativity as well. We are created in God's image to be creative in turn (Gen 1:26–27). Creativity is one of the most godlike things humans can do.

God's Spirit is the agent of creativity. The Holy Spirit inspires artistic creativity. It is the Spirit who inspires freshness, newness, innovation; the bringing into existence of what never before existed. Artistic creativity captures people's attention and challenges the status quo.

Creativity is the opposite of conformity. Creativity breaks through slavish adherence to tradition or convention. Where things have grown stale or clichéd, the Spirit breathes vigor and freshness. Artists are often in the vanguard of social and cultural change. But creativity is not iconoclasm. Creativity is bringing into existence. Iconoclasm is the destroying of what exists.

Unlike God's creative activity, human artistry is not *ex nihilo*. "God makes each thing and all things out of nothing," says New Zealand poet James K. Baxter. "Nobody else can. We make something out of something—houses out of timber, or bread out of wheat."[10] Human creativity uses preexisting materials, or reveals antecedent influences. We can see in works of human creativity elements of borrowing or allusion to earlier artists. Nevertheless, the artifacts of human creativity are also novel and innovative. Without the creative work of the artist, they would not exist. They are unprecedented and unparalleled, revealing unique aspects of the artist's personality.

## Creativity as Artistry

Tom Smail describes the Holy Spirit as "the artist of the Trinity."[11] An artist conceives an idea in their mind and brings it to completion in a realized form in a work of art. Artistic creativity is a movement from conception to realization. What first comes to mind in the artist's imagination has to be brought into existence through the exercise of technical skill.

---

10. Baxter, *Autumn Testament*, 48 (*Complete Prose*, 3:480). In contrast, Baxter adds: "The devil . . . makes a nothing out of nothing: that is, a lie. He has nothing positive to contribute, only wars, quarrels, lies, ulcers, deformations, the absence of good."

11. Smail, *Like Father, Like Son*, 186.

An artist is therefore a person who has both the imagination to conceive a work of art and the technical skill to bring it to accomplishment. Along with the power of creative imagination, technical prowess is necessary. Mastery of the required skills is essential to artistic achievement—whether with words (in poetry, literature, or drama), with the voice and instruments (in music), with paints and pigments (in the visual arts) or with materials (in sculpture, architecture, and the plastic arts).

Since we do not have access to the minds of the biblical artists, it may be appropriate to illustrate the creative process with a later documented example. Creativity, like many scientific discoveries, begins with something akin to a spiritual inspiration, which often comes in a flash and as a whole. Roger Penrose records the staggering ability that Mozart had to envisage an entire work of music, to conceive it as a whole in his mind. Mozart said, "It does not come to me successively, with various parts worked out in detail, as they will later on, but [it is] in its entirety that my imagination lets me hear it."[12]

Yet this inspiration has to be elaborated and worked out. Though endowed with this prodigious ability, Mozart needed a keyboard to work out his musical thoughts. Like every artist, he faced the technical challenge of laying out his ideas in finished form. Ulrich Konrad has studied Mozart's method of composition. His earliest sketches are in casual handwriting and give just snippets of music. More advanced sketches cover the melody line and often the bass, leaving other lines to fill in later. What Mozart called his "draft score" was good enough for him to consider complete and enter in the personal catalog of his works. But the draft score did not include all the notes of the composition. He still needed to flesh out the internal voices, fill out the harmony, and create the completed score, which he was careful to write out in a legible hand.[13]

One of the marks of a great artist is the combination of technical and artistic skill. Today there is much mediocre work that passes for art, as well as technical brilliance in the service of a dehumanized vision. Great artists can be recognized by their painstaking care in working with their materials, as well as by their cleverness in making connections that arrest the reader, viewer, or listener.

Acclaimed examples of artistry would be the textures in the garments of Rembrandt's *The Night Watch* (1642) or *The Jewish Bride* (1666), or the reflections in Vermeer's paintings, such as his *Woman Reading a Letter* (1662). Modern art often excels in technical skill, while depicting what is debased or dehumanized. An example would be Salvador Dali's *Raphaelesque Head Exploding* (1951): a very clever painting, comparing a disintegrating human head to a domed building or cathedral. Dali is saying that as the unifying role of Christendom has disintegrated

---

12. Quoted by Penrose, *The Emperor's New Mind*, 547, 576, citing French fellow mathematician Jacques Hadamard, *Psychology of Invention*, 16.

13. Ulrich, *Mozarts Schaffensweise* [Mozart's Method of Composition], 103.

in secular culture, so has the concept of a unitary human person disintegrated under scientific investigation into a bundle of chemical and electrical impulses.

Much modern art is technically brilliant, but not beautiful. Often the brilliance of contemporary art is in the service of what is ugly, debased, and inhuman, or at best a critique of a dehumanized culture. A great deal of modern art is inspired by human rather than divine inspiration—it is dehumanizing rather than ennobling and uplifting.

This is the theme of H. R. Rookmaaker's book *Modern Art and the Death of a Culture*. Rookmaaker sees the work of a modern artist like Francis Bacon, for example, as "great cries of despair for lost values and lost greatness, for a humanity deprived of its freedom, love, rationality, everything that the great humanist painters had celebrated for centuries."[14] By contrast, one of the distinctively Christian marks of Rembrandt's art is its humanity—its depiction of ordinary human beings, portraying but not gloating over their frailty and weakness.[15] In his later years, the Bible was one of only two books Rembrandt possessed.[16] It informed his worldview and his art. Apart from his many self-portraits, and the occasional commission like *The Night Watch*, Rembrandt concentrated on biblical themes. But the Bible not only provided his subject matter. It suffused his realism with tenderness, humanity, and compassion.

## Poetic and Musical Inspiration

Other forms of artistic creativity are mentioned in the Bible. Music, poetry, and songwriting are paramount in the career of the shepherd-king David, just as parable and storytelling feature in the ministry of the prophets and of Jesus. This, too, is attributed to the inspiration of the Holy Spirit. The Bible tells how Samuel took a horn of oil and anointed David, "and from that day on the Spirit of the Lord came powerfully upon David" (1 Sam 16:13).

The drama of God's Spirit lies at the heart of the skillfully written succession narrative in Samuel—itself a work of art, a brilliant example of history writing and perhaps its earliest example.[17] The story explains how the kingship passed from the house of Saul to the house of David. It describes how "the Spirit of the Lord departed from Saul" and as a result, how the king used to suffer from bouts of melancholy and depression. Saul's attendants suggest that they find someone who could play music to soothe his troubled emotions. So young shepherd David is brought into Saul's court to play the lyre for him. Whenever melancholy came upon Saul, "David

---

14. Rookmaaker, *Modern Art*, 174.
15. See Yule, "Icons as Christian Art," 203.
16. Visser 't Hooft, *Rembrandt*, 15.
17. Rad, "Beginnings of Historical Writing," 166–204.

would take up his lyre and play. Then relief would come to Saul; he would feel better, and the evil spirit would leave him" (1 Sam 16:23).

God's Spirit anointed David not only for leadership and governance, but also for musicianship with stringed instruments like the harp and lyre, and for creative songwriting and poetry as we find in the Psalms. "The Spirit of the Lord spoke through me," he says (2 Sam 23:2). With his creative artistry inspired by the Spirit, David is the forerunner of the use of the folk arts in worship and church renewal. What was born in the rustic solitude of minding flocks of sheep became the lasting heritage of Jewish and Christian worship.

When David brought the ark to Jerusalem (1 Chr 15:1—16:43), he inaugurated a curious and momentous interlude in the history of Israel's worship. He placed the ark in a simple tent on Mount Zion, while Zadok and his fellow priests continued the daily sacrifices in the tabernacle at Gibeon. His action introduced a period of glorious, inspired, informal worship in Israel, marked by singing, stringed instruments, tambourines, dancing, and rejoicing, in which women took part as well as men. It was in this context that David's personal skill as a musician was communicated to an entire community of worshipers, giving birth to the psalter as Israel's songbook or "book of praises" (*sepher tehillim*), its Hebrew title. In turn, the rise of the psalter bequeathed to the Christian church its great heritage of psalmody and praise.

David's placing of the ark in a tent on Mount Zion created an interim situation in which the ark (representing the immediate presence of God) and the altar (representing the Mosaic sacrifices) were separated. During David's rule in Jerusalem, the sacrifices continued to be performed in the tabernacle at Gibeon until the consecration of Solomon's temple, when ark and altar were reunited (2 Chr 5:2–14).

In this fascinating interlude, the Davidic worshiper offered to God sacrifices of praise ("the fruit of lips that openly profess his name," Heb 13:15), rather than animal sacrifices. Worship involved the playing of musical instruments, singing, dancing, and infectious joy, little mentioned in earlier descriptions of Israelite worship. Psalm 68 was composed to celebrate this festive movement from Mount Sinai to Mount Zion, from Mosaic sacrifices to Davidic praise.

Inspired by the experience and joy of God's nearness, the charismatic renewal movement took up the theme of "Davidic worship": worship with Hebrew rhythms in the immediate presence of the Lord. In the forefront of this phenomenon were Toronto- and later Jerusalem-based musicians Merv and Merla Watson, cofounders of the International Christian Embassy, Jerusalem in 1980 and its annual Feast of Tabernacles celebration.[18]

---

18. See Watson and Watson, *Songs from Jerusalem*, Vols. 1 and 2. The ICEJ's other founders were Jan Willem van der Hoeven, warden of the Garden Tomb, and George Giacumakis, director of the American Institute of Holy Land Studies, now Jerusalem

Inspired by the prophetic vision of the Gentile nations coming up to worship God in Jerusalem in the latter days (Zech 14:16), the Watsons began the Feast celebration in 1979. It has become the most colorful and most notable expression of Davidic worship. Before starting it, Merv and Merla contacted a leading rabbi in Jerusalem for advice. Surprised, he said to them, "Our prophets declare that in the Messianic times, Gentiles will come to Jerusalem to celebrate this feast with us. When you asked me today how to celebrate Sukkot, I am hearing the footsteps of Messiah, that he is coming."[19]

## Renewal of the Folk Arts

Today, wherever the Spirit of God is poured out in the church, the church is rejuvenated, made new. What is old, familiar, tired, and stale becomes refreshed, invigorated, and enlivened. There is a surge of creativity. Above all, there is a recovery of participatory music and art forms.

The 1970s saw an extraordinary revival of folk music and the folk arts in the charismatic renewal movement. There was a flowering of music with folk rhythms and directness of expression, in the Jesus People movement, the music of groups like the Second Chapter of Acts and the Fisherfolk, and the revival of Jewish worship by the Watsons. There was even a revival of worship dance—something unheard of in Victorian Christianity, but not absent from the Bible! There was a resurgence of drama, mime, and puppet shows in worship and evangelism—including the open-air theater provided by the Riding Lights Theatre Company that made David Watson's ministry in St. Cuthbert's and St. Michael-le-Belfrey next to York Minster world famous. There was a revival of the visual arts, in what was still largely a pre-television culture.

The finest flower of this awakening of Christian worship and expression came from the Post Green Community in Dorset, England and the Community of Celebration on the isle of Cumbrae, Scotland.[20] Their experience was enshrined in a large book, *The Folk Arts in Renewal*, by Patricia Beall and Martha Keys Barker. It was the fruit of ten years' experience in new expressions of worship and praise, inspired by the Holy Spirit at the height of the charismatic renewal movement. "The materials in this book," Beall writes, "are the treasures we have unearthed both in our community workshops and through the travelling ministry of the Fisherfolk."[21] It contained readings on drama, improvisation workshops, creativity, dance, music, songwriting, and worship.

This renewing work of the Holy Spirit is much-needed in the arts in today's church and society. We have all but lost the artistic and musical freshness that the charismatic renewal movement rediscovered in the 1970s. What was cutting edge then, has grown stale today. The culture of many churches has moved from acoustic instruments and participatory congregational worship, including singing in tongues, to amplified performance music for audience entertainment but with little or no opportunity for congregational participation. At the same time, pop culture is

---

University College (King, "The Feast," 8).

19. Bühler, "Footsteps of Messiah."
20. Durran, *Wind at the Door*.
21. Beall and Barker, *Folk Arts in Renewal*, "Introduction."

moving in the direction of totalitarianism—a conformist, sexualized, herd-mentality, meeting in large-scale orgiastic events dominated by loud, rhythmic music and the idolizing of celebrities.

In such a situation, we need a fresh move of God's Holy Spirit to bring a further renewal of personal creativity and enrichment of the arts in the Christian community. For where the Spirit of the Lord is, there is true freedom (2 Cor 3:17).

## Empowering Leaders

The Old Testament not only presents the Holy Spirit as the inspirer of creative artists but also as the enabler of selected leaders. This too has prophetic implications, anticipating later developments.

## All God's People Prophets?

Numbers 11 contains one of the great stories of the Old Testament. It tells how a harried Moses complained to God about his workload and job conditions. God took some of the Spirit that was on Moses and put it on seventy of Israel's elders so that they could share in the leading of the people and Moses would not have to carry the burden alone (Num 11:16–17, 24–30).

There is a touch of humor in the story. Two elders—Eldad and Medad—did not assemble at the tabernacle with their colleagues when this redistribution of the Spirit took place. When the Spirit rested on the assembled elders, the two recalcitrants also began to prophesy. A young man rushed up to report that something unusual was happening. "Eldad and Medad are prophesying in the camp." The Spirit had even come on the two individualists who hadn't gathered with their colleagues at the tent of meeting!

Their report did not faze Moses. Unlike the disciples who told Jesus that someone who was not a member of their group was casting out evil spirits (Luke 9:49–50), he showed none of the possessiveness that mars the ministry of some church leaders today, and none of the defensiveness that characterizes some anti-charismatics. "Are you jealous for my sake?" he asked. "I wish that all the Lord's people were prophets and that the Lord would put his Spirit on them!" (Num 11:29).

The Holy Spirit is so wonderful that it is hard to imagine why anyone would not want to experience the Spirit's blessings, joys, gifts, and graces! Would that all God's people were prophets and that the Lord would put his Spirit on them all!

## Empowering Israel's Leaders

Compared with what we now enjoy in Christ, the Old Testament records three significant limitations in describing the activity of the Holy Spirit. These are important to note, to appreciate how unique are the privileges granted to believers now through faith in Jesus Christ.

### 1. *The Spirit Was for Leaders Only*

In the Old Testament, the Spirit was a source of inspiration for leaders. Even when the Spirit that was on Moses was distributed to others, it was to enable these seventy elders to share in the leadership of God's people. The extension of the Spirit's empowerment to Moses was granted to other leaders only, not to the wider community of Israel. Moses longed for all God's people to experience the Holy Spirit—but that wish would not begin to be granted till the day of Pentecost.

### 2. *The Spirit Rested on, Not in Those Leaders*

The Bible's language is precise. The Old Testament uses the preposition *on*, not *in* when describing the Holy Spirit's empowerment of people. "I will take some of the power of the Spirit that is *on* you and put it *on* them" (Num 11:17). "The Lord . . . took some of the power of the Spirit that was *on* him and put it *on* the seventy elders" (Num 11:25a). "When the Spirit rested *on* them, they prophesied" (Num 11:25b). This characteristic is particularly vivid in the case of Gideon, where the Hebrew text says that the Spirit of the Lord "*clothed*" him or "wrapped itself around him" (*labshah*, Judg 6:34).[22]

*On*, not *in*. This language denotes an external endowment of the Spirit's power, not an internal indwelling of the Spirit's presence, as happens when we believe in Jesus. There are two modes of the Holy Spirit's activity: *empowerment* and *indwelling*. Both are real, but they are distinct. The empowerment of the Spirit is for leadership and ministry—to make us effective in God's service. The indwelling of the Spirit is for relationship and intimacy—to give us a close and personal relationship with God. We need to distinguish the Spirit's empowerment from the indwelling of the Spirit that occurs when we become a Christian. The latter is for salvation; the former is for service.

---

22. I remember the New Zealand Old Testament scholar, George A. F. Knight, paraphrasing this verse: "The Spirit of the Lord wrapped itself around Gideon like a cloak."

The only exceptions to this pattern, approaching a presence of the Spirit *in* people in the Old Testament, are two sages whose wisdom is attributed to the *rûach* of God. After Joseph had interpreted Pharaoh's dream, Pharaoh asked his officials, "Can we find anyone like this man, one in whom is the Spirit of God?" (Gen 41:38). Similarly, after Daniel interpreted his dream, King Nebuchadnezzar says that "the spirit of the holy gods is in him" (Dan 4:8). Both tributes come from pagan rulers who had been challenged by dramatic events to recognize God's hand at work. By the time of the New Testament, wisdom comes to be associated more with the divine *Logos* (John 1:1–4), through the personification of wisdom in Proverbs 8:22-23, "The Lord brought me forth as the first of his works, before his deeds of old; I was formed long ages ago, at the very beginning, when the world came to be," though the association with the Spirit continues in the word of wisdom (*logos sophias*).

### 3. The Spirit's Endowment Was Temporary, Not Permanent

The Old Testament describes the endowment of the Spirit for leadership and service as being for a limited time only, not a permanent or enduring one. In the days of the Old Testament, the Spirit came as a special empowerment upon selected individuals to lead the nation at times of national crisis. God raised up leaders like Joshua (Num 27:15–23), Othniel (Judg 3:9–10), Gideon (Judg 6:33–35), Samson (Judg 14:6, 19), Saul (1 Sam 10:10–13), and David (1 Sam 16:13), and anointed them with his Spirit to lead his people for a time.

The Spirit came on these leaders with a charismatic endowment of power for their particular task or mission. When that task was accomplished, the Spirit's empowerment was withdrawn. It would not be until the coming of Jesus Christ that the Spirit would dwell in and remain permanently on a human being. The permanent indwelling of the Spirit is something that Jesus inaugurates and alone makes possible.

The impermanence of the Spirit's empowering is especially evident in the case of Samson, who "did not know that the Lord had left him" (Judg 16:20), and Saul, from whom "the Spirit of the Lord had departed" (1 Sam 16:14). But the impermanence does not minimize the reality and significance of the Spirit's anointing for leadership and service. This is particularly evident in the case of Gideon. The Spirit takes a shy, reserved person and transforms him into a courageous leader who destroys his father's idols and leads the oppressed and demoralized Israelites to a great victory over the marauding Midianite invaders. Gideon led them in a revival of faith in God and a stunning victory over their enemies. He did so not by human strength or wisdom, but with a force of only three hundred fighters, by following a divinely given strategy, and through the guidance of God's Spirit by way of a vision, a dream, and confirmatory miracles (Judg 6–7).

## Charisma and Character

Two Old Testament stories contrast dependence on the Holy Spirit with reliance on human resources or human strength.

### *The Story of Samson*

Samson was a man greatly gifted by God, but who fooled around and squandered his gifts (Judg 13–16). The Spirit of God from early in his life endowed him with superhuman strength. But many times we see Samson wasting this precious anointing in foolish exploits, loutish stunts, petty vendettas, and playing loose and fast with women. He never achieved his great potential. He is a lasting lesson to us that charisma must be matched by character.

### *The Story of Saul*

Saul's loss of the anointing of the Spirit, and the transference of the anointing and the kingship to David, is one of the most tragic stories in the Bible (1 Sam 9 through 2 Sam 9). The contrast between these two people is a contrast between "the flesh" and "the spirit." Saul was a physically handsome and imposing man, who stood "head and shoulders" above his fellow Israelites (1 Sam 9:2; 10:23, NRSV). But David, agile and small of stature, was "a man after God's own heart" (1 Sam 13:14).

Saul was a man of the flesh. Like many well-endowed people, he grew self-reliant and proud. He became moody, despondent, obsessive, and jealous of David's successes.

David, by contrast, was a man of the Spirit. Despite his faults, he loved God, was a pioneer of praise worship, was admired as a team leader, showed immense flair and courage, and led Israel in many victories in battle. He defeated the giant Goliath with a sling and a single stone when Saul and the Israelites were cowering intimidated in their tents. He introduced praise in the immediate presence of God on Mount Zion, inaugurating Israel's psalter and foreshadowing our contemporary experience of charismatic worship.

# 4

# Jesus and the Holy Spirit

*The first indication in the Bible that God's Spirit will dwell permanently in human beings is in the messianic prophecies of the Old Testament. The New Testament shows how these prophecies are fulfilled by Jesus. At his baptism by John the Baptist, the Holy Spirit descends on Jesus to equip him for his healing ministry and saving death. In this event, Jesus is inaugurated as Messiah. From this point on the Spirit indwells him fully, marking him—in a reality overlooked by the church's traditional Christology—as the Spirit-filled human being and baptizer in the Spirit, the one qualified to communicate the Spirit to others.*

THE MOST SUCCINCT AND illuminating summary in the Bible of Jesus' life and ministry is the one given by Peter in his explanation to the Gentile enquirer Cornelius, a devout Roman officer who came to him seeking to learn more about God. Peter's account emphasizes the role of the Holy Spirit in Jesus' public ministry:

> God anointed Jesus of Nazareth with the Holy Spirit and power, and . . . he went around doing good and healing all who were under the power of the devil, because God was with him. (Acts 10:38)

This anointing of Jesus with the power of the Spirit took place at his baptism by John the Baptist. Peter says it was the secret of his good works and his ministry of healing and deliverance.

## The Spirit before Christ

### Empowering Israel's Leaders

Before the coming of Jesus, as we have seen, the Spirit came as a special empowerment upon selected individuals chosen by God to lead the nation of Israel at times of national crisis. Examples were Joshua, who led Israel in its conquest of the promised land; Gideon, who led a demoralized Israel in a great rout of the Midianite invaders from trans-Jordan; Samson, the erratic playboy who led raids against their Philistine conquerors from the coastal plain; and Saul and David, Israel's first kings.

We saw that there were two noteworthy characteristics of this empowerment: it was *impersonal*, an endowment of power for service, and it was *impermanent*, withdrawn when the task was accomplished, or, in the case of Saul, when he turned from God's purpose and lost his anointing. In each of these people, the Spirit of God came with a charismatic endowment of power for a particular task, which was withdrawn when that task was forfeited or accomplished.

### Indwelling Israel's Messiah

There is one notable exception to this picture in the Old Testament, and it is to be found in the group of Old Testament prophecies that foretell the coming of Israel's Messiah, God's chosen and "anointed" future world leader.

The word "Messiah," from the Hebrew *Māshiach*, means, "anointed one." The reference is to the commissioning, with the pouring on of anointing oil, of the priests of Israel (Lev 8:12; 10:7; 21:10, 12) or its kings (1 Sam 10:1; 16:13; 1 Kgs 1:39). This commissioning conferred God's authority on the priests or kings for their sacred office. It is the kingly rather than the priestly role which is emphasized in Israel's messianic prophecies, though the priestly one will emerge after Jesus' death. The Old Testament hope for the Messiah springs from the expectation of a kingly rule which will be forever, foreshadowed in the remarkable prophecy of Nathan to King David. "I will raise up your offspring to succeed you, your own flesh and blood, and I will establish his kingdom.... Your house and your kingdom shall endure for ever before me; your throne shall be established for ever" (2 Sam 7:12, 16). In Nathan's prophecy, it is not just a dynasty, but an individual who is promised. The idea of the Messiah and his worldwide reign of justice, peace, and prosperity is developed by the Psalms and prophets, especially in the Solomonic psalm, Psalm 72, and by the prophet Isaiah.

There are three messianic prophecies, all from the book of Isaiah, and all speak of the special role the Holy Spirit will play in the life of this coming leader.

The first is from Isaiah 11:1–4:

> A shoot will come up from the stump of Jesse;
> from his roots a Branch will bear fruit.
> The Spirit of the Lord will rest on him—
> the Spirit of wisdom and of understanding,
> the Spirit of counsel and of might,
> the Spirit of knowledge and fear of the Lord—
> and he will delight in the fear of the Lord.
> He will not judge by what he sees with his eyes,
> or decide by what he hears with his ears;
> but with righteousness he will judge the needy,
> with justice he will give decisions for the poor of the earth.

This passage speaks descriptively in the third person. The Spirit of the Lord *"will rest on him,"* as a permanent factor in his life and as a source of wisdom, counsel, and impartiality in his administration of justice.[1]

The second passage is Isaiah 42:1–4:

> Here is my servant, whom I uphold,
> my chosen one in whom I delight;
> I will put my Spirit on him,
> and he will bring justice to the nations.
> He will not shout or cry out,
> or raise his voice in the streets.
> A bruised reed he will not break,
> and a smoldering wick he will not snuff out.
> In faithfulness he will bring forth justice;
> he will not falter or be discouraged

---

1. Some commentators link this prophecy with the seven spirits or sevenfold Spirit in the book of Revelation (Rev 1:4; 3:1; 4:5; and 5:6), the seven branches of the lampstand or menorah (Exod 25:31–40; Rev 4:5), and the seven colors of refracted light. The image of spectral light is particularly suggestive of diversity in unity. The sevenfold gifts of the Spirit—wisdom, understanding, counsel, fortitude, knowledge, piety, and fear of the Lord—were often mentioned by patristic and medieval writers.

till he establishes justice on earth.

In his law the islands will put their hope.

In this passage, God speaks in the first person of a chosen servant in whom he would delight, and on whom he would put his Spirit to bring justice to the nations and the distant islands, not with force, but with gentleness.[2]

The third messianic prophecy is Isaiah 61:1–3:

> The Spirit of the Sovereign Lord is on me,
>
> because the Lord has anointed me
>
> to proclaim good news to the poor.
>
> He has sent me to bind up the brokenhearted,
>
> to proclaim freedom for the captives
>
> and release from darkness for the prisoners,
>
> to proclaim the year of the Lord's favour
>
> and the day of vengeance of our God,
>
> to comfort all who mourn,
>
> and provide for those who grieve in Zion—
>
> to bestow on them a crown of beauty
>
> instead of ashes,
>
> the oil of joy
>
> instead of mourning,
>
> and a garment of praise
>
> instead of a spirit of despair.

Here too, the Holy Spirit is the wellspring of the mission and ministry of the Messiah. Because the Holy Spirit is "on" him and has "anointed" him, the Messiah will have a ministry to the poor, to the brokenhearted, to captives, to prisoners, and to the downtrodden of the earth.

Uniquely, this is the only messianic prophecy that speaks of the Messiah in the first person, completing a sequence of the three prophecies. In the first, the Messiah is spoken of in the third person. In the second, God speaks in the first person about the Messiah as an object of his delight. In the third, the Messiah speaks in the first person about himself: "The Spirit of the Sovereign Lord is on *me*."

In the synagogue of his hometown of Nazareth, Jesus took the Isaiah scroll, unrolled it, looked up this prophecy, read it, and declared it to be

---

2. Not lording it over and brutalizing people, like Gentile tyrants, but exercising justice with gentleness and mercy, as Jesus taught his followers (Luke 22:25).

fulfilled in the hearing of his listeners (Luke 4:18–19).[3] As Messiah, Jesus offers a new intimacy with God, a presence of the Holy Spirit which is permanent and personal, bringing healing through the Spirit's anointing and inaugurating a season of good news and grace.

The content of these messianic prophecies is different from what we have observed elsewhere in the Old Testament. In them, the Spirit's relationship to the Messiah is personal, not impersonal, and permanent, not temporary. The messianic prophecies describe the Spirit as dwelling permanently on this special individual, the chosen leader of God's people.

## Jesus and the Spirit

In fulfilling these messianic prophecies, Jesus inaugurates a new relationship between the Holy Spirit and humanity. His installation as Messiah reveals that he is the special recipient of the Holy Spirit, who is thus qualified to be the unique giver of the Spirit to others. John the Baptist, whose historical mission it was to introduce the Messiah to the world, is the one who first recognized and spoke of these two aspects of Jesus' messiahship.

### Jesus as Receiver of the Spirit

The word "Christ" (*Christos*) is the Greek equivalent of the Hebrew word *Māshiach*, "Messiah," meaning "anointed one" (Luke 2:11, 26). "Christ" is not Jesus' surname. It is his title and function. Jesus is the promised Messiah—the leader who is anointed and empowered by the Spirit of God for his mission to Israel and the nations. "God anointed [*echrisen*] Jesus of Nazareth with Holy Spirit and power [*pneumati hagio kai dynamei*]" (Acts 10:38). This anointing is both the meaning of the term "messiah" and what constitutes Jesus as Messiah.

John's Gospel tells us that John the Baptist recognized Jesus as the Messiah by the fact that the Spirit came on him at his baptism in the Jordan River and *remained* on him. John testified: "I saw the Spirit come down from heaven as a dove and remain on him. And I myself did not know him,

---

3. Significantly, Jesus stops reading after proclaiming "the year of the Lord's favor," and does not pronounce "the day of vengeance of our God." It seems that he was consciously inaugurating the era of his own ministry of grace and mercy, and postponing the day of God's judgment. Joachim Jeremias sees this as the offence which provoked the violent reaction of his audience. "The good news was their stumbling block, principally because Jesus had removed vengeance on the Gentiles from the picture of the future" (Jeremias, *Jesus' Promise to the Nations*, 45.)

but the one who sent me to baptize with water told me, 'The man on whom you see the Spirit come down and remain is the one who will baptize with the Holy Spirit.' I have seen and I testify that this is God's Chosen One" (John 1:32–34).

All four Gospels record the Spirit's descent on Jesus. Myk Habets notes that three of the evangelists, drawing on Isaiah 42:1, record that the Spirit came "upon him" (*ep auton*, Matt 3:16, Luke 3:22, John 1:32). But Mark says the Spirit entered "into him" (*eis auton*, Mark 1:10).[4] The Spirit descends, comes upon and enters into Jesus. Thus the relationship of the Spirit to Jesus is not an external one, but a permanent indwelling.

So with Jesus, a new relationship of God's Spirit to humanity begins. All the Spirit, the totality of the Spirit without limitation, rests on and dwells in his human person. John says, "God gives [him] the Spirit without limit. The Father loves the Son and has placed everything in his hands" (John 3:34–35). Paul says, "God was pleased to have all his fullness dwell in him" (Col 1:19), and adds, "For in Christ all the fullness of the Deity lives in bodily form" (Col 2:9). So Jesus is not only the Son of God. He is the completely Spirit-filled human being.

## Jesus as Giver of the Spirit

Because he is the Anointed One, the Spirit-filled Messiah, Jesus is also the Anointing One, the one who baptizes others with the Holy Spirit. John the Baptist was told by God, who sent him to baptize, "The man on whom you see the Spirit come down and remain is the one who will baptize with the Holy Spirit" (John 1:33). So John the Baptist said, "I baptize you with water. But one who is more powerful than I will come, the straps of whose sandals I am not worthy to untie. He will baptize you with Holy Spirit and fire" (Luke 3:16). John recognized that the empowerment and fullness of the Spirit that Jesus has himself received, he will impart to others.

Jesus, too, made this clear at the messianic feast, the Feast of Sukkot or Tabernacles. At the high point of the festival, when water was poured out and prayers were made for rain, Jesus stood up and said, "Let anyone who is thirsty come to me and drink. Whoever believes in me, as the Scripture has said, rivers of living water will flow from within them." John, the Gospel writer, adds, "By this he meant the Spirit, whom those who believed in him were later to receive" (John 7:37–39).

---

4. Habets, *The Anointed Son*, 135. Cf. Hawthorne, *The Presence and the Power*, 127.

It is because Jesus is the Spirit-anointed Messiah, the Spirit-filled man, that he is qualified and equipped to be the Baptizer in the Spirit, the one who imparts the Holy Spirit to others.

This truth, clearly attested in the Gospels, never featured in the classical two-nature formulations of the church's Christology in the fourth and fifth centuries. Pentecostal scholar Frank Macchia suggests that the early theologians were wary of highlighting Jesus' reception of the Spirit at the Jordan because of its role in the adoptionist heresy.[5]

There are certain similarities with views later condemned as adoptionist. The *Shepherd of Hermas* (c AD 150) argued that Jesus was a virtuous man chosen by God, united with the Spirit, who was adopted by God as a Son and exalted to Lordship. Theodotus (c AD 190) said that Jesus was a man born of a virgin through the operation of the Holy Spirit, whose piety of life was approved by God when the Holy Spirit descended on him at his baptism, giving him power for his ministry, and who was declared to be Son of God by his resurrection. The Synod of Antioch condemned such views in AD 268, because they did not recognize the continuing divine identity of the incarnate Jesus and looked on him merely as an inspired man. The adoptionists, though, claimed that their views had once been dominant in Rome and had been handed down by the apostles.[6]

The recovery of the understanding of Jesus as the Spirit-anointed and Spirit-baptizing man was due to the nineteenth-century Scottish minister Edward Irving (1792–1834). Much misunderstood and maligned in his time, Irving is now recognized as a remarkable precursor of the modern charismatic renewal movement.[7] Alasdair Heron observes that those who seek an adequate basis for a Pentecostal theology could benefit from studying him.[8] Unlike Theodotus, who regarded Jesus as a "mere man" (*psilos anthropos*), Irving maintained that Jesus was indeed the Son of God. But being the Son of God, he divested himself of his divine prerogatives of innate holiness and the power to work miracles when he "made himself nothing" to become incarnate as a human being (Phil 2:6–7). In his incarnate life he achieved holiness not because of his inherent virtue as the Son of God, but as a human being, by resisting the Tempter and overcoming temptation. Likewise, he performed miracles not by his innate power as the Son of God, but as a human being endowed with the Holy Spirit.

In 1833 Irving was accused of heresy and deposed by the Presbytery of Annan from the Church of Scotland ministry for denying the sinlessness of Jesus' humanity. He strenuously denied this charge. His contemporaries failed to grasp what he was maintaining about Jesus overcoming sin in the flesh. "The point at issue is simply this," he explained during the controversy, "whether Christ's flesh had the grace of sinlessness and incorruption from its own nature, or from the indwelling of the Holy Ghost; I say the latter."[9] This accords with the account of Jesus' obedience in the book of Hebrews. He was "tempted in every way, just as we are—yet he did not

---

5. Macchia, *Jesus the Spirit Baptizer*, 190.
6. Vos, "Adoptionism," 13–14.
7. Strachan, "Theological and Cultural Origins," 17–28; Roxborogh, "As at the Beginning," 17–23.
8. Heron, *The Holy Spirit*, 111.
9. Quoted by MackIntosh, *Person of Christ*, 277.

sin" (Heb 4:15). It was "through the eternal Spirit" that he "offered himself unblemished to God" (Heb 9:14).

Irving set forth his views in *The Orthodox and Catholic Doctrine of Our Lord's Human Nature* (1830). His opponents, he says, "argue for an inherent holiness; we argue for a holiness maintained by the person of the Son, through the operation of the Holy Ghost." "All creation is sinful," he acknowledged. "The person of the Son of God was born into it, he restrained, withstood, overcame this co-operation of a sinful creation, conquered the conqueror, and won it back to God.... This is the great theme which we maintain."[10] Irving held that Jesus was indeed sinless. But his sinlessness was not innate, in virtue of his divinity. Having emptied himself of his divine prerogatives, his sinlessness was acquired and achieved, by actively resisting temptation and overcoming sin. If he had not done this in our fallen humanity, our fallen humanity would not have been redeemed and reconsecrated to God.[11]

In *Christ's Holiness in Flesh* (1831), Irving approached Jesus' signs, wonders, and miracles in the same way. He saw them not as the exercise of innate divine power, but as being accomplished by Jesus through the power of the Holy Spirit imparted to him by God the Father at his baptism. "From the time of his baptism with water and the Holy Ghost, he became the man of the Spirit, . . . and now his work was to contend with spiritual wickedness in all these forms, with Satan personally, with demons inhabiting men, with diseases, with storms and tempests and every created thing." Jesus received "the adoption of Son of God publicly at his baptism, and is now to use his body for the more glorious end of commanding and subduing the rebellious creation, . . . which also was an original design in the creation of man, to have dominion."[12] From his baptism onwards, Jesus is the Spirit-filled man who overcomes the destructive activity of Satan and liberates afflicted people by his miracles of healing and deliverance.

## Jesus Our Prototype

Because Jesus is the preeminent Spirit-filled and Spirit-imparting human being, he is also the prototype of the Spirit-filled person. As Gerald Hawthorne points out, Jesus is not only our Savior. He is "the supreme example . . . of what is possible in a human life because of his own total dependence upon the Spirit of God."[13] Indeed, he is not only our example. He is our incentive to live a Spirit-filled life and to exercise a Spirit-empowered ministry.

10. Irving, *Our Lord's Human Nature*, x–xi; quoted by Strachan, *Theology of Edward Irving*, 37. I had long discussions with Gordon Strachan about Irving's Christology in 1971, during my years of postgraduate study at New College, Edinburgh, when he was working on his doctorate on Irving.

11. Irving's emphasis is reminiscent of the formula of Gregory of Nazianzus in the fourth century: "What has not been assumed has not been healed" (Gregory, *Ep.* 101.32).

12. Irving, *Christ's Holiness in Flesh*, 24–26; quoted by Strachan, *Theology of Edward Irving*, 50. Cf. Gen 1:26, 28; Ps 8:6; 1 Cor 15:27; Eph 1:22; Phil 3:21a.

13. Hawthorne, *The Presence and the Power*, 234. The Catholic theologian Heribert Mühlen also affirms that "Jesus' baptism of the Spirit" is the "prototype of our renewal

When I was young, I used to think that Jesus was holy and sinless because he was the Son of God. I thought that Jesus healed the sick, cast out evil spirits, and worked miracles because he was God's Son; that it was his divinity that gave him this innate holiness and power. Thinking like this, I drew the conclusion: he was God; it was a pushover for him. But I am not God. I am just a human being. Therefore, I cannot be holy like Jesus or heal the sick like Jesus.

Since being baptized in the Holy Spirit, I have come to see that the Scriptures teach a different view of Jesus. My charismatic view is quite different from my childhood one. Jesus is and remains forever the unique and only begotten Son of God. But immortality, immunity from weakness and temptation, and the ability to work miracles were the very prerogatives of being the Son of God that he laid aside when he "emptied himself" (*heauton ekenōsen*) and became a human being like us (Phil 2:6–7, RSV).

Having relinquished these abilities when he became incarnate, Jesus won them back and received them back as a human being, in the limitations of our humanity, by the same means that are available to us. Besides his devout upbringing, these included his submission to his parents, his growth in learning, his acquired knowledge of the Scriptures, his worship of God, his life of prayer, his discernment of God's call, his obedience to the Father, his resisting the Tempter, his refusing society's expectations, and his overcoming temptation. All this was made possible through the impartation of the Holy Spirit at his baptism, by his active obedience to the Father throughout his life and ministry, by his faithfulness to death, and by his trust in God's ultimate vindication.

Jesus, the Son of God, became fully human, like us in all respects except that he did not sin. As a human being, he experienced all that we experience, including temptation and death, except that, unlike us, he overcame sin and triumphed over death. As the book of Hebrews says, "For we do not have a high priest who is unable to empathize with our weaknesses, but we have one who has been tempted in every way, just as we are—yet he did not sin" (Heb 4:15).

Gerald Hawthorne's contribution to what may be called a charismatic Christology has been developed as a contribution to New Testamant scholarship without reference to Edward Irving and seemingly without knowledge of his earlier contribution. In broad outline, though, it provides independent support for Irving's arguments. Hawthorne wants to avoid any association with the radical kenotic Christologies put forward by the nineteenth-century continental theologians. Instead, he associates more with such British thinkers as Vincent Taylor and Brian Hebblethwaite. In becoming a human being, Hawthorne says, "The Son of God willed to renounce

---

in the Spirit" (Mühlen, *Charismatic Theology*, 92).

the exercise of his divine powers, attributes, prerogatives, so that he might live fully within those limitations which inhere in being truly human."[14]

The incarnation means that the Son of God fully entered our humanity. "The Word *became flesh*" (John 1:14, my emphasis). This means that the Son of God was incarnate as a Jewish man within all the social, cultural, political, and religious distinctives of his place and time.[15] More generally, as Hawthorne explains, it means that the Son of God was incarnate within all the limitations of our human condition:

> God the Son... actually thought and acted, viewed the world, and experienced time and space events strictly within the confines of a normally developing human person. Under these conditions of humanness it is possible to dare to say that God—God the Son—learned as we learn, felt as we feel, laughed as we laughed, was surprised as we are surprised, suffered to the full our sorrows and disappointments, hurt as we hurt, died as we die. "He wove up his life, as each of us must, out of the materials that were to hand."[16]

An entirely different view of Jesus is presented in the apocryphal *Infancy Gospel of Thomas*, dating from a late Syriac manuscript of the sixth century. One of its stories describes Jesus making clay birds. Jesus claps his hands, and his birds spring to life and fly away.[17] This gratuitous and fanciful act, also recorded in the Qur'ān (5:110), where Jesus breathes on them rather than claps his hands,[18] presents Jesus as a larger-than-life and precocious child. It underlines, by contrast, the appropriateness and sobriety of Luke's account of Jesus' childhood and the miracle stories in the canonical Gospels. The Gospel miracles are never described as acts of self-display. They are always performed for a particular purpose or in response to human need. They are not represented as issuing from a mythical demigod, but from a sympathetic human being who operates in a power greater than his own. Invariably such deeds raise questions about his identity and authority. "Who is this? Even the wind and waves obey him!" (Mark 4:41). "Who gave you authority to do this?" (Mark 11:27).

In the New Testament Jesus is not only presented as our Savior but as our ministry exemplar, our pattern for Christian living and service. How he lived and overcame temptation, how he ministered and healed the sick, how he suffered and served God faithfully to the end is how we as Christians are meant to live and minister in the power of the Spirit. As the Scottish charismatic theologian Tom Smail says in his excellent discussion of this issue, "In both Christ and us the Spirit is working with the stuff of our common

---

14. Hawthorne, *The Presence and the Power*, 208.

15. As emphasized by David Flusser in *The Sage from Galilee*, and the Jerusalem School of Synoptic Research, over against the Gentilized picture of Jesus that has prevailed through the centuries.

16. Hawthorne, *The Presence and the Power*, 210, quoting Farrer, *Celebration*, 89.

17. James, *Apocryphal New Testament*, 49.

18. Parrinder, *Jesus in the Qur'ān*, 83–85.

humanity; because he is man and we are men, it becomes possible and credible that what the Spirit did first in him, he should be able to do again in us."[19]

## The Case of Mary Campbell

There is a little-known historical incident that illustrates the implications of such a charismatic view of Jesus.[20] Mary Campbell (1806–39) was a devout, theologically literate young woman dying of an incurable lung disease. She came under the influence of Edward Irving's teaching about the humanity of Christ and the power of the Holy Spirit in 1829 in Fernicarry, on the Gare Loch, in southwest Scotland.

She reasoned, if Jesus as a human being like me preached and performed mighty deeds by the power of the same Holy Spirit who is promised to me, then I, in the same humanity as his and by the same Spirit, ought to do the same works which he did and even greater works as he promised (John 14:12).

Having thought this through and come to this conviction, one Sunday in March 1830, while praying with a sister and a woman friend, the enfeebled Mary Campbell spoke "in an unknown tongue, to the astonishment of all who heard, and to her own great edification and enjoyment in God."[21]

Some days later, James McDonald, a thirty-year-old family friend, wrote Mary Campbell a letter describing how he had prayed for the healing of his sister Margaret. James described coming to his sister's bedside and commanding her, in a free rendering of Psalm 20:8 (KJV): "Arise and stand upright!" As Mary came to the part of the letter where this command was described, "every word came home with power," and she rose from her couch healed.[22]

The next morning James was at the Port Glasgow dock to meet the ferry from the Gare Loch. Imagine his surprise to see Mary Campbell, who had come to tell him what had happened![23]

---

19. Smail, *Reflected Glory*, 63.

20. David Dorries notes that the revival associated with Mary Campbell "cannot be found in most textbooks, not even those focussing on revival movements" (Dorries, "West of Scotland Revival," 1192).

21. Irving, "Recent Manifestations of Spiritual Gifts," 759–60, quoted by Strachan, *Theology of Edward Irving*, 66.

22. Norton, *Memoirs of James and George Macdonald*, 109–10, quoted by Strachan, *Theology of Edward Irving*, 67–68.

23. Dallimore, *Life of Edward Irving*, 105–6.

# 5

# The Spirit in Christ and Christians

*Jesus came as the Lamb of God to take away sins, and as the Baptizer in the Spirit to equip his followers for God's service. These two roles correspond to the two modes of the Spirit's activity in Jesus, enabling his human incarnation and empowering his public ministry. The Spirit is the agent of Jesus' virgin birth and of the Christian's new birth or regeneration. The Spirit anointed Jesus before his public ministry and empowers Christians for effective service. This parallel between the Spirit's role in Jesus and in Christians offers a way to resolve misunderstandings between evangelicals and Pentecostals over the work of the Holy Spirit. But the conflation of these two realities has the effect of quenching expectation that there is more of the Spirit to be experienced in our lives.*

## The Spirit in Christ

### The Spirit and Jesus' Birth

THE INFANCY NARRATIVE IN Luke's Gospel, tenderly written by a medical doctor and historian, describes how Jesus was miraculously conceived by the power of the Holy Spirit, although his mother Mary was a virgin. The angel said to her, "The Holy Spirit will come on you, and the power of the Most High will overshadow you. So the holy one to be born will be called the Son of God" (Luke 1:35).

So Jesus, God's Son, owed his human life on earth to the supernatural action of the Holy Spirit. Acting on Mary at his conception, the Holy Spirit makes her child the Son of God in human form. The Spirit enables the miraculous birth and incarnation of the Son, giving to Jesus' humanity a capacity for God that our unaided fallen human nature does not possess. The Spirit initiates the restoration of our humanity to God.

> Caesarea is the most likely location for the writing of the first part of Luke-Acts, Luke's two-part history of the origin of the Christian movement, where he could have conducted his research during the two-year delay of Paul's case. Where Matthew gives Joseph's viewpoint of Jesus' birth, Luke gives that of Mary, suggesting that he interviewed her at this time. The infancy narratives breathe the simple piety and national culture of a devout Jewish home. As a medical doctor Luke would have had the respect and discretion to conduct an interview about childbirth. He mentions Jesus' circumcision and even the detail of swaddling cloths or diapers, the kind of things a doctor would notice. Such color and attention to detail confirm we are dealing with Jewish historical reality, not Hellenistic mythology, in the account of Jesus' conception. Moreover, Luke shows more interest in the Holy Spirit than Matthew and Mark, the other synoptic writers.[1]

## The Spirit and Jesus' Baptism

But Jesus was not only born of the Holy Spirit. Luke goes on to describe how, when he was "about thirty years old," Jesus was impacted by the Holy Spirit at his baptism by John the Baptist, before he began his public ministry.

John the Baptist's appearance was a revival of prophecy after a silence of four centuries. He even resembled the Old Testament prophets. He lived and dressed like the prophet Elijah. His stirring revival preaching called on his hearers to return to God and prepare for the one who was to come, drawing vast crowds from the surrounding region and from the city of Jerusalem (Matt 3:5; Mark 1:5). Though Jesus called him the greatest man who ever lived (Matt 11:11; Luke 7:28), he still does not receive the recognition he deserves as the originator of the Christian movement. John preached up the wave that Jesus surfed. He even bequeathed to Jesus his first disciples (John 1:35–42).

There is a startling dissonance in Jesus' request for baptism at the hands of John the Baptist. John's baptism was "a baptism of repentance for the forgiveness of sins" (Luke 3:3). It was for people whose lives were at

---

1. This section draws on the insights of the charismatic Bible teacher David Pawson, *Unlocking the Bible*, 829–35.

variance with God's will, who had done wrong, who were conscious of their wrongdoing and were turning from it. Indeed, John required of his candidates evidence of changed lives (Luke 3:8, 10–14). But Jesus' life was not at variance with God's will. He had done no wrong. He did not need to repent. He had no sins to be forgiven. He did not need to change his way of life. So why was he baptized?

It would seem that in associating with those who were being baptized, Jesus chose to identify with fallen human beings, with those he had come to save. His baptism was his identification with sinners, the beginning of his assuming the role of our Savior and sin-bearer. As Frank Macchia says, "He stepped into solidarity with sinners in their need to repent, or in their fallenness. . . . He did not need to repent or convert; but he stepped into those waters of repentance in identification with those who did."[2]

Jesus' baptism was a further stage in his self-emptying, a necessary step to becoming our Savior. He had to identify with sinners before he could make atonement for our sins. As Paul later explains, he who was without sin became sin for us (2 Cor 5:21). Jesus' baptism was an extraordinary act of self-humbling. Symbolically, he took this step of identification with humanity at the lowest point on earth.[3]

John the Baptist remonstrated with Jesus and tried to deter him from being baptized, recognizing that this was inappropriate for the holy one of God. In reply, Jesus stressed that it was right and fitting, "proper for us to do this to fulfill all righteousness" (Matt 3:15). Heribert Mühlen suggests that Jesus wanted to signify at the beginning of his public activity that his vocation was not an assertion of his own will or initiative, but a response to his Father's call. "Jesus lets John's baptism happen to him as something he . . . *accepts*, in order to testify that he is proclaiming, not himself, but the Father."[4] By being baptized, Jesus accepts his Father's will and calling.

In turn, God the Father dramatically acknowledges, in speech and sign, this act of surrender and consecration by Jesus. "As he was praying, heaven was opened and the Holy Spirit descended on him in bodily form like a dove. And a voice came from heaven: 'You are my Son, whom I love; with you I am well pleased'" (Luke 3:21–22). By this symbol and affirmation, the Father publicly authenticated Jesus as the unique bearer of the Spirit. It is as if a dad were to say to his son: "Great move, boy! Right on!"

---

2. Macchia, *Jesus the Spirit Baptizer*, 232, drawing on Barth, *CD*, IV, 4, 59.

3. Similarly he will disclose that he is the Spirit-anointed Messiah at Caesarea Philippi, the source of the River Jordan, and reveal his divine glory on Mount Hermon, the highest place in Israel. Even the geography of the Gospels has meaning in the saga of the world's redemption.

4. Mühlen, *Charismatic Theology*, 96–97.

Jesus' experience at the Jordan must have been decisive for his awareness of divine sonship and of being the unique bearer of the Spirit. Michael Green observes that "the content of this voice is even more amazing than its occurrence," and is a "combination of two famous Old Testament texts."[5] The first part, "You are my Son," echoes Psalm 2:7, where God addresses the king as "my Son," affirming Israel's messianic hope for a ruler who would make the nations his inheritance and the ends of the earth his possession. The second part, "with you I am well pleased," alludes to Isaiah 42:1, "Here is my servant, whom I uphold, my chosen one, in whom I delight."

The divine affirmation that begins Jesus' ministry encourages him in the dual role of the messianic Son and the Suffering Servant—the first time these two roles had ever been combined. Jesus must have meditated on these words as he pondered the nature of his ensuing mission. In contrast to current messianic expectation, he would have realized that the path of the conquering world ruler would be that of service, through gentleness and justice, suffering and sacrifice, identification with sinners and atonement of their sins. On him the Father would lay the iniquity of us all (Isa 53:6).

Myk Habets says, "With the anointing of the *ruach* of God, Jesus's relationship to God is clearly authenticated as one of Sonship, and God's relationship to Jesus, as one of Father." He also recognizes that there is "an incipient Trinitarianism" in the account of Jesus' baptism: "God speaks and the Spirit descends on the man Jesus."[6] Eastern Orthodox iconography acknowledges this by depicting the historical event of Jesus' baptism as the "New Testament Trinity."[7]

From this point on, Jesus is described as being "full of the Holy Spirit" (Luke 4:1). After a period of fasting and temptation, engaging the prince and principalities of darkness, he emerges from anonymity and begins his public ministry in Galilee "in the power of the Spirit" (Luke 4:14). The result is immediate effectiveness: authoritative teaching, a power encounter, a miracle of deliverance, healings, and spontaneous popular acclaim (Luke 4:31–41). The empowerment of the Spirit propels Jesus from a private life of anonymity into a public ministry with little time for himself.

## The Spirit and Jesus' Messiahship

The descent of the Holy Spirit at his baptism marks Jesus' commissioning as Messiah, God's anointed leader. His messianic ministry begins from this point. In Gerald Hawthorne's perceptive observation, he "came to the Jordan as Jesus of Nazareth and left it as the Messiah of God."[8] Hawthorne believes that Jesus had no idea ahead of time that this event would be the

---

5. Green, *Holy Spirit*, 33–34.

6. Habets, *The Anointed Son*, 137.

7. See Yule, "Icons as Christian Art," 209.

8. Hawthorne, *The Presence and the Power*, 134.

decisive break with his hometown and his family, that this would be his stepping out of obscurity onto the stage of history into a mission of ultimate significance.[9]

The Hebrew term *Māshiach* and the Greek *Christos* mean "anointed one." Just as the kings of Israel were anointed with oil and commissioned for their task, so Jesus, the long-expected Messiah-deliverer, is anointed with the Spirit of God at his baptism and equipped with power and authority for his divine mission. It was the permanence of this endowment of Spirit that indicated to John the Baptist that Jesus was the Messiah, the uniquely Spirit-filled and so Spirit-imparting man. John had been told by God, "The man on who you see the Spirit come down *and remain* is the one who will baptize with Holy Spirit" (John 1:33).

From this point on in his life, Jesus is conscious of being the Lord's Messiah, enjoying an intimate and personal relationship with God's Spirit. Heribert Mühlen says, "We may assume that the prophetic-charismatic endowment of Jesus made its complete breakthrough at his baptism in the Jordan, for it is from that point that he came on the scene as the Spirit-filled prophet, bearing witness publicly to his unique Abba-experience."[10]

Jesus returns to Galilee "in the power of the Spirit, and news about him spread through the whole countryside" (Luke 4:14). In the synagogue of his hometown, Nazareth, he selects and reads the only messianic prophecy where the Messiah speaks in the first person, indicating his awareness of fulfilling this role. "The Spirit of the Lord is on *me*, because he has anointed *me*" (Luke 4:18–19, quoting Isa 61:1–2).

## The Spirit and Jesus' Ministry

The impartation of the Spirit also marks the beginning of Jesus' ministry. After this event, he begins to exercise a new power to expel evil spirits and heal the sick (Mark 1:21—2:12; Luke 4:31–41; 5:17–26). As a result, his fame spreads and crowds gather wherever he goes. He calls his disciples, who will lead his movement when he is no longer here, and begins to teach about the growth of the kingdom of God, from small beginnings to a world-changing enterprise.

Gerald Hawthorne describes the decisive change that came as a result of Jesus being filled with the Holy Spirit. "According to the Gospel writers, Jesus, from the moment the Spirit descended to him, became aware of a new power within him, a power to save, to heal, to bind the strong man and overturn his evil designs (Matt 12:29). He became aware of having a new authority to teach and preach (Mark 1:22), to release . . . those held captive by sin (Matt 9:6),

---

9. Hawthorne, *The Presence and the Power*, 131–32.
10. Mühlen, *Charismatic Theology*, 92.

to command unclean spirits to come out of tortured people (Luke 4:36). He became aware that from this moment a new age had dawned, that the old age was on its way out, that the time (*kairos*), God's time, was now being fulfilled, that the kingdom of God was at hand (Mark 1:15)."[11]

The kingdom of God becomes the distinctive theme of Jesus' preaching. The inbreaking of God's rule is reinforced by his ministry of exorcism. The presence and activity of God's Spirit is decisive in this demonstration of God's authority. As Jesus explains when his ministry of deliverance was being questioned and misrepresented, "If it is by the Spirit of God that I drive out demons, then the kingdom of God has come upon you" (Matt 12:28). He rejects the accusation of his critics that he was casting out demons by Beelzebul, the prince of demons, in the strongest terms as a "blasphemy against the Spirit" (Matt 12:31).

Jesus was aware that the power of the Spirit was the decisive factor in his demonstration of the kingdom of God. "Here the presence of the kingdom (which constitutes the distinctive note in Jesus' proclamation) is defined in terms of the effective power of the Spirit working uniquely through Jesus. The end-time rule of God can be said to be already operative because the end-time power is evidently at work conquering demonic power. There were other exorcists, but their work did not bear the same significance (Matt 12:28; Luke 11:19). Jesus' exorcisms were so effective that he was able to conclude that his was the power of the end-time rule of God."[12]

There is a curious reference in Luke's Gospel that only makes sense if we take Jesus' empowerment by the Holy Spirit seriously. Luke records on one occasion that "the power of the Lord was with Jesus to heal the sick" (Luke 5:17). This suggests that even Jesus knew seasons of greater anointing. The Holy Spirit, as John O'Donnell recognizes, "did not indwell him in a static way. The Spirit's presence was dynamic and made itself felt in the humanity of Jesus at significant moments of his life and ministry."[13]

Because the Jewish leaders who assembled on this occasion came from throughout the entire country, Messianic Jewish teacher Arnold Fruchtenbaum believes this was an official delegation summoned by the Sanhedrin to check out Jesus' messianic credentials, following his performance of an earlier miracle, the healing of a Jewish leper (Matt 8:2–4; Mark 1:40–45; Luke 5:12–16). "One day Jesus was teaching, and Pharisees and teachers of the law were sitting there. They had come from every village of Galilee and from Judea and Jerusalem" (Luke 5:17). If Fruchtenbaum is right, this incident has particular importance in validating Jesus' authority.[14]

---

11. Hawthorne, *The Presence and the Power*, 133.
12. "*Pneuma*," in *NIDNTTE* 3:810.
13. O'Donnell, "In Him and over Him," 31, quoted by Habets, *The Anointed Son*, 139.
14. Fruchtenbaum, *Yeshua*, 281–83. I thank Lindsay Robertson for helping me

This was the occasion when a paralyzed man was lowered through a hole in the roof because his friends had no other way of getting him to Jesus because of the size of the crowd, swelled by the official delegation. It is amusing to think of these important dignitaries being caught up in the falling dust and debris! Fruchtenbaum points out that Jesus used a form of rabbinic logic called *kal v'chomer*, "from difficult to easy." By doing the harder (healing the paralytic), he proved that he had the right to say the easier ("your sins are forgiven").[15] In this impressive manner, he demonstrated his divine authority as God's agent and Messiah to forgive sin. Luke the doctor wishes to emphasize that this momentous miracle and demonstration in the presence of the Jewish leaders was made possible by a special measure of the power of the Spirit.

Later, Peter, when summarizing Jesus' ministry for the Gentile convert Cornelius, explains that the Holy Spirit was the source of his extraordinary ministry and the reason for its effectiveness. "God anointed Jesus of Nazareth with the Holy Spirit and power, and . . . he went around doing good and healing all who were under the power of the devil, because God was with him" (Acts 10:38). Though Jesus was the Son of God (John 1:34), he ministered in dependence on the Holy Spirit, not out of his divine nature.

It is the anointing of the Holy Spirit that constitutes Jesus as Israel's Messiah, God's anointed world ruler. In contrast to the earlier charismatic leaders and kings of Israel, the presence of the Holy Spirit in Jesus is both *permanent* and *personal*. This fulfills what was foretold in messianic prophecy and inaugurates a new relationship between the Spirit and humanity. The Spirit makes him the Spirit-filled man and the Baptizer in the Spirit. As Messiah, he receives the fullness of the Spirit from God. As the Baptizer, he is qualified to impart this fullness to others (John 1:33; Luke 3:16).

## Jesus' Twofold Work

John the Baptist's historical role was to introduce Jesus to the world. His prophetic announcement intimates that Jesus would accomplish a twofold work. As the Lamb of God, he would take away the world's sin. As the Spirit-filled man, he would baptize his followers with Holy Spirit (John 1:29–34). Jesus would die for our salvation *and* equip us for his service.

The first aspect of Jesus' work is primarily negative. His death on the cross as the sinless Lamb of God was to "*take away* the sin of the world" (John 1:29). He came to remove all that has corrupted people's lives. The second aspect of Jesus' work is primarily positive. As the Spirit-filled man on whom the Spirit came down and remains, he "*will baptize* with Holy

---

locate this reference.

15. Fruchtenbaum, *Yeshua*, 285–86.

Spirit" (John 1:33). He came to immerse or fill his followers with his Holy Spirit.

| Table 1 Jesus' Twofold Work | |
|---|---|
| To "take away sin" | To "baptize with Holy Spirit" |
| Savior from sins | Baptizer in the Spirit |
| The negative aspect of his ministry | The positive aspect of his ministry |
| A work of emptying and removal | A work of filling and renewal |
| Involves our cleansing | Involves our consecration |
| Bestows forgiveness | Bestows fruitfulness |
| Took place at Calvary | Took place at Pentecost |
| The result of Jesus' incarnate and earthly life | The result of Jesus' ascended and heavenly life |
| "I will cleanse you from all your impurities" (Ezek 36:25) | "I will put my Spirit in you" (Ezek 36:27) |
| "Without the shedding of blood there is no forgiveness" (Heb 9:22) | "Apart from me you can do nothing" (John 15:5) |
| The evangelical aspect of the gospel | The Pentecostal aspect of the gospel |
| Necessary for eternal salvation | Normative for effective service |

The evangelical wing of the Christian church rightly emphasizes Jesus' role as Savior. Unless Jesus had lived a perfect life as the sinless Lamb of God, made himself responsible for our wrongdoings, and offered his life as a sacrifice for the sins of the world, there could be no forgiveness of sins. This is necessary for our eternal salvation. But Jesus' role as Baptizer in the Spirit, rightly emphasized by the Pentecostal wing of the church, continues to be overlooked by many evangelicals. Yet this dimension is equally necessary if we are to be effective in Christian service.

"You will receive power when the Holy Spirit comes on you," said the risen Jesus to his disciples, "and you will be my witnesses in Jerusalem, and in all Judea and Samaria, and to the ends of the earth" (Acts 1:8). Such a mission, the progressive transformation of the whole world, is an enormous challenge. "A powerless church can hardly consider it," says Clark Pinnock. "It presupposes the anointing and empowerment of the Spirit."[16]

God never intended us to serve him in our own strength. To think otherwise is an expression of deep-seated pride and self-sufficiency. God

---

16. Pinnock, *Flame of Love*, 147.

intends us to serve in his strength—in the power and fullness of the same Spirit who rested on Jesus, by whom he performed his miracles of healing and did his mighty works. Unless we are baptized in (or with) Holy Spirit, we are powerless to do what Jesus did, let alone the even greater works that he promised we would do when he left the limitations of this life and returned to his Father (John 14:12).

There is no shortcut to success in the Christian life. We must be emptied of what is impure and unclean before we can be filled with what is pure and holy. Without cleansing, there can be no consecration. Without forgiveness, there can be no fruitfulness. Unless we put off the old life, we cannot put on the new (Eph 4:22–24). As Jesus made clear in his analogy of the vine and the branches, God must prune the deadwood in our lives to make us fruitful and productive (John 15:1–8). "There is no way to Pentecost except by Calvary."[17]

A story from my childhood may serve to illustrate this twofold work of Jesus. I grew up in a small rural township in the south of New Zealand, where there was no town water supply. Our water was collected from the house roof or pumped from an underground bore. It was stored in two large linked tanks, each holding 600 gallons (2,700 liters) of water, which sat on a wooden tank stand behind the house.

One day we complained about the taste of the water. My Dad climbed up to have a look. Floating on the surface were the decomposed remains of a dead blackbird! So Dad put on his swimming togs, got into the putrid tank, and removed the bung from the bottom. Water poured out, all over the back lawn! As it drained out, and we played mudslides on the grass, Dad got a scrubbing brush and cleaned the slime off the sides of the tank. When it was clean and empty, he put back the bung, turned on the pump, and began to fill the tanks with clean water from the bore. The pump toiled away for several days till they were full again.

This is a picture of what Jesus came to do. According to John the Baptist, Jesus entered our corrupt and putrid world to *take away sin* (John 1:29) and to *fill us with Holy Spirit* (John 1:33). Both are an essential part of the Christian message. Jesus' taking away sins is a work of removal—like emptying the impurities from the tank. Jesus' baptizing with Holy Spirit is a work of renewal—like filling the tank with fresh water. It is not God's intention that a Christian be clean but empty, saved but ineffective. God wants to fill all believers with Holy Spirit—with his life-giving resources for effective service.

---

17. Smail, *Reflected Glory*, 105 (an interpretation given of Smail's first public utterance in tongues).

## The Spirit in Christians

### The Spirit and Christian life

John's Gospel says that Christian believers are "born of God" (1:13) or "born of the Spirit" (3:5, 8). John does not mention the virgin birth. But it seems clear from his language that he wishes to establish an analogy between our new birth as Christians and the special nature of Jesus' birth. Just as Jesus' birth as a human being originated in a miraculous conception by the Holy Spirit without normal human procreative activity, so Christians are "born anew" or "born from above" (John 3:3, 7; cf. Titus 3:5) through a miracle of divine agency, the action of the Holy Spirit. It is this new birth by the Spirit that makes us "children of God" and gives us a share in God's "eternal life"—central themes in the Johannine writings (John 1:12; 3:16; 1 John 3:1–2).

There is a clear parallel between Jesus' birth and the new birth or regeneration of a Christian believer. Both are the result of a divine agency and initiative accomplished by the Spirit. Jesus was conceived by the Holy Spirit. He who was the Son of God owed his existence as a human being to an act of God's Spirit. Similarly, Christians are "born anew," "born from above," by the action of the Holy Spirit. We who are human owe our participation in God's life to the Spirit. Jesus' natural environment was heaven. He needed a supernatural birth by the Holy Spirit to become a child of Mary and share in our humanity. Our natural environment is earth. We need a supernatural birth to become children of God and share in God's divine life.

> The careful language of John's Gospel underlines the parallel between Jesus' virgin birth and our new birth as Christians. The Holy Spirit is the agent of both. Without a miracle wrought by the Spirit, Jesus, who is divine by nature, could not have become a human being. In the same way, without a miracle of the Spirit's mysterious activity in our lives, we who are human by nature could not receive divine life and become "children of God" (John 1:12–13). This Johannine passage specifically and comprehensively rules out human lineage and action, using terms—natural descent (*ex haimatōn*), sexual desire (*thelēmatos sarkos*), and male agency (*thelēmatos andros*)—that suggest a direct analogy with the virgin birth, which John otherwise does not mention in his Gospel. As William Temple says, "Nothing can explain the quite peculiar phrasing of this passage except the supposition that it refers to the Virgin Birth of our Lord."[18]
>
> Against such evidence, Presbyterian theologian Dale Bruner rejects the analogy between the virgin birth of Christ and the regeneration of Christians, dismissing it without further comment as "unfortunate and christologically inappropriate."[19] Tom Smail disagrees, saying that "the parallel is very much to the point." He adds, "The making of a Christian, like the making of the

---

18. Temple, *Readings*, 13.
19. Bruner, *Theology of the Holy Spirit*, 222.

Christ, is a creative miraculous act of the Holy Spirit, giving our nature a capacity for God that in its fallenness it does not have, and cannot give itself."[20]

According to Jesus, to enter the "kingdom of God"—the realm where we experience God's reality—we need a new birth (John 3:3, 5–8). This is not just a new or second birth but a birth "from above" (*anōthen*). The Greek phrase "is designedly ambiguous and suggests also a transcendent experience *born from above*" as well as *born anew*.[21] "Flesh gives birth to flesh," says Jesus, "but the Spirit gives birth to spirit" (John 3:6). As the Good News Bible translates this passage: "A person is born physically of human parents, but . . . born spiritually of the Spirit." We receive human life and enter the human family by natural birth. We receive eternal life and enter God's family by supernatural birth. The agent of this regeneration is the Holy Spirit, for only God can give eternal life, the life of God himself.

## The Spirit and Christian Service

It is surely notable that Jesus, even though he owed his life to the Holy Spirit, did not begin his ministry until he was filled with the Spirit. The same is true of his apostles. He told them to stay in Jerusalem and not begin the great task of world evangelization until they had been "clothed with power from on high" (Luke 24:49). It would be the Holy Spirit's power which would equip them in this great task to be his witnesses "to the ends of the earth" (Acts 1:8).

Just as the Holy Spirit empowered Jesus for his itinerant public ministry of healing the sick, casting out evil spirits, and preaching the good news of the kingdom of God, so God provides us with the necessary resources of the Spirit to make our Christian witness effective. Recognizing that Jesus ministered in the power of the Spirit should be a vital incentive for us as Christians to be filled with the Holy Spirit too. At the very least, it should give pause for thought: if he, the incarnate Son of God, needed the enablement of the Spirit for his ministry, how much more do we mere humans! God never intended us to serve him in our own unaided strength. Through Jesus, God has provided the baptism and fullness of the Holy Spirit so that we can serve him in the Spirit's power and effectiveness.

## The Dual Role of the Spirit

The Holy Spirit's twofold role in the life and ministry of Jesus parallels the two essential things that the Spirit desires to do in our lives as Christians: *to*

---

20. Smail, *Reflected Glory*, 82–83. (Smail cites the wrong page number in Bruner's book.)

21. "*Anōthen*," BDAG 92.

*give us new birth* (John 3:1-8) and *to baptize us with Holy Spirit* (Luke 3:16). The New Testament makes it clear that these are two distinctive operations or modes of the Spirit's activity in our lives, and that Jesus is our pattern for both. As they are distinct and important in the life and ministry of Jesus, so they are for us as Christians.

Though he dismisses the appropriateness of the analogy of the Spirit's role in Christ and Christians, Bruner gives a clear and even persuasive presentation of it. But his statement is interspersed with pejorative comments that predispose his readers to reject it. I have put these in square brackets, to give the argument its proper force. "The Messiah himself ... passed through two great experiences with the Spirit: conception, enduement with power. The Messiah's career serves then as the perfect model for all later Christians [who wish to be more than Christians in name or conception only]. This model should teach Christians to [be dissatisfied with being merely Christians; they should strive to] come to the place reached by their Lord, and by all the earliest Christians, the place where the Spirit can[, a second time, intersect their lives and] give them power to fulfill their specific, God-designed tasks."[22] When the gratuitous innuendos are removed, this is as good a summary of my viewpoint as I could compose myself.

I speak of two modes or operations of the Spirit, not a "second blessing." Clark Pinnock notes that the description of charismatic empowerment as a "second blessing" arises because of the neglect of this aspect in Christian initiation. The problem is less with the Pentecostal terminology than with the defective counsel of the historic churches regarding the full reality of initiation as described in the New Testament. Conversion, he says, "is too often unempowering and not experientially life-changing. In such cases it is usually not the second blessing that is abnormal, but the deficient initiation."[23]

The parallelism between the role of the Spirit in Christ and the role of the Spirit in Christians should be recognized by Christian theology and evangelism. It is patently obvious, yet it is ignored or ridiculed. It should be viewed as an accepted datum of theology, because it forms a christological pattern and prototype of the Christian life. It should also feature as a controlling factor in evangelistic counseling, to ensure that new converts are properly grounded, fully initiated into all that God offers them, and not deprived of divine resources to maximize their effectiveness.

Ideally, new Christians should be encouraged to be baptized with the Spirit when they are counseled for salvation. They should be told that there are two things the Holy Spirit wishes to do in their lives: firstly, to bring about their new birth, giving them a share in Christ's life, and secondly to bestow on them new power, making them effective in Christ's service. They

---

22. Bruner, *Theology of the Holy Spirit*, 68. The double entendre in the use of the word "conception" is particularly regrettable, for it reflects badly not only on the Christians so described, but also on Jesus.

23. Pinnock, *Flame of Love*, 169.

should be told that the former is *necessary* for eternal salvation, and that the latter is *normative* for effective service.

Just as Jesus was born of the Spirit, but did not begin his ministry until the Spirit came upon him, so every new Christian should be instructed to seek his means of divine empowerment, and invite the Spirit to come on them. When they are born anew, they will enjoy the Spirit's *presence*; when they are baptized in Holy Spirit, they will experience the Spirit's *power*. Their faith should be encouraged by telling them that what the Spirit can do in and through them will be immeasurably greater and more wonderful than anything they can do in their own unaided abilities.

## Conflating these Realities

This christological pattern and prototype of the Christian life is overlooked in two influential modern works on Christian initiation. Both conflate the distinctive regenerative and empowering modes of the Spirit's activity into a single action and identify the baptism of the Holy Spirit with regeneration. The effect of such identification is to quench expectation that there is more of the Spirit to be experienced in one's later Christian life.

Karl Barth does so in the last fragment of the *Church Dogmatics* to be published before his death. He rightly defines conversion, in a brief but powerful section on the beginning of the Christian life, as "the divine change," "impossible with men but possible with God," "in which a man becomes God's friend instead of his enemy, a man who lives for him instead of being dead for him."[24] He recognizes that what makes this divine change possible is the Holy Spirit. The Holy Spirit gives a person "the freedom, ability, willingness and readiness" to live for God, makes a person "open, seeing, hearing, comprehending" of all that Jesus Christ has done for them, bearing witness with our human spirit that we are children of God (Rom 8:16).[25]

All this is what I, in common with evangelical theology, understand as regeneration. But Barth uses "the baptism with the Holy Spirit" as an omnibus term for all that is involved in the beginning of the Christian life, including its charismatic dimension. "We thus regard it as legitimate to understand by the baptism of the Holy Ghost, without prejudice to its special meaning and scope, the divine preparation of man for the Christian life in its totality."[26] Barth includes within this "the fullness of the *charismata* of the one community."[27]

Barth describes the *charismata* of 1 Corinthians 12 and Romans 12 briefly, but in a way that is consistent with their meaning in the charismatic renewal movement, which was just beginning when he wrote. "Through their distribution each individual Christian—independently

---

24. Barth, *CD*, IV, 4 (1969), 13.
25. Barth, *CD*, IV, 4, 27–28.
26. Barth, *CD*, IV, 4, 31.
27. Barth, *CD*, IV, 4, 38.

of the particularity of his natural character or personal concerns—receives his own special spiritual power and therewith his own special task in the total life and ministry of the community."[28]

Barth distinguishes baptism with the Holy Spirit from baptism in water. In so doing he takes a courageous stand against baptismal regeneration—the view of the historic churches of Christendom that water baptism makes one a Christian, rather than the Spirit's agency in regeneration and awakening personal faith in Christ.[29]

But Barth combines the Spirit's role in regeneration with the Spirit's role in giving the *charismata*, using "baptism with the Holy Spirit" as a general initiatory term. As we will see in chapter 7, this term does not appear in the New Testament, which always uses the verbal form "baptize in Holy Spirit" to convey the dynamism of one's initial charismatic empowerment, as distinct from the Spirit's role in regeneration. The term "baptize in Spirit" is always used of an endowment of power, not to describe the new birth.

In his book *Baptism and Fulness: The Work of the Holy Spirit Today*, John Stott also identifies baptism in the Spirit with regeneration. Stott, like Barth, rightly affirms that "the Christian life is life in the Spirit." "It would be impossible to be a Christian," he says, "let alone live and grow as a Christian, without the ministry of the gracious Spirit of God." The new birth "is a birth of the Spirit," and the Spirit "comes himself to dwell within us." These realities are "the common possession" of all Christians.[30]

But when it comes to baptism in the Spirit, Stott claims that the phrase "to have been 'baptized' with the Spirit is a vivid figure of speech for to have 'received' the Spirit." Thus he regards baptism in the Spirit as an experience "which all Christians have had" at the time of their conversion, regardless of whether they show any evidence of it or not.[31] Like Barth, Stott's interpretation consists in collating all the references to the activity of the Spirit in Christians, without regard to their different circumstances, under the omnibus term "baptism of the Spirit." "All Christians receive the Spirit at the very beginning of their Christian life."[32] What of postconversion experiences of the Spirit? Stott is adamant. Because "baptism with the Spirit" is an initiatory term, "it cannot be the right expression to use for them."[33]

Stott's examination of particular cases smacks of special pleading. The nuanced and varied situations described in the book of Acts are forced into a theological schema. The two-stage experience of the one hundred and twenty on the day of Pentecost (Acts 2:1–13) was "due simply to historical circumstances." The two-stage experience of the Samaritan believers at the hands of the apostles was to ensure that the ancient division between Jews and Samaritans would not continue in the church (Acts 8:14–17). The two-stage experience of the Ephesian "disciples" is illusory because they had not even been converted (Acts 19:1–7).[34] Against the evidence of these

28. Barth, *CD*, IV, 4, 38.

29. The conflation of Spirit baptism with water baptism is also rejected by Dunn, *Baptism in the Holy Spirit*, 19, 227–28; and Macchia, *Jesus the Spirit Baptizer*, 194.

30. Stott, *Baptism and Fulness* (1975), 19. Stott specifically denies rumors that his views have changed since the publication of the first edition (1964), 9.

31. Stott, *Baptism and Fulness*, 21.

32. Stott, *Baptism and Fulness*, 36.

33. Stott, *Baptism and Fulness*, 44.

34. Stott, *Baptism and Fulness*, 28–36. Stott's "fundamental principle" of biblical interpretation, reflected in his understanding of these passages, is "to begin with the

texts, Stott concludes that "neither a two-stage experience nor laying on of hands is the norm for receiving the Spirit today."[35]

Another well-known London preacher, Dr. Martyn Lloyd-Jones, has trenchantly criticized the identification of baptism in the Spirit with regeneration. "There is nothing... that so 'quenches' the Spirit as the teaching which identifies the baptism of the Holy Ghost with regeneration. It is said that the baptism of the Holy Spirit is 'non-experimental,' that it happens to everyone at regeneration.... So we say, 'Ah well, I am already baptized with the Spirit; it happened when I was born again, at my conversion; there is nothing for me to seek, I have got it all.' Got it all? Well, if you have 'got it all,'... why are you so unlike the New Testament Christians?"[36]

Such teaching, says Lloyd-Jones, "is false." It destroys expectancy and quenches the Spirit, because it deprives believers of any expectation and motivation that there is more of God to be sought and experienced in the Christian life. "The apostles were regenerate before the day of Pentecost. The baptism of the Holy Ghost is not identical with regeneration; it is something separate. It matters not how long the interval between the two may be, there is a difference.... But if you say that they are identical, you do not expect anything further."[37]

From the Catholic viewpoint, Gregorian University theologian Francis Sullivan also questions the assumption that in baptism, the sacrament of initiation, "we receive a 'total gift of the Spirit,' including all the graces and charisms that we are ever going to have, and that subsequently all that happens is that some or all of these gifts 'break through into conscious experience.'"[38] He does not accept that Catholic theology requires us to believe that new sendings of the Spirit can only take place through the sacrament of baptism. Indeed, he quotes St. Thomas Aquinas to the contrary.

To the question whether we can speak of a sending of the Spirit to a person in whom the Spirit is already indwelling, Aquinas answers: "There is an invisible sending also with respect to an advance in virtue or an increase of grace... as, for instance, when a person moves forward into the grace of working miracles, or of prophecy, or out of the burning love of God offers his life as a martyr, or renounces all his possession, or undertakes some other such arduous thing."[39] Sullivan, who quotes this passage, concludes, "There is no reason why Catholics, who believe that they have already received the Holy Spirit in their sacramental initiation, should not look forward to new sendings of the Spirit to them."[40]

It is surely significant that Jesus taught the importance of expectancy if we are to grow in spiritual experience. "Blessed are those who hunger and

---

general, not the special" (31). This is particularly inappropriate when dealing with the Holy Spirit, who not only blows where he wills, but whose ministry is to human beings in the particularity of their pastoral circumstances and to persons in their uniqueness and individuality.

35. Stott, *Baptism and Fulness*, 33.
36. Lloyd-Jones, *Christian Warfare*, 280.
37. Lloyd-Jones, *Christian Warfare*, 280.
38. Sullivan, *Charisms and Charismatic Renewal*, 69.
39. Aquinas, *Summa Theologiae*, I, q.43, a.6, ad 2um.
40. Sullivan, *Charisms and Charismatic Renewal*, 71.

thirst for righteousness, for they will be filled" (Matt 5:6). "Ask and it will be given to you; seek and you will find; knock and the door will be opened to you. For everyone who asks receives; the one who seeks finds; and to the one who knocks, the door will be opened" (Matt 7:7–8; cf. Luke 18:1–8). "Let anyone who is thirsty come to me and drink" (John 7:37).

I can testify that it was only because of persistent seeking that I was baptized in the Holy Spirit, in what I later discovered to be a classic instance of a midlife post-conversion experience as a mature Christian.[41]

---

41. For this phenomenon, see Lawson, *Deeper Experiences of Famous Christians*, which describes the experiences of Girolamo Savonarola, Madame Guyon, Francois Fénelon, John Bunyan, John Wesley, George Whitefield, Charles Finney, George Müller, Francis Ridley Havergal, A. J. Gordon, D. L. Moody, William Booth, and Johann Christoph Blumhardt.

# 6

# The Spirit as Presence and Power

*In his farewell discourse, Jesus said that he must go away so that "another Paraclete" could come, who would not only be "with" his followers but "in" them. Jesus makes it clear that the coming of the Holy Spirit is dependent on his ascension or return to the Father. The Spirit was not given when he was on earth, but when he ascended to heaven; when the localized presence of his incarnate life was replaced by the universal presence of his ascended state. A surprising feature of New Testament references to the Spirit, obscured in translation, is the use or omission of the definite article, the former pointing to the Spirit's presence or indwelling and the latter to the Spirit's power or enabling. This distinction is reflected in Paul's teaching about the Spirit's "fruit" and "gifts."*

THE MOTTO OF THE international Christian organization, the Navigators, is "To know Christ and make him known." This motto summarizes what Jesus teaches about the role of the Holy Spirit. According to Jesus' farewell discourse, his "last will and testament" before he died (John 14–16), the role of the Holy Spirit is to make Christ known to us, and to enable us to make Christ known to others:

"He will glorify me because it is from me that he will receive what he will make known to you.... The Spirit will receive from me what he will make known to you" (John 16:14–15).

When the Advocate comes, whom I will send to you from the Father—the Spirit of truth who goes out from the Father—he will testify about me. And you also must testify . . ." (John 15:26–27).

The Spirit makes Christ real to us and helps us make Christ real to others.

## An Abiding Presence

It was just hours before his death that Jesus gave this teaching about the Spirit. He explained to his disciples that he would soon leave them. But he would not leave them as orphans (John 14:18). He had to go away so that the Spirit could come to them (John 16:7). He promised that he would not leave them alone without his presence, to continue his work in their own strength. He would send "another *Paraclete*" to help them (John 14:16–19).

The word *Paraclete* which Jesus uses here to refer to the Holy Spirit (translated "Advocate" in the New International Version), comes from two Greek words—*para*, "beside," and *kaleō*, "to call." The Holy Spirit is the one who is called to stand beside us, a person summoned to our aid, someone who appears on our behalf.[1] The word suggested a defence counsel in a legal trial and was often translated *advocatus* ("advocate") in Latin translations. It means an "advisor," "advocate," "defender," "helper," or "assistant," rather than the term "comforter" used in the King James Version. The Spirit will speak on our behalf, assist us to give an account of our faith, especially when it is difficult to do so when we face opposition or persecution.

Jesus said he would send us "*another* Paraclete"; that is, another helper than himself. When Jesus was alive, he was present with his disciples, training them to continue his work when he had gone. During his ministry, while with them physically, he could only be in one place at a time. He could not be with people in Galilee and Judea, in Capernaum and Jerusalem, at the same time.

But after his death, Jesus promised that "another Paraclete" would come, the Holy Spirit, who would not be limited to one time and place, but will be with believers "forever" as a universal spiritual presence (John 14:16). Jesus could not remain on earth permanently, and even if he could

---

1. "*Paraklētos*," BDAG 766: "one who is called to someone's aid," "one who appears in another's behalf," "mediator," "intercessor," "helper."

have, he could only be in one place at a time. God's abiding and universal presence is only possible if Jesus' physical presence is replaced by the spiritual presence of the Holy Spirit.

"The Paraclete is the presence of Jesus when Jesus is absent," says Raymond Brown.[2] There is a sense in which this is so. Yet such language must be used with care, for the Spirit is not a second Jesus. In speaking of the Spirit as "*another* Paraclete" (John 14:16), Jesus himself draws attention to the distinctiveness of the Spirit, both in the nature of his person and in the form of his activity. The Spirit will point to Jesus and remind Jesus' followers of his teaching (John 14:26; 15:26). But the Spirit is not identical with Jesus. The Spirit is unique, different, and in some way, "other." John McIntyre, noting the precision of John's language, says, "There is nothing vague or shadowy here; rather are we in the presence of the whole power of God operating in a third way, completing the work of the Son as the Son has perfected the work of creation."[3]

"Unless I go away," Jesus says, "the Paraclete will not come to you; but if I go, I will send him to you" (John 16:7). More is involved in this saying than merely that "the earthly ministry of Christ must be completed before the Spirit comes."[4] Jesus here says that "the departure of the Incarnate Son to the Father was a necessary condition of the coming of the Spirit from the Father."[5] It is "as if the one were somehow impossible without the other, as if the Ascension, the withdrawal from the space-time in which our present senses operate, of the incarnate God, were the necessary condition of God's presence in another mode."[6] Without the ascent of the Son, there could be no descent of the Spirit.

Writing from the perspective of Jesus' resurrection and ascension, the Gospel writer says there was "no Spirit," no coming or outpouring of the Spirit, until Jesus had been glorified. Explaining the meaning of Jesus' words at the Feast of Tabernacles about "streams of living water flowing from within" the believer, John says that "he said this about the Spirit, whom those who believed in him were later to receive. For there was no Spirit yet, because Jesus was not yet glorified" (John 7:39, literal translation).[7] John is aware of the difference between the limited physical presence of Jesus during his earthly life and the universal presence that comes with the Holy Spirit.

Moreover, Jesus says there will be a change in the mode of God's presence among believers, a change from "with" to "in." Before Jesus' baptism, the Spirit came only occasionally *on* selected individuals. During Jesus'

---

2. Brown, "The Paraclete in the Fourth Gospel," 128.
3. McIntyre, *Shape of Pneumatology*, 71.
4. Hendry, *Holy Spirit*, 22.
5. Swete, *Holy Spirit in the New Testament*, appendix E, 373.
6. Lewis, *Reflections on the Psalms*, 106.
7. Yves Congar favors punctuating this passage so that "'the rivers of living water' flow from the heart of the Messiah, not from the believer" (Congar, *I Believe in the Holy Spirit*, 1:50). But the more natural rendering affirms that those who quench their spiritual thirst at the spring of the Messiah "will become themselves fountains for the spiritual refreshment of others" (Temple, *Readings*, 130).

public ministry, the Spirit was *with* the disciples and the crowds, present and active in his ministry. After his departure, there would be a brief moment when the disciples would be orphaned, and *without* the Spirit, then Jesus promised that the Spirit would be not just "*with*" them but "*in*" them (John 14:17).

Jesus promised that after he rose from the dead and ascended into heaven, they would realize that he is in the Father, they are in him, and he is in them. The Spirit would make the presence of Jesus and the Father real to believers, and Jesus and the Father would make their home in them (John 14:20, 23).

There is a clear trinitarian implication in these Johannine verses, even an anticipation of the *perichoresis* or mutual indwelling of the triune persons in one another. It is not possible to regard the doctrine of the Trinity as a post-biblical invention, a metaphysical departure from the simplicities of the apostolic faith. The nature of such biblical texts required its development.[8] These verses even suggest that the Pauline "in Christ" passages are to be viewed perichoretically as intercommunion of persons, certainly not as an annihilation of personal identity.[9]

The New Testament emphasizes the difference between Jesus' limited, localized presence during his earthly ministry and the unlimited, universal presence he has as the ascended Lord. The Spirit is not given by the earthly Jesus but poured out by the ascended Christ after he has completed his ministry on earth, triumphed over sin, death, and the devil, and exchanged his mortal body for a resurrected, heavenly one. As Peter says, explaining the phenomena of the day of Pentecost, "Exalted to the right hand of God, he [Jesus] has received from the Father the promised Holy Spirit and has poured out what you now see and hear" (Acts 2:33). The earthly Jesus is in one place at any given time, but the presence of the ascended Christ "fills the whole universe" (Eph 4:8–10) and "is all, and is in all" (Col 3:11).

Thus the "incomparably great power" at work in believers is not merely that of their Master during his Galilean ministry. It is, rather, the power that God exercised in raising Jesus from the dead and exalting him to the heavenly realms, placing all things under his authority, making him ruler of everything, and filling all creation with his presence (Eph 1:19–23). This is why Jesus promises his followers that they will not only do what he has been doing; "they will do even greater things than these," because he is "going to the Father" (John 14:12).

The New Zealand Brethren elder Frank Garratt was one of the earliest members of a historic Christian denomination to be baptized in the Holy Spirit (see appendix 2). As a result of his experience—over against the Brethren movement's cessationism—he became convinced that this dispensation is governed by "the exaltation of Jesus to God's right hand and the outpouring of the Holy Spirit." He became convinced that the church must grasp the implications of these twin interconnected realities: "the enthroned Christ and the outpoured Spirit."[10] This conviction underlay his extensive deliverance ministry.

8. See Wainwright, *Trinity in the New Testament*.

9. This has relevance for the disagreement between John Zizioulas and Vladimir Lossky, discussed in chapter 11 below.

10. Reported by his son, Ian Garratt, at a charismatic leaders' consultation,

## A Continuing Teacher

Jesus is soon to be arrested; his teaching is drawing to a close. But in his farewell testament he promises his disciples that the Holy Spirit will carry on his teaching role among them and through them. "The Paraclete, the Holy Spirit, whom the Father will send in my name, will teach you all things and will remind you of everything I have said to you" (John 14:26).

The detailed preservation of so much of Jesus' teaching in the four Gospels is a remarkable fulfillment of this promise. So too is the Spirit's inspiration of people today. We can trust the Holy Spirit to help us remember, act upon, and do the works of Jesus today.

Jesus elaborates on the continuing teaching role of the Holy Spirit (John 16:8–15):

- The Spirit convicts people of sin (16:8–9), exposing what is opposed to God's way of life.
- The Spirit convinces people of righteousness (16:8, 10), inspiring them to pursue a way of life pleasing to God.
- The Spirit brings judgment (16:8, 11), showing that God calls evil (and the Evil One) to account.
- The Spirit guides believers into all truth (16:13).
- The Spirit reveals things to come (16:13).
- The Spirit makes real in our experience the full reality of who Jesus is (16:14–15).

In this way the Spirit continues the work of Jesus after he has left this earth, convicting the world of sin, righteousness, and judgment, empowering Christians and reminding us of everything that he taught and said. The joy of this reality is something that no one can take away (John 16:22, 24).

Every Christian has a responsibility to bear witness to Jesus. The Spirit assists our witness but does not supplant it. "When the Paraclete comes, whom I will send to you from the Father—the Spirit of truth who goes out from the Father—he will testify about me. And you also must testify" (John 15:26–27). The Spirit is not a substitute for our preparation, discipline, or hard work, but cooperates with our redeemed faculties and enhances our human endeavors. Jesus' promise particularly applies to extreme situations when we are under pressure or persecution for our testimony to him (Matt 10:17–20).

---

Wellington, 31 August 2019.

## An Acting Person

The Paraclete sayings, together with what Jesus says about the Spirit as our teacher, provide clear evidence of the personhood of the Holy Spirit. Whatever else the Spirit is, he is "another" being with personal qualities like those of Jesus. He "teaches," "reminds," "convicts," "judges," "guides," "reveals," "communicates." These are characteristics of a personal agent, not of a merely impersonal force or influence.

The highest conception of God in Hinduism is that of an impersonal absolute, *Brahman*. Among those who have reflected on the distinctiveness of Christian pneumatology, therefore, the Indian theologian Ivan Satyavrata is very sensitive to the way in which the New Testament represents the Holy Spirit as a person. It is a clear point of differentiation from monistic views of "spirit." "The Gospel of John," Satyavrata says, "refers to the Spirit in clearly personal terms. The Spirit variously teaches and reminds (14:26), testifies (15:26), and guides and speaks (16:13). When Jesus refers to the Spirit . . . as *allos paraclētos* (another Advocate, NRSV) in 14:16, he clearly implies that he himself is the present *paraclētos* (Advocate). The Spirit was thus regarded as a person in the same sense that Jesus was."[11]

Satyavrata draws attention to John's distinctive use of the personal pronoun when referring to the Spirit. When he first introduces the Spirit in John 14:17, he uses the more grammatically correct neuter pronoun "it" (*auto*) when referring to the Spirit (*pneuma*), a neuter noun. Repeatedly after that he uses the personal masculine pronoun "he" (*ekeinos*) when referring to the Spirit (14:26; 15:26; 16:8, 13, 14), although he should more accurately use the impersonal neuter pronoun. "John clearly wants his readers to view the Holy Spirit as 'he' and not 'it.'"[12]

Two other sayings of Jesus also refer to the Spirit as a person. In the first (Mark 3:29; cf. Matt 12:31 and Luke 12:10), Jesus warns his hearers of the serious consequences of blaspheming against the Holy Spirit. In the second (Mark 13:11; cf. Matt 10:20 and Luke 12:12), Jesus assures his disciples that the Spirit will help them by speaking through them when they have to testify in times of persecution. "Thus," says Satyavrata, "Jesus clearly regarded the Holy Spirit as a personal being who could be blasphemed against, and on occasion, could speak through people."[13]

Satyavrata also draws attention to passages in the book of Acts and in the writings of Paul that provide evidence of the personal activities and character of the Holy Spirit. On numerous occasions in Acts the Spirit is said to speak (1:16; 8:29; 10:19; 11:12; 13:2; 28:25). The Spirit sends (13:4), prevents (16:6–7), appoints (20:28), bears witness (5:32; 20:23), and is conscious of what is good (15:28). The Spirit can be lied to (5:3), tested (5:9), and resisted (7:51). According to Paul, the Spirit testifies (Rom 8:16), intercedes (Rom 8:26), knows (1 Cor 2:11), distributes (1 Cor 12:11), gives life (2 Cor 3:6), cries out (Gal 4:6), and can be grieved (Eph 4:30; cf. Isa 63:10).[14]

---

11. Satyavrata, "The Spirit Blows," 38. Cf. Satyavrata, *The Holy Spirit*, 75.
12. Satyavrata, *The Holy Spirit*, 75.
13. Satyavrata, "The Spirit Blows," 38.
14. Satyavrata, "The Spirit Blows," 38.

All these descriptions speak of a conscious, knowing, thinking, acting subject of a kind we regard as having personal qualities and characteristics. They suggest that the Spirit is a person. Many of these passages—such as Jesus' statements about the Spirit's relationship to the Father (John 14:26; 15:26), or Paul's description of the Spirit as a participant in God's self-knowledge (1 Cor 2:11)—also point to the divinity of the Spirit.

## An Enabling Power

Jesus never intended that we should have to be his followers and witnesses on our own. He promised the Holy Spirit, the third person of the Trinity, who comes from the Father and bears witness to him, to be our personal assistant in this task. The same Spirit that anointed Jesus as Messiah and empowered his ministry is promised by Jesus to be our helper in turn, present and active in our lives. The Spirit has a divine origin and a Christ-centred mission. He comes "from the Father" and is sent by the Father in Jesus' name (John 14:26; 15:26).

Jesus said, "It is for your good that I am going away. Unless I go away, the Paraclete will not come to you; but if I go, I will send him to you" (John 16:7). He said this because the Spirit could not become universally available until the physical limitation of his human life on earth had ended. Before the Holy Spirit could be poured out in power on earth, Jesus' humanity had to be glorified by ascending into heaven. The mission of the Spirit could not begin until the ministry of the Son had finished.

According to John's Gospel, Jesus' giving of the Spirit has a sacramental character. In a very real sense, Jesus instituted two sacraments at the end of his life, not just one as commonly thought: the sacrament of his body, the consequence of his death, and the sacrament of his Spirit, the outcome of his ascension.

- Before his crucifixion, he gathered his disciples, broke bread, gave it to them and said, "Take, eat, this is my body." He blessed a cup, gave it to them and said, "Take, drink, this is my blood" (Matt 26:26–28; Mark 14: 22–24; Luke 22:17–20).

- Before his ascension, he met with his disciples, breathed on them and said, "*Take* Holy Spirit.[15] If you forgive anyone's sins, their sins are forgiven; if you do not forgive them, they are not forgiven" (John 20:22–23, adapted).

---

15. The same command, *labete*, is used in both situations.

Jesus breathed on them, in what can be described as a sacramental or prophetic act that remembers a past event and prefigures a future one. His action echoes the breath of the Spirit which animated human life at its creation (Gen 2:7). His action was fulfilled when a wind "came from heaven and filled the whole house" where the believers were worshiping on the day of Pentecost (Acts 2:2). Jesus' command omits the definite article, and he gives a direct order, using the aorist tense, indicating a single act of receiving: "Take Holy Spirit."

It astonishes me that Jesus' action has never qualified as a dominical sacrament because it has all the defining elements of what constitutes one. It is an "outward and visible sign of an inward and spiritual grace." It announces an imparting of divine grace: "Take Holy Spirit." It is an act of *anamnēsis* or remembrance, reminiscent of the divine breath that gave life to humans at the beginning and constituted them as living beings (Gen 2:7). It has a prophetic foreshadowing, fulfilled when the rushing wind entered the house, and the Holy Spirit rested on the believers on the day of Pentecost (Acts 2:2). There is even a potential real presence, with salvific consequences. Would it be too testing of our faith, too disruptive of our safe worship services, too risking of the Spirit to admit that this meets the requirement of a sacrament instituted by our Lord himself? Would our churches be so ignored by an indifferent society if we risked such action and trusted the Spirit for the outcome?

I think of the impact of the first John Wimber conference in New Zealand, "Signs and Wonders and Church Growth," on 18–21 August 1986. At the end of his opening session, Wimber calmly invited the Holy Spirit to come. After a few minutes of silent expectancy, the Spirit moved in waves of joy across the crowd of 2,200 in the Assembly of God auditorium in Beaumont Street, Auckland. None of us had seen anything like this before. It was as tangible as a stadium wave. My friend Neven MacEwan was spontaneously healed of a damaged sternum dating from his days as an All Black rugby lock. He heard it crack into place.[16] Another friend, Spreydon Baptist pastor Murray Robertson, normally phlegmatic and unemotional, was so overcome in the Spirit he had to be assisted from the auditorium at the end of the evening. When Wimber heard about it he called him "the first Baptist holy-roller!"[17]

This action implies that our cooperation is required. Jesus breathes out; the disciples have to breath in. There is no place for passivity in receiving the Spirit. Just as we must actively receive the bread and wine of his body and blood, so we need to partake actively of Holy Spirit, to receive divine empowerment for our witness and service.

Jesus commissions us to carry on his ministry in the world. He imparts his Spirit to empower us in this great task. Our responsibility is to receive

---

16. Neven MacEwan, conversation with the author, 12 July 2018. The incident is not mentioned in MacEwan's moving memoir of sporting success, moral failure, and Christian redemption, *When the Crowd Stops Roaring*.

17. Murray Robertson, personal testimony, charismatic leaders' consultation, Wellington, 31 August 2019.

and act on this inspiration. Life in the Spirit involves not a passive response, but a deliberate effort, reception, and outworking.

Passivity is the enemy of the spiritual life. So often Western theology, with its tragic polarization of divine grace and human free will, has dismissed the notion of our cooperation with God as "Semi-Pelagianism." But the Christian life consists in us being "coworkers with God" (*sunergoi theou*, 1 Cor 3:9; 2 Cor 6:1). The experience of being baptized in the Spirit brings this element to the forefront of Christian experience.

Indeed, understanding such synergy is essential for our living in the Spirit. To speak in tongues, we must speak. To prophesy, we must articulate the thoughts or impressions the Spirit brings to mind. To heal the sick, we must step out in faith and pray for sick people. I compare this to power steering in a vehicle. The hydraulics do nothing if I do not turn the steering wheel. But the instant I do, the power is there to assist my action. This simultaneity of human and divine action is fundamental in our experience of the Holy Spirit. "He distributes his energy in proportion to the faith of the recipient," says Basil, "not confining it to a single share."[18]

## Indwelling and Empowering

The parallel with Jesus mentioned in the previous chapter shows that there are two modes of the Holy Spirit's activity in Christians: we are *born* of or regenerated by the Spirit, resulting in the Spirit's personal presence or *indwelling*; and we are *baptized* in or reinvigorated by the Spirit, leading to the Spirit's impersonal assistance or *empowering*.

We saw that this complementary understanding clarifies what has been a source of unnecessary conflict between evangelical and Pentecostal Christians. Over against classical Pentecostal teaching, this parallelism shows that being born anew of the Spirit is what makes us Christian and that baptism with Holy Spirit is not necessary for salvation. In contrast to conservative evangelical teaching that a person needs nothing more of the Holy Spirit once they become a Christian, it shows that being baptized in Holy Spirit is essential for effective Christian service. The biblical pattern is that new birth in the Spirit is necessary for *salvation*; being baptized in Spirit is normative for *service*.

The Bible consistently describes the presence or indwelling of the Spirit by use of the preposition "*in*," and the power or empowering of the Holy Spirit by the preposition "*on*." The Spirit's indwelling is absent from the Old Testament, except for the first time in the prophecies of Ezekiel that God will put his Spirit "in" people (Ezek 36:26–27; 37:14), foreshadowing the great change that took place in the relation between God and human beings with the incarnation of Jesus Christ.

---

18. Basil, *On the Holy Spirit*, 9.22.

By contrast, the Old Testament is replete with instances where the Holy Spirit "came (up) on" people (e.g. the seventy elders, Num 11:17, 25, 26, 29; Samson, Judg 14:6, 19, 15:14; Saul, 1 Sam 10:6, 10–11; and David, 1 Sam 16:13). Two famous Old Testament prophecies foretell that God will one day pour out his Spirit "on the people of Israel" (Ezek 39:29) and "on all people" (Joel 2:28). In the New Testament the Holy Spirit "descended on" Jesus at his baptism (Luke 3:22), tongues of fire "came to rest on" each of the apostles when the Holy Spirit came at Pentecost (Acts 2:3), and the Holy Spirit "came on" the Roman centurion and his household at the beginning of the Gentile mission (Acts 10:44–45; 11:15).

## Person and Power

A surprising clue to the distinction between the Holy Spirit as a person and the Holy Spirit as an influence or power exists in the Greek New Testament, but is universally overlooked in Bible translations. This is the presence or absence of the definite article in references to the Spirit. A few scholars had noticed it, but its significance was not fully appreciated until the advent of the charismatic renewal movement brought a reexamination of these passages.

In the Greek New Testament, texts referring to the divine personality and personal feelings of the Holy Spirit consistently use the definite article, e.g., "Whoever blasphemes against *the* Holy Spirit will never be forgiven" (Mark 3:29). "*The* Spirit of truth . . . will guide you into all the truth" (John 16:13). "No one knows the thoughts of God except *the* Spirit of God" (1 Cor 2:11). "Do not grieve *the* Holy Spirit of God" (Eph 4:30).

By contrast, passages referring to the filling, empowerment, influence, or impact of Holy Spirit on people typically omit the definite article in the original Greek, e.g., "He will baptize [immerse] in Holy Spirit" (Luke 3:16). "Receive Holy Spirit" (John 20:22). "They were all filled with Holy Spirit" (Acts 2:4). "Did you receive Holy Spirit when you believed?" (Acts 19:2). "Be filled with Spirit" (Eph 5:18).[19]

Not even Robert Young's *Literal Translation of the Bible* (1862; rev. ed., 1887) makes this distinction. The first person to spot it seems to have been the Cambridge scholar (later bishop of Durham) B. F. Westcott in 1881, in his note on John 7:39: "Up to that time the Spirit had not been given, since Jesus had not yet been glorified." The Greek of this passage is curious. Literally translated it reads ". . . for there was no Spirit yet, because Jesus was not yet glorified." Westcott comments, "The addition of the word *given* expresses the true form of the original, in which *Spirit* is without the article . . . When the term occurs in this form, it marks an operation, or manifestation, or gift of the Spirit, and not the personal Spirit."[20]

19. For a list of all the theologically significant texts, see appendix 1 below.
20. Westcott, *St. John*, 123.

Early in the twentieth century the careful English scholar H. B. Swete also saw this distinction. He concluded that texts with the definite article, "*the* Holy Spirit," refer to "the Holy Spirit considered as a Divine Person," whereas texts omitting the definite article refer to "Holy Spirit" as "a gift or manifestation of the Spirit in its relation to the life of man."[21] More recently D. Pitt Francis reexamined all eighty-nine New Testament references to the Holy Spirit and found "that 'power' references (49) do not contain the definite article, but the references to the Holy Spirit as a person (40) invariably do."[22] The article is required when the Spirit is spoken of as a person but omitted when the reference is to the operation, manifestations, or gifts of divine Spirit as a power or influence operative in people's lives.

So close is the relationship between the divine Spirit and the human spirit when the former is acting on the latter, that it is sometimes difficult to decide which is which. Swete observes, "In the Pauline Epistles it is often a point of great difficulty to determine whether the action of the Spirit of God upon the human spirit or the human spirit under the power of the Spirit of God is intended when *pneuma* is anarthrous [lacking the definite article]." He concluded that it is safest to give Paul's references to "Spirit" without the definite article the thought of "the human spirit awakened, guided, and inhabited by the Spirit of Christ, but never losing sight of the Power by which the spiritual element in man is what it is."[23]

For this reason, Nikos Nissiotis cautions against assuming a trichotomist view of our human constitution. "It would be a wrong interpretation of the biblical understanding of the nature of man to introduce here without qualification the trichotomy—body, soul, spirit—in order to explain the constitutive elements of human nature. The operation of the Spirit becomes a third element in a human being, but as an operation from outside man."[24]

It is extraordinary that the Christian community continues to be presented with Bible translations that efface this crucial distinction about the person and activity of the Holy Spirit. To translate New Testament references to the Holy Spirit according to the use or omission of the definite article would be a contribution to global ecumenical understanding. It would help to overcome the tragic and unnecessary polarization between Pentecostal and evangelical Christians in their views of the Holy Spirit.

Each of these large and Bible-believing constituencies bears witness to a half-truth. Evangelicals rightly affirm the Holy Spirit to be a person. Pentecostals rightly affirm the Holy Spirit to be a power. The New Testament reveals the Holy Spirit to be both a person and a power. It is no longer excusable that Bible translations suppress this fundamental truth.

---

21. Swete, *Holy Spirit in the New Testament*, appendix P, 396.

22. Francis, "The Holy Spirit," 136–37. See also David Pawson's excellent study of the New Testament passages on conversion, *The Normal Christian Birth*, appendix 2, "'Spirit' without the Definite Article," 320–24. "*Pneuma*," BDAG 834–35, also distinguishes references with and without the article.

23. Swete, *Holy Spirit in the New Testament*, 397–98.

24. Nissiotis, "Doctrine of the Trinity," 50–51.

It should go without saying that the power of the Spirit is not an abstract brute force but the expression of personal love. Anthony Thiselton has a timely warning about this. He expresses concern that some sections of the renewal movement use "power" "as if it denoted sheer force." He finds problematic the titles of John Wimber's books, *Power Evangelism* (1985) and *Power Healing* (1986),[25] though I see these titles as a literary device and think this is unfair to Wimber. He notes that Karl Barth avoided this problem by rendering the word *dynamis* not as "power" but as "effectiveness" or "effective action."[26] Thiselton himself defines the Greek term *dynamis* as "competence to perform a given function."[27] It involves "*ability, effectiveness*, and *heightened capacity*, not raw power."[28] The power of the Spirit is given to us so that we may do God's work with God's enabling and in God's way. This involves the exercise of power with gentleness and consideration, ministering to others as we would like to be ministered to ourselves.

## The Fruit Tree and the Christmas Tree

The use or omission of the definite article—a little-known grammatical feature of the Greek text of the New Testament—is consistent with the well-known New Testament imagery of the Holy Spirit's "fruit" and "gifts." The former is a naturally occurring process of growth, the latter a serendipitous distribution of grace.

The Holy Spirit's *indwelling* of believers, following their new birth, is described by the New Testament in *organic* analogies. Like a living organism, the indwelling of the Spirit imparts life, growth, and fruitfulness.

Jesus compared the relation of believers to himself as branches to a vine. "No branch can bear fruit by itself; it must remain in the vine. Neither can you bear fruit unless you remain in me. I am the vine; you are the branches. If you remain in me and I in you, you will bear much fruit; apart from me you can do nothing" (John 15:4–5). Similarly, Paul spoke of the indwelling of Christ's life in us through the Spirit as producing in us "the fruit [singular] of the Spirit": "love, joy, peace, forbearance, kindness, goodness, faithfulness, gentleness, and self-control" (Gal 5:22–23).

Like a fruit tree, these results of the indwelling life of the Spirit in the believer take time to ripen. Sanctification and godliness, progress in Christian living, takes time, patience, and perseverance to produce. Holiness is not instant, but progressive, achieved by our obedience and cooperation with God's grace. As John Stott points out, the fruit of the Spirit is

---

25. Thiselton, *The Holy Spirit*, 498.
26. Thiselton, *The Holy Spirit*, 105, citing Barth, *Resurrection*, 18.
27. Thiselton, *The Holy Spirit*, 498.
28. Thiselton, *The Holy Spirit*, 12.

supernatural in its origin and natural in its growth.[29] It is the transforming effect in our character of God's indwelling Spirit.

By contrast, the Holy Spirit's *empowering* of believers, following their baptism in the Spirit, is described in an entirely different way. The gifts of the Spirit that result are like the gifts on a Christmas tree.

The New Testament term for the "gifts" of the Spirit is *charismata*, a diminutive form of the Greek word for "grace," *charis*. Charismatic gifts or charisms of the Holy Spirit are what Fuller Theological Seminary theologian Russell Spittler calls "gracelets." A gracelet, he says, "is a droplet of divine grace, a tiny and often temporary manifestation of God's unmerited favor given to an individual believer mostly for the benefit of others in the congregation. . . . A *charisma* is a miniature manifestation of divine grace."[30]

Charisms are "favors," expressions of God's grace, freely given to any believer without regard to personal maturity, merit, holiness of life or length or quality of Christian experience. The gratuitous nature of these gifts explains what is offensive to some evangelicals: that immature Christians who exercise faith can employ charismatic gifts and sometimes be greatly used by the Holy Spirit.

At the same time, the New Testament emphasizes that the exercise of spiritual gifts is not a mark of maturity. Jesus warned that he would not acknowledge those who prophesied or performed miracles in his name but had no ongoing relationship with himself (Matt 7:21-23). In his discussion of the gifts of the Spirit Paul likewise sets the priority of selfless, Christlike love above the exercise of spectacular charisms like tongues, prophecy, insight, or faith (1 Cor 13:1-2), while recognizing and encouraging their responsible use (1 Cor 12:4-11; 14:1-5, 26-33, 37-40).

A poignant illustration of the difference between the gifts and personal maturity is the archetypal Jesus People evangelist, Lonnie Frisbee. Frisbee was the spiritual fuse that ignited two global movements: first Calvary Chapel, through his role in the large open air baptisms in the Pacific Ocean at Corona del Mar, which featured in *Time* magazine on 21 June 1971,[31] then calling down the Holy Spirit when the Spirit first impacted the nascent Vineyard movement in

---

29. Stott, *Baptism and Fullness*, 78-79. Stott sees Paul's list of the fruit of the Spirit as comprising three triads: "love, joy, peace" involve our relationship with God; "patience, kindness, goodness" our relationship with other people; and "faithfulness, gentleness, and self-control" our relationship with ourselves (77).

30. Foreword to Griffin, *Gracelets*, 1. Arnold Bittlinger defines a *charisma* as "the concrete realization of divine grace" (Bittlinger, *Gifts and Ministries*, 16). Most, but not all, charisms are temporary. Celibacy, the ability to be sexually continent, is also described as a *charisma* in 1 Cor 7:7.

31. See the wonderful photograph in Jones, "The Jesus People," *DPCM* 492—an article dropped entirely from *NIDPCM*.

the Canyon High School gymnasium, Yorba Linda, on 11 May 1980.[32] A free spirit from a broken home and with little education, Frisbee was sexually violated in his childhood. His dramatic conversion while on a drug trip seemed to overcome this, but he later became involved in homosexual liaisons and died of AIDS in 1993. As a result, Calvary Chapel and the Vineyard distanced themselves from him and effectively wrote him out of their histories. Wimber only refers to "a young man."[33] He is not mentioned in the *Dictionary of Pentecostal and Charismatic Movements* or its sequel. Researcher David Di Sabatino, who seeks to give him due recognition, presents him as a gifted, tragic, Samson-like figure.[34]

## Evangelical and Pentecostal

The conclusion to be drawn from this survey is that the Bible has both "evangelical" and "Pentecostal" elements in its description of the activity of the Holy Spirit. The evangelical emphasis on new birth through the Holy Spirit and the Pentecostal emphasis on being baptized in Holy Spirit are both parts of the scriptural record, and both belong *together* in Christian experience.

| Table 2 Two Aspects of the Spirit's Activity ||
|---|---|
| The evangelical aspect | The pentecostal aspect |
| Holy Spirit's role in Jesus' birth | Holy Spirit's role at Jesus' baptism |
| Holy Spirit "in" a person | Holy Spirit "on" a person |
| Born anew by the Holy Spirit | Baptized in Holy Spirit |
| Regeneration | Reinvigoration |
| Christian conversion | Heightened capacity |
| New life in Christ | New effectiveness for Christ |
| Necessary for salvation | Normative for service |
| The presence of the Spirit | The power of the Spirit |
| Abiding presence | Enabling power |
| Personal intimacy | Impersonal activity |
| With the definite article in Greek | Without the article in Greek |
| Fruit of the Spirit | Gifts of the Spirit |

---

32. Vividly described by Carol Wimber, who was present and gives the correct date (Wimber, *John Wimber*, 147–49).

33. Wimber, *Power Evangelism*, 36.

34. See the award-winning DVD, *Frisbee* (2006).

| Analogy of the fruit tree | Analogy of the Christmas tree |
|---|---|
| Organic growth | Undeserved gift |
| Builds character | Bestows *charismata* |
| Explains how godly believers may lack effectiveness (e.g., the Ephesians in Acts 19:1–7) | Explains how effective believers may lack holiness (e.g., Samson in Judg 16–19) |

Separation of these two streams has resulted in unnecessary polarization between Bible-believing Christians, with consequent damage to Christian unity, biblical holiness, and evangelistic effectiveness. What God has joined, let no one separate! Christians are to "follow the way of love *and* eagerly desire gifts of the Spirit" (1 Cor 14:1).

# 7

# The Doorway to Life in the Spirit

*At the heart of the experience of the early Christians was the dynamic event described as being "baptized in Holy Spirit." Neglected in traditional Christianity and many contemporary forms of Christian initiation, but mentioned by John the Baptist, Jesus, and the apostles, the New Testament presents it as a foundational experience of continuing validity, the doorway to the realm of the Spirit. Presented as a distinct experience which the recipient is conscious of receiving, it leads to an awareness of the transcendent life, power, presence, and guidance of the living God. Being baptized in Holy Spirit awakens an awareness of spiritual gifts and introduces the Christian to a life of effectiveness in God's service.*

BAPTISM IN (OR WITH) Holy Spirit is a distinct spiritual experience whose biblical basis is found in the preaching of John the Baptist, Jesus, and the apostles. The New Testament does not use the noun "baptism in the Holy Spirit," but only the verbal form "baptize with Holy Spirit" (omitting the definite article, as in other "power" references). This feature of the terminology points to a dynamic experience, not a spiritual or theological concept. It denotes a dynamic, not a doctrine.[1]

---

1. I agree with Peter Hocken's assessment of baptism in the Holy Spirit as the

The Bible bears witness to four aspects of being baptized in or with Holy Spirit.

## It Is a Valid Experience

At the beginning of his ministry, Jesus was baptized in the River Jordan by John the Baptist. John said of Jesus, "I baptize you with [or in] water. But one who is more powerful than I will come, the straps of whose sandals I am not worthy to untie. He will baptize you with [or in] Holy Spirit and fire" (Luke 3:16). Most Christians know John 3:16. Why do they not know Luke 3:16?

Three years later, in his last words to his apostles before he ascended into heaven, Jesus said, "Do not leave Jerusalem, but wait for the gift my Father promised, which you have heard me speak about. For John baptized with [or in] water, but in a few days you will be baptized with [or in] Holy Spirit" (Acts 1:4–5). The gift the Father promised is Holy Spirit. The gift would come from Jesus, as John the Baptist promised. Our reception of that gift is being baptized with Holy Spirit. Both of these passages mention "Holy Spirit" without the definite article, emphasizing the Spirit's power rather than the Spirit's personality. The gift is an endowment of power to enable Christians to serve Jesus more effectively.

This promise was fulfilled on the day of Pentecost in Jerusalem. The Bible says of the apostles and their associates, "All of them were filled with Holy Spirit and began to speak in other tongues [or languages] as the Spirit enabled them" (Acts 2:4). As a result, a vast crowd gathered. Peter said to them, "Repent and be baptized, *every one of you*, in the name of Jesus Christ for the forgiveness of your sins. And you will receive the gift of the Holy Spirit. The promise is *for you and your children and for all who are far off— for all whom the Lord our God will call*" (Acts 2:38–39, my italics).

The promise of the Holy Spirit has not ceased to be valid, as evangelical and Reformed Christians have often maintained.[2] Rather, this passage

---

"foundational grace" or "foundational spiritual reality" of the Pentecostal-charismatic movement, from which all its other characteristics derive (Hocken, *Azusa, Rome, and Zion*, 66). But in this chapter I am concerned to expound the biblical character and validity of this foundational phenomenon, not its wider ramifications.

2. The classic presentation of the cessationist position is that of the Calvinist Princeton theologian B. B. Warfield, *Counterfeit Miracles* (1918), reissued as *Miracles: Yesterday and Today, True and False* (1953). An early refutation of such views was Miller, *Pentecost Examined* (1936). More recently, cessationism has been effectively answered by Kraft, *Christianity with Power* (1989), Ruthven, *On the Cessation of the Charismata* (1993), Deere, *Surprised by the Power of the Spirit* (1993), and Long and McMurry, *Collapse of the Brass Heaven* (1994). I have had conversations with Chuck Kraft and Brad Long on this subject.

shows that the promise applies not just to Peter's hearers, but throughout time and space. It was not only for the generation of the apostles but extends to later generations ("for you and your *descendants*").[3] It was not just for Jewish believers, but for all peoples of the earth ("for all who are far off"), just as the prophet Joel foretold (Joel 2:28, 32; Acts 2:17, 21).

To be baptized with Holy Spirit is something God intends all Christians to experience, across the centuries and around the world. It is a valid experience for today.

## It Is an Initiatory Experience

The term "baptize" suggests a first or initial experience, an initiation into the realm of the Holy Spirit. To be baptized in Holy Spirit, says the early Catholic charismatic writer Steve Clark, "is an introduction to the life of the Spirit. It is a beginning, a doorway, to the life of the Spirit."[4] The experience of being baptized in Holy Spirit opens up a whole new realm of transcendental experience that has never previously entered our human understanding (1 Cor 2:9–10).

The realm of the Spirit is not vague or nebulous but can be experienced by human beings. As the biblical accounts testify, the Spirit can be "heard," "seen," and expressed in speech. On the day of Pentecost, the apostles and their fellow believers "were all together in one place" (Acts 2:1–4), when suddenly they *heard* a sound like the rush of a strong wind that came from without and entered the room. They *saw* "what seemed to be tongues of fire that separated and came to rest on each of them." They "began *to speak* in other tongues [or languages] as the Spirit enabled them."

This was the opposite of what happened in Jesus' initiation in the Spirit. When the Spirit came on Jesus at his baptism, it was in a concentrated, physical form with the appearance of a dove or a homing pigeon (Luke 3:21–22). The totality of the Spirit was concentrated in Jesus (Col 2:9). But when the Spirit was outpoured on the apostolic community at Pentecost, the Spirit was distributed on all the believers present. The tongues of fire "separated and came to rest on each of them." Each, individually, received a distinctive, personal experience of the Spirit.

This suggests that the entire community of believers need to be living in agreement for the fullness of the Spirit to be expressed. No one individual believer has all the Holy Spirit. We need to be dwelling in unity and giving

---

3. "In a more general sense the plural is used for *descendants, posterity*" ("*Teknon*," AG 816).

4. Clark, *Baptized in the Spirit*, 22.

and receiving our personal gifts of the Spirit for the full character of Jesus to be expressed, for the body of Christ in its fullness to be manifest. Being baptized in Holy Spirit has implications for Christian unity.

The biblical account shows that as they were filled with Holy Spirit, each of the believers "began *to speak in other tongues* as the Spirit enabled them" (Acts 2:4). Speaking in tongues through the enabling of the Spirit is evidence of being baptized with Holy Spirit. When you pour water into an urn or a pump pot, you know that it is full when it overflows. The overflow of a human being is the mouth. What is inside is what comes out. You can tell that there is a lot that is unpleasant in many people because what comes out is swearing, crudity, and foul language. In the same way, you can tell when a person has been filled or baptized with Holy Spirit. They begin to speak in tongues, praise God, prophesy, and overflow with joy and wholesome speech. The vocal gifts of the Spirit are signs of the fullness of the Spirit.

The book of Acts goes on to describe the "Gentile Pentecost" when the first non-Jewish believers were baptized in Holy Spirit. In the home of the Roman military officer Cornelius in Caesarea the Jewish believers who accompanied Peter "were astonished that the gift of the Holy Spirit had been poured out even on Gentiles. For they heard them speaking in tongues and praising God" (Acts 10:45–46). Here speaking in tongues was unmistakable evidence to the Jewish believers who accompanied Peter that the members of Cornelius's household had also experienced Spirit baptism as they had. Peter later gave an account of his experience to the apostles and believers in Jerusalem. "As I began to speak, the Holy Spirit came on them as he had come on us at the beginning" (Acts 11:15).

John Stott comments that the coming of the Spirit of God as described in Acts 2:1–4 "was accompanied by three supernatural signs: a sound, a sight and strange speech.... These three experiences seemed like natural phenomena (wind, fire and speech); yet they were supernatural both in origin and in character. The noise was not wind, but sounded like it; the sight was not fire but resembled it; and the speech was in languages which were not ordinary but in some way 'other'. Again, three of their higher senses were affected, in that they heard the wind-like sound, saw the fire-like apparition and spoke the 'other' languages. Yet what they experienced was more than sensory; it was significant. So they sought to understand it. 'What does this mean?'... If so, the noise like wind may have symbolised *power*,... the sight like fire *purity*,... and the speech in other languages the *universality* of the Christian church."[5]

5. Stott, *The Spirit, the Church, and the World*, 62–63. Peter Hocken shows that this search to understand a prior God-given experience is also characteristic of contemporary charismatic experience: "People were first baptized in the Spirit, and then they faced the question of its meaning and what to do with it" (Hocken, "Charismatic Movement," *DPCM* 158.) The present book, too, is an example of Anselm of Canterbury's

Luke says that the early believers "*began* to speak in other tongues [or languages of some kind] as the Spirit enabled them" (Acts 2:4). The contemporary experience of charismatic Christians when baptized with Holy Spirit is consistent with this description. A person initiated in the things of the Spirit does not immediately speak with fluency in unknown tongues or languages. Rather, he or she "*begins*" to speak, sometimes hesitantly and stumblingly, and then grows in confidence as they continue to exercise the gift. There is a dual agency at work. God gives spiritual gifts, but we must appropriate them and put them to use. Like all learned skills, we grow in confidence and fluency by exercising them.

## It Is a Distinct Experience

The New Testament shows that baptism in Holy Spirit is a conscious experience that is distinct from a person's conversion or experience of salvation, though ideally and with proper counsel, it should accompany conversion. The story of the group of believers in Ephesus described in Acts 19 indicates that people can genuinely believe in Jesus Christ yet not have had the experience of being baptized in or with Holy Spirit. The account suggests that you can tell if a person has had this experience or not. If a person has not received Spirit baptism, the responsible thing to do is to remedy this defect by laying hands on them and praying that they would receive it.

You can tell the difference between an ordinary glass tumbler and a crystal glass by tapping them and listening to the sound they make. Crystal goes "ding." An ordinary glass goes "dong." When Paul met these believers in Ephesus, he recognized that something was lacking in their Christian experience. They went "dong," not "ding." "Did you receive Holy Spirit when you believed?" he asked them. They answered, "No, we have not even heard that there is Holy Spirit."

So Paul placed his hands on them. As he did so, "the Holy Spirit came on them, and they spoke in tongues and prophesied" (Acts 19:1–7). In the early church, the usual way Christians helped someone to receive the Spirit was through prayer with the laying on of hands.[6] When Paul did so, these believers consciously experienced the Holy Spirit. This experience remedied what they previously lacked. The evidence of their Spirit baptism was speaking in tongues and "prophesying," speaking under the inspiration of the Spirit. It was a distinct and conscious experience, with audible evidence.

---

classic summary of theological enquiry as "faith seeking understanding" (*fides quaerens intellectum*).

6. John Stott denies that the laying on of hands "is the norm for receiving the Spirit today" (Stott, *Baptism and Fullness*, 33), despite the evidence of Acts 8:17–19; 9:17; 19:6; and his experience of episcopal ordination. One can only assume that none of those he pastored experienced this blessing and encouragement at his hands.

As theologian Francis Sullivan says, "Some such experiential evidence of the outpouring of the Spirit was normal and expected in New Testament times."[7]

Roland Allen, a man famous for his reenvisaging of the church's mission from his study of the book of Acts, comments on the "peculiar definiteness" of the New Testament's references to Spirit baptism. "The gift which the apostles received was a definite gift received at a definite time. It was not the experience of a vague influence which they felt more or less markedly at different times: it was a definite fact concerning which they could name the time and place. Later the Holy Spirit was given to many others, but always this peculiar definiteness marked the coming of the gift."[8]

Likewise, discussing what it means to be baptized in the Spirit, Steve Clark observes: "From the passages in the New Testament, it is clear that when people are baptized in the Spirit, they know it.... They can recognise it not only in themselves but also in others. The result of being baptized in the Spirit is that the Spirit enters their lives and begins to make things happen in a way that they can experience."[9] Conversely—and this would appear to have been the condition of the believers Paul met in Ephesus (Acts 19:1–7)—"If there are no traces at all of the presence of the Spirit in him, he has not been baptized in the Spirit."[10] The pastorally responsible thing is then to pray with laying on of hands that the person may experience what he or she is lacking.

David Pawson, in *The Normal Christian Birth* (1989), argues that in the New Testament "Christian initiation is a complex of four elements—repenting towards God, believing in the Lord Jesus, being baptized in water and receiving the Holy Spirit,"[11] and that our regular instruction for new Christians should teach this and make this clear. In the mid-1980s, before the publication of Pawson's book, I received a stunning prophecy from the Holy Spirit: "I am sick and tired of my people having to shop around from church to church to get fully converted. Stop dividing what I have joined. From now on, I want every church in every place to offer the whole package to every convert." From that point on, I built my New Christians' Classes around those four ingredients: repentance from sin, faith in Jesus, baptism in water, and being filled with Holy Spirit.

## It Is a Profound Experience

At the beginning of 1 Corinthians, Paul speaks about the role of the Holy Spirit in revealing God to us. God is transcendent, beyond all human

---

7. Sullivan, *Charisms and Charismatic Renewal*, 67.

8. Allen, "Pentecost and the World," 9. Reuben A. Torrey had also taken this view: "The baptism with the Holy Spirit is a definite experience of which one may and ought to know whether he has received it or not" (Torrey, *What the Bible Teaches*, 270, quoted by Bruner, *Theology of the Holy Spirit*, 335).

9. Clark, *Baptized in the Spirit*, 19, cf. 21.

10. Clark, *Baptized in the Spirit*, 37.

11. Pawson, *The Normal Christian Birth*, 11.

experience. Therefore, the only way that we human beings can know God is if God makes himself known to us. This is what the Holy Spirit does. The Spirit is what Bishop John Taylor called "the go-between God."[12] He is the person of the Godhead whose role is to reveal God or make God known to us.

Paul quotes from the prophet Isaiah to make this essential point.

> What no eye has seen,
> what no ear has heard,
> and what no human mind has conceived—
> the things God has prepared for those who love him . . .

"These," he says, "are the things God has revealed to us by his Spirit" (1 Cor 2:9–10, quoting Isa 64:4). The realm of God is beyond everyday human experience: unseen, unheard, unthought by human beings. Yet this realm of God—unimaginable, mysterious, and utterly glorious—is what the Holy Spirit introduces us to. It is no wonder that the baptism in the Holy Spirit is a profound and overwhelming experience.

The word used of this experience suggests its overwhelming nature: the word "baptize." It is a pity that this word has never been translated in our English Bibles. When we say, "baptize" we are speaking Greek. Many misunderstandings about baptism would vanish if this word were translated into plain English, instead of being transliterated letter for letter from the original Greek.

"Baptize" is simply a transliteration of the Greek word *baptizō*, which does not in any way explain its meaning. In secular Greek literature, *baptizō* means to "dip, immerse, plunge, sink, drench, overwhelm,"[13] "to put or go under water."[14] Euripides in *The Orestes* uses a different word, *baptō* when water splashes into a ship; but the word *baptizō* when a vessel sinks![15] *Baptō* would describe the Team New Zealand America's Cup yacht that took on water in Auckland's Hauraki Gulf in 2003. But *baptizō* would describe the Australian America's Cup yacht *One Australia* that broke in two and sank off San Diego in 1995!

Since baptism means immersion or submersion, to be baptized in or with Holy Spirit is to be submerged or overwhelmed by the reality of the Holy Spirit. A person baptized in Holy Spirit has an overwhelming sense of God's presence and reality. He or she speaks with joy and inspiration,

---

12. Taylor, *The Go-Between God*.
13. "*Baptizō*," AG 131, which thereupon treats the New Testament usage as "only in a ritual sense" and itself uses the transliteration "baptize."
14. "*Baptizō*," BDAG 164.
15. Watson, *One in the Spirit*, 68.

praising God using words they have never learned before, and speaking prophetically about realities they have never experienced before and may not comprehend for many years to come.

The Catholic theologian Heribert Mühlen rightly emphasizes the significance of the metaphorical expression "baptism of the Spirit." "We are plunged—so to speak—into the Holy Spirit as into a vital element; we move in him like a fish in water; breathe him in as we breathe in the air around us; are filled with him, filled to repletion, as a vessel is filled up. . . . In baptism of the Spirit we are plunged into the divine *power*."[16]

Charismatic Presbyterian theologian J. Rodman Williams notes that this has been the correct understanding of many Pentecostals. "Since the essential meaning of baptism is immersion, Pentecostals often emphasize that to be baptized in the Holy Spirit is to be immersed in the Holy Spirit. This signifies a total submergence within the reality of the Holy Spirit so that whoever is so baptized has a vivid sense of the Spirit's presence and power. . . . Immersion, similar to that in water but in the reality of the Spirit, is a central emphasis in Pentecostalism."[17] Williams also quotes the testimony of an early Catholic charismatic: "Talking about a baptism, it was just like I was being plunged down into a great sea of water, only the water was God, the water was the Holy Spirit."[18]

When I was baptized in the Holy Spirit, on 30 October 1981, this was my experience too. I spoke in tongues. My striving ceased, and I began to feel a deep inner peace, assurance, and contentment. The experience in my heart was like bubbles aerating a fish aquarium! It was as if I was surrounded by the Holy Spirit and being refreshed by a wonderful new inner reality!

Moreover, I began to discern things I had never learned. Biblical passages about what God was doing to prepare the world for the return of Jesus began to light up, reshaping my thinking about the Christian hope. It took me a long time to get my mind around what I was being shown and to integrate it into my understanding. It was more than fifteen years before I felt the confidence to write about it, in my little booklet on *The Return of Jesus*. It was thirty-five years before I published a full account, in my book *Restoring the Fortunes of Zion*, on the restoration of Israel in modern history and biblical prophecy. Both publications present a restorationist, millennial understanding of eschatology free from the speculations and limitations of popular dispensationalism.[19]

---

16. Mühlen, *A Charismatic Theology*, 95.

17. Williams, "Baptism in the Holy Spirit," *DPCM* 41, *NIDPCM* 355.

18. Ranaghan and Ranaghan, *Catholic Pentecostals*, 16, quoted by Williams, "Baptism in the Holy Spirit," *DPCM* 41, *NIDPCM* 355.

19. I was once accused of dispensationalism by the General Secretary of the NZ Church Missionary Society. I replied that I was not a dispensationalist and that my views were probably little different from the restorationists who originally founded the

Because this experience of the Spirit is so real and overwhelming, the New Testament describes it in many different ways. It is a "filling" or a "being filled" (Acts 2:4; 9:17), an "outpouring" or a "pouring out" (Joel 2:28–29; Acts 2:17–18, 33; 10:45), a "falling on" or a "coming upon" (Acts 1:8; 8:16; 10:44; 19:6), an "empowerment" or a "receiving power" (Luke 5:17; Acts 1:8). With one exception, it is not the terminology that is important, but the reality that these terms point to. The exception is that the New Testament uses the verbal form of these terms, not nouns, indicating that we are dealing with a dynamic experience, not a doctrinal concept.

> Rodman Williams comments, "All of this terminology—baptising, filling, outpouring, falling, coming on—suggests a total experience of the presence of the Holy Spirit. In one sense it is an immersion, a submergence within (baptized), in still another it is an invasion from without (outpouring, falling upon, coming on)."[20] The experience of the Spirit described in this language "is not some kind of mystical participation in the immanent presence of God. Rather, the language suggests a profound experience of the transcendent God coming powerfully to people."[21] It is not a subjective possibility but an objective certainty; not the realization of some innate spiritual potential within human beings, but a transcendent divine reality, the life and grace of the living God being imparted to his adopted sons and daughters.
>
> Is it significant that John Stott should title his non-charismatic book on the Holy Spirit *Baptism and Fullness*, two nouns that do not occur in the New Testament in association with the Holy Spirit? This book has a strong doctrinal or didactic emphasis, as opposed to experiential. The New Testament always uses the verbal forms, *baptize* and *fill*, in connection with the Holy Spirit,[22] suggesting the dynamic nature of the Spirit's activity (Matt 3:11; Luke 3:16; Acts 11:16; Luke 1:15, 41, 67; Acts 2:4; 4:8, 31; 9:17; 13:9; Eph 5:18). As David Pawson points out, "'Baptized' has an initiatory nuance; it seems to have been used only once in any individual's experience, of their first 'filling' (no one is said to have repeated 'baptisms' in the Spirit). 'Filled,' however, is used of subsequent outpourings of the Spirit."[23]

These biblical terms indicate the invasion of a person's life by God's Holy Spirit; an initiation into a reality so glorious that it cannot be grasped in any single term or description. They point to the Holy Spirit overwhelming us and taking control of our life, yet respecting our integrity, cooperating with our freedom, and fulfilling our deepest longings.

---

CMS in 1799, the organization he purported to represent (Yule, "Letter to the Editor," 6). Peter Hocken was coming to similar views (Hocken, *Challenges*, 129–37; Hocken, *Azusa, Rome, and Zion*, 147–61), but he died before I could discuss this with him.

20. Williams, "Baptism in the Holy Spirit," *DPCM* 42, *NIDPCM* 356.
21. Williams, *Renewal Theology*, 2:198.
22. As correctly noted by Pawson, *The Normal Christian Birth*, 66 and 68 respectively.
23. Pawson, *The Normal Christian Birth*, 68.

To be baptized in Holy Spirit is to enter into a new realm of experience of God's reality and a new effectiveness in God's service. We become aware of spiritual gifts and their role in serving God and ministering to others. We discover that they are the doorway to a life of effective service specially suited to our personality and aspirations; a life of "good works" that God has "prepared in advance for us to do" (Eph 2:10). The important thing is not to quibble about the terminology, but to enter into this marvelous experience and through it appropriate all that God wishes to impart to enrich our relationship with him and our service of his kingdom.

# 8

# Spiritual Gifts as Charisms of the Trinity

*Being baptized in Holy Spirit opens up an awareness of spiritual gifts and their role in edifying the believer and building up the Christian community. The New Testament mentions three categories of spiritual gifts. Some scholars merge them into a single gift inventory. But the three types of gifts, distinguished by the apostle Paul, reflect the different roles of the three persons of the Trinity. Manifestation gifts, the charismata proper, are the Holy Spirit's tools for effective ministry. Ministry gifts are the leaders the risen and ascended Lord provides to equip his body, the church. Motivational gifts reveal the Father's special providence in our personal makeup and calling. By recognizing and participating in these gifts, we gain a sense of personal involvement in God's purposes and fulfillment in his service.*

## Tokens of Providence

ONE OF THE MAIN reasons why people do not embrace the activity of the Holy Spirit is that they do not know how the Holy Spirit works. They have no firsthand experience. This is why Paul says, even to the Corinthian Christians, that he does not want them to be "uninformed" about "the gifts of the Spirit" (1 Cor 12:1). Many Christians do not know what spiritual gifts are, how they operate, what they are for. Paul writes with a pastoral concern that we might have a practical working knowledge of the Holy Spirit's gifts. By learning how the Holy Spirit works and by cooperating with the Spirit, we may become more effective in our work for God and more fulfilled in our particular sphere of service.

The word that Paul uses for the "gifts" of the Holy Spirit in Romans 12:6 and 1 Corinthians 12:4 is the plural Greek word *charismata*, from which we get the term "charismatic." Its singular, *charisma*, is Paul's "distinctive term for the manifold outworking of divine grace in individual Christians through the one Spirit," a "spiritual endowment for service in the life of the community."[1] *Charisma* comes from the Greek *charis*, meaning, "grace." As we have seen, Russell Spittler calls them "gracelets." They are specific, personalized expressions of God's grace.

It is important to recognize the gratuitous nature of spiritual gifts. Like gifts on a Christmas tree, they are given, not earned. They are free expressions of God's favor, granted to each one personally. They are not the result of holiness, or a reward for good behavior. God gives them generously, whether we deserve them or not.

But like the gifts on a Christmas tree, they have to be unwrapped, appreciated, and put to use. As we use them, we discover that a loving Father has given them to us with a view to our unique personality, interests, and calling. They reflect the Father's providential purpose for our lives. When we begin to use them we experience joy at being in touch with God, awe at the personal nature of God's love, and a sense of fulfillment in being useful in God's service.

Evangelicals, who emphasize the importance of holiness and godly character, need to understand the gratuitous nature of spiritual gifts. They are offered to all believers, regardless of maturity. They can be exercised by anyone who is open to the Spirit, even by immature Christians. So Paul is also concerned to help such Christians to grow in maturity and learn to operate in the gifts with sensitivity to others. Pentecostal and charismatic Christians, who stress the importance of spiritual gifts, need to grow in character and holiness and exercise the gifts in love (1 Cor 13:1–3). They are not for personal kudos or self-display.

Steve Clark says, "The work of the Spirit in us . . . is a gift. A gift can be given right away, all at once. And because it is a gift and not something that we have to grow into, it can be given at the beginning of the process of spiritual maturity as well as any place along the way." This is why it needs to be recognized that "a person who has been baptized in the Spirit still needs to

---

1. "Charis, Charisma," *NIDNTT* 4:660.

go through a process of spiritual maturing. One of the greatest dangers facing people who have experienced a filling with the Spirit is the misconception that they have arrived at spiritual maturity because of it. . . . Spiritual maturity comes to us through a process of effort and dedication. . . . The gift of the Spirit, on the other hand, comes to us through asking faith. It is a gift. . . . No amount of dedicated service can earn it."[2]

In 1 Corinthians 13:1–3 Paul gives a further list of charisms: speaking in tongues, prophecy, insight into mysteries, faith that can move mountains, giving away all one's possessions, and giving one's life in martyrdom. Without love, he says, the exercise of these gifts is worthless. Paul is not dismissing their value. He is saying that if the person exercising the gifts does so without love, it is of no benefit to them.

## The Nature of Spiritual Gifts

The term "spiritual gifts" comes from 1 Corinthians 12:1. Paul introduces his guidance to the Christian community in Corinth with the words, "Now concerning spiritual gifts." Literally translated, "concerning spiritual matters" (*peri ton pneumatikon*), he is referring to matters that involve the direct inspiration or activity of the Holy Spirit.

The way that Paul introduces the subject of "spiritual gifts" in 1 Corinthians suggests that it was the Corinthians themselves who had raised the matter with him. It appears, from chapter 7 onwards, that Paul has been giving his solutions to problems that the Corinthians had raised in earlier correspondence with him. He opens chapter 7 with a phrase that could be translated, "Now concerning the matters you wrote about," and repeats this phrase at 7:25, 8:1, 12:1, and 16:1. In 12:1, Paul responds to questions "concerning spiritual gifts." There is general agreement among commentators that Paul is dealing with an exaggerated emphasis on speaking in tongues and an inconsiderate use of this gift in worship in the Christian community in Corinth.

The phrase *ton pneumatikon* (1 Cor 12:1) is usually translated "spiritual gifts." This has become the accepted generic term for God's gifts, which I follow in this chapter. A more literal translation is "matters of the Spirit." Gregorian University theologian Francis Sullivan suggests that the closest English equivalent is "gifts of inspiration."[3] Paul begins the chapter by contrasting how the Corinthians were inspired in their pagan rites before they became Christians, which involved ecstatic states and the overriding of their personalities, with their present inspiration by the Holy Spirit that "Jesus is Lord," which presupposes their free cooperation (1 Cor 12:2–3; 14:32; 2 Cor 3:17). In the next three chapters, he discusses how to express the Spirit's inspiration in Christian worship and the life of the community.

Various ways have been proposed of classifying spiritual gifts. Compilers of modern spiritual gifts inventories often gather them into a single comprehensive list. This overlooks their distinctive origin, nature, and

---

2. Clark, *Baptized in the Spirit*, 46–48.
3. Sullivan, *Charisms and Charismatic Renewal*, 21.

significance. Arnold Bittlinger suggests a fourfold classification: "gifts of proclamation" (prophecy, teaching, words of wisdom or knowledge), "gifts of service" (administration of money, stewardship of possessions, acts of mercy, leadership), "gifts of special power" (faith, healing, exorcism, miracles), and "gifts of prayer" (praying or singing in the Spirit, interpreting, giving thanks).[4] I prefer the threefold classification that Paul himself makes when introducing them. "There are different kinds of gifts (*charismata*), but the same Spirit distributes them. There are different kinds of service (*diakoniai*), but the same Lord. There are different kinds of working (*energēmata*), but in all of them and in everyone it is the same God at work" (1 Cor 12:4–6).

In this threefold classification, Paul identifies three kinds of spiritual gifts. The first are the charismatic gifts proper, the *charismata* (singular *charisma*), which are the result of the immediate inspiration of the Holy Spirit, distinct from human talents and natural abilities. These are the "charisms" that he goes on to discuss in 1 Corinthians 12 and 14. He distinguishes them from the second kind of gifts, *diakoniai*, the "ministries" given by the risen and ascended Lord for the building up of his church, which he discusses in Ephesians 4. These, in turn, are different from *energēmata*, the primary "activities" or callings of Christian believers, gifts that are of a more psychological or vocational nature and do relate to human abilities, which he discusses in Romans 12.

All the gifts have in view the distinctive contribution each member makes to the Christian community, the body of Christ. In 1 Corinthians 12, Paul begins with the gifts and moves to the body of Christ. In Romans 12:3–8, he moves from consideration of the body of Christ to the gifts. In Ephesians 4:10–13, he begins with the gifts of the risen and ascended Lord and moves to their role in building up the body of Christ.

Francis Sullivan notes, "For Paul the charisms are the principle of differentiation in the body of Christ. It is the charisms that determine which function each member is to have, and that enable each member to have that function."[5] "Without the charisms," he notes, "one could no longer speak of the Christian community as a body, because it would lack a principle of differentiation, essential to every living body."[6] This draws our attention to the distinctive role of the Holy Spirit as the agent of personal differentiation.

This threefold classification of the gifts has a trinitarian pattern. Each category of gifts has its origin in one of the three persons of the Trinity and reflects the distinctive role that person plays in the divine economy. Paul

---

4. Bittlinger, *Gifts and Ministries*, 17.
5. Sullivan, *Charisms and Charismatic Renewal*, 19.
6. Sullivan, *Charisms and Charismatic Renewal*, 20.

attributes the *charismata* to the immediate inspiration of the Holy Spirit, the ministries for building up the body of Christ to the Son, and our distinctive activities or vocations to the providence of God the Father.

It may be asked why Paul should introduce three classes of gifts then only expound one. This is because the situation he was addressing in the Corinthian church involved the first category only, the exercise of specifically charismatic gifts. The threefold summary in 1 Corinthians 12:4–6 reveals that he had a more comprehensive grasp of the subject, but the situation in Corinth meant it was appropriate only to discuss the *charismata* with them. Later, he will explain the ministry gifts in his letter to the Ephesians, when talking about the relationship between the risen and ascended Christ and the Christian community (4:7–13). He will deal with the motivational or vocational gifts when discussing how believers may know God's "good, pleasing, and perfect will" in their lives, as he introduces the pastoral section of his letter to the Romans (12:1–8).

I had developed this trinitarian classification of spiritual gifts before I discovered that Francis Sullivan had made passing reference to it, without elaborating on it further. "Paul uses three terms: *charismata* (gifts), *diakoniai* (services), and *energēmata* (workings), and seems to attribute the charisms to the Spirit, the services to the Lord Jesus, and the workings to God the Father." Rather than seeing them as "three distinct categories of gifts," he prefers to see them as three aspects of a single phenomenon: "all these grace gifts (*charismata*) are meant for service (*diakonia*) and all are workings of divine power (*energēmata*).[7]

Arnold Bittlinger, too, recognizes the trinitarian pattern of Paul's thought. "Behind this whole activity stands the triune God who works 'all in all' (1 Cor 15:28): the God who encounters us as *pneuma*–Spirit, as *kyrios*–Lord, and as *theos*–God." Even the emphasis on unity and variety is trinitarian. On the one hand, Paul emphasizes unity: "the *same* Spirit, the *same* Lord, the *same* God." On the other, he stresses variety: "there are *varieties* of gifts, *varieties* of service, *varieties* of working" (1 Cor 12:4–6, RSV). "The nature of God is infinite variety," says Bittlinger. "God is not uniform; he is many-sided."[8]

Paul's threefold classification of spiritual gifts is practical, clarifying, and illuminating. It illustrates his remarkable theological understanding, complemented by his pastoral insight and sensitivity. It helps us understand the varied nature of God's gifts, how they relate to each of us personally and to our fellow Christians, and how they build up the church. Understanding the gifts and how they operate has brought a sense of personal fulfillment to many Christians, in their service of others and the church.

The foregoing threefold classification of spiritual gifts contrasts with what has become the standard approach of evangelical scholars, which is to list them all together in a single spiritual gifts inventory. This tends to result in treating supernatural gifts as if they were the same as natural talents.

---

7. Sullivan, *Charisms and Charismatic Renewal*, 29.
8. Bittlinger, *Gifts and Graces*, 21.

In 1974, C. Peter Wagner published his first account of spiritual gifts, designed to harness them for church growth.[9] In 1979, he adapted his inventory to include the insights of Richard F. Houts, a professor at North American Baptist Theological Seminary. The resulting "Wagner-Modified Houts Questionnaire" has become the standard spiritual gifts inventory, comprised of 125 questions correlated to twenty-five gifts, including celibacy, intercession, and voluntary poverty.

An example of Wagner's reduction of specifically charismatic gifts to personal attributes in general is his treatment of the gift of knowledge. Wagner assimilates this to knowledge in general, more typical of the ministry gift of a teacher like himself. "The gift of knowledge is the special ability that God gives to certain members of the body of Christ to discover, accumulate, analyze, and clarify information and ideas which are pertinent to the well being of the body."[10]

This is at variance with how the word of knowledge is understood and functions in Pentecostal and charismatic circles. A word of knowledge is a Holy Spirit inspired insight, usually into something about a person, or about what God is doing in a meeting, that could not be known by natural means. It often indicates God's intention to perform certain healings. From his extensive experience of the healing ministry, Fr. John Rea, SM, says, "often when the Holy Spirit exercises a word of knowledge it means there is an anointing on a gathering for that kind of healing."[11]

The definition of spiritual gifts and their relationship to natural abilities needs careful handling. James Dunn rightly says that the *charismata* are *"not to be confused with human talent and natural ability*; nowhere does charisma have the sense of the human capacity heightened, developed or transformed." He acknowledges that the *charismata* are expressed through an individual's "disposition and temperament" and "make use of natural abilities." But in Paul's usage the *charismata* proper are *"always* God acting, *always* the Spirit manifesting himself." For Paul, *"every* charisma was supernatural."[12]

Arnold Bittlinger's view that spiritual gifts lead "natural endowments" to "blossom forth"[13] is therefore not true of the *charismata* proper (1 Cor 12:7–11), which are miraculous graces of the Holy Spirit beyond any normal human ability to perform. His comment, strictly speaking, applies to the gifts listed in Romans 12:4–8, which I class as "motivational gifts" and which do relate closely to our natural aptitudes.

---

9. Wagner, *Your Spiritual Gifts*.

10. "Wagner-Modified Houts Questionnaire," definition C. Anthony Thiselton, too, defines what he calls a "communication of knowledge" as "knowledge of basic Christian truths" or "instruction in the basic truths of the gospel" (Thiselton, *The Holy Spirit*, 88).

11. Rea, *Witness to Wonders*, 17.

12. Dunn, *Jesus and the Spirit*, 255 (italics original).

13. Bittlinger, *Gifts and Graces*, 72.

Francis Sullivan also argues that the *charismata* "presuppose, build upon, and perfect the natural capacities that are already present."[14] The example he gives, that of teaching, properly belongs in the list of motivational gifts, where it is true that a person may be endowed with a natural capacity to teach, and the charism for teaching may add "a new willingness to employ this capacity" and a "new effectiveness in teaching." One can see this in a great Bible teacher like David Pawson, whose teaching often had a prophetic quality. But it is straining the facts to argue that more supernatural charisms, such as healing and miracles, "add a great deal to the natural capacities of the person who is used as an instrument of such gifts."[15] No human being possesses a natural ability to heal the sick or work miracles. That is why Jesus' mighty deeds raised the question of who he was (Mark 4:41), and why signs and wonders play such an important part in evangelism (Rom 15:18–19).

## Manifestation Gifts

Manifestation gifts are the *charismata* proper, the dynamic gifts exercised in Christian meetings or pastoral ministry. Of the seventeen occurrences of the word *charisma* (plural *charismata*) in the New Testament, all but one (1 Pet 4:10) are in the letters of Paul, seven in his correspondence with the Corinthians. Such charisms are distributed: "Each of you has your own gift from God; one has this gift, another has that" (1 Cor 7:7). The point is reiterated in Paul's rhetorical question: "Do all work miracles? Do all have gifts of healing? Do all speak in tongues? Do all interpret?" (1 Cor 12:29–30). As Francis Sullivan observes, "One person receives this gift, another that, and there is no one charism that everyone needs to have or should expect to have."[16]

Manifestation gifts are the nine specifically charismatic gifts best known from Pentecostal and charismatic gatherings (1 Cor 12:7–11): giving a word or message of knowledge (*logos gnōseōs*), giving a word or message of discernment (*logos sophias*), the gift of faith (*pistis*), gifts of healings (both terms plural, *charismata iamatōn*), deeds of power (also plural, *energēmata dynameōn*, "miracles, wonders"), prophesying (*prophēteia*), distinguishing between spirits (*diakriseis pneumatōn*), various kinds of tongues (*glossōn*), and interpretation of tongues (*hermēneia glossōn*).

---

14. Sullivan, *Charisms and Charismatic Renewal*, 13.
15. Sullivan, *Charisms and Charismatic Renewal*, 13.
16. Sullivan, *Charisms and Charismatic Renewal*, 18.

These are called "manifestation gifts" because they "show forth" or "make known" God's reality in a dynamic way in the context of a Christian meeting or a pastoral situation, though they are not limited to such settings. Paul explains, "Now to each one the manifestation (*phanerōsis*) of the Spirit is given, for the common good (*pros to sympheron*)" (1 Cor 12:7, RSV, NIV). Francis Sullivan prefers to translate *pros to sympheron*, "for a useful purpose," since charisms are often for the direct benefit of individuals and only indirectly for the community as a whole. They are "manifestations of the Spirit for a useful purpose."[17]

Sullivan describes the charismatic gifts as "an immediate intervention of the Spirit, in which he exercises his sovereign freedom to allot his gifts as he wills and to whomever he wills, in a way that cannot be foreseen or controlled by man."[18] They are the manifestation or outworking of the presence of the Holy Spirit in and through believers and in the lives of people to whom they minister. God gives such gifts as they are needed in any situation, whether in a worship service, in a ministry setting, or in personal counsel.

Manifestation gifts, the charismatic gifts in the strict sense, are dynamic. They are given by the Spirit as and when required, for example, as a gift of healing for someone sick, as a gift of discernment for someone needing guidance or reassurance, or as a prophetic insight for personal encouragement or rebuke. Christians have only one primary motivational gift, but as they are open to the Holy Spirit, they can be the channel for any number or combination of manifestation gifts. Such gifts are not "on tap," but are given by the Holy Spirit in particular situations on an "as required" basis. Because of their effectiveness, such gifts are to be eagerly desired (1 Cor 12:31). They are to be exercised, not in competition but in love (1 Cor 13:1–3), for the mutual upbuilding of the Christian community.

In his book, *Releasing Spiritual Gifts Today*, James Goll discusses the nine manifestation gifts in three groups: "Revelatory Gifts," "Power Gifts," and "Vocal Gifts." "Revelatory Gifts" are the three gifts that "reveal": discerning of spirits, word of wisdom, and word of knowledge. "Power Gifts" are the gifts that "do": faith, healings, and workings of miracles. "Vocal Gifts" are the gifts that "speak": tongues, interpretation of tongues, and prophecy.

---

17. Sullivan, *Charisms and Charismatic Renewal*, 22, 78.
18. Sullivan, *Charisms and Charismatic Renewal*, 12.

## Particular Charismata

### 1. Words of Knowledge and Wisdom

We have already seen that a *word* or *message of knowledge* (*logos gnōseōs*) is a gift of insight that cannot be known by natural means, usually into a person's life or what God is doing in a meeting. Closely related is a *word* or *message of wisdom* (*logos sophias*, 1 Cor 12:8). This is a God-given insight to provide an instantly recognizable solution to a difficult situation. It calls to mind Solomon's proposal to divide a baby to show which of two quarrelling women was the true mother (1 Kgs 3:25), and Jesus' promise that when Christians are brought to trial, God would give "words and wisdom" to respond (Luke 21:15).

The most unusual word of knowledge I have ever had came to me when waking up one morning. The letters "LPG" came clearly to my mind. I dismissed the thought. A couple of days later I felt convicted. "Rob, you can't expect the Lord to show you people's needs on Sunday and dismiss what he shows you during the week." So I rang my garage mechanic. "Rob, how interesting you should phone!" he said. "The Liquid Fuels Authority has a special promotion at the moment. They're offering free installation of LPG systems in motor vehicles, charging only $500 for the components." With liquid petroleum gas (LPG) costing only half the price of petrol, its installation saved us thousands of dollars during our most expensive family years.

Once, in a pastoral situation, I had a striking experience of the word of wisdom. A young woman came to my office, confused and desperate. Two young men were interested in her. She didn't know what to do. Without premeditation, a solution popped into my mind. "Play difficult to get. Ask for time out, and watch the reaction." Some time later she came back, beaming. One young man had been angry and demanding, not wanting to accept her request. The other was a complete gentleman. He honored her decision, left her alone, and treated her with dignity and respect. She had her answer! Later, I had the joy of celebrating their marriage!

### 2. Faith to Move Mountains

Both Bittlinger and Sullivan point out that the gift of *faith* (*pistis*, 1 Cor 12:9) is not to be confused with "saving faith," the faith exercised in becoming a Christian (John 3:16), by which "the righteous will live" (Rom 1:17) and without which "it is impossible to please God" (Heb 11:6). Nor is it the faithfulness which as a fruit of the Spirit (Gal 5:22) every Christian should display. Rather, the gift of faith is the faith that Jesus spoke of, the specific "faith that can move mountains" (Matt 17:20; 1 Cor 13:2), given as a gift of divine grace to individuals at particular times. It is a gift of confidence that God will intervene in a specific situation.[19]

In 1996, during my second visit to Harvest International Ministries Bible School at Kostelec nad Orlicí in the Czech Republic, I had a dramatic illustration of this gift. The Bible School was threatened with closure by the district authorities because of fecal contamination of its water supply. I felt led to suggest that they should follow the example of Elisha (2 Kgs 2:19–22) and pray over the wellhead. After some debate and equivocation over this proposal, the leaders of the Bible School finally agreed. On 26 November I went out in the snow with the Old Testament lecturer Michal Krchňak and several students. We threw salt down the two wells and prayed over them for the cleansing of the water.

Nine days later, on 6 December, the senior student Stefan Vrubel burst into my room waving a piece of paper. "Rob, it's a great miracle!" He was holding a scientific report from the District Hygiene Station at Rychnov nad Kněžnou. It reported a drop in microorganisms in the water from 200 to 4, of fecal coliform material from 31 to 0, and even an improvement in the chemical composition of the water! The Bible School could stay![20]

### 3. Healings and Miracles

Paul does not speak of the gift of *healing* in the singular. Both substantives he uses are plural. The literal translation is "gifts of healings" (*charismata iamatōn*). Sullivan rightly notes, "Paul does not speak of anyone as having 'the gift of healing' (which would suggest a habitual power to heal people), but he sees each healing as a distinct charism or gift of grace."[21] The implication of Paul's language, which is repeated three times in this chapter (1 Cor 12:9, 28, 30), is that each healing is a specific instance of God's solicitude.

Paul's use of the plural also includes another phenomenon observed by those in the healing ministry today, that different people seem to be used in different areas of healing. Derek Prince, for example, found that God used him to heal back problems by lengthening legs and bringing them into alignment. Fr. John Rea, a New Zealand Marist priest with extensive experience in the healing ministry, found that God used him extensively in the healing of hand injuries following the healing of the damaged fingers of Sarah McCracken, an accomplished violinist, which had been crushed in a bus door. He also found that God also gave him a special effectiveness in praying for infertile couples to have children.[22]

---

19. Bittlinger, *Gifts and Graces*, 32; Sullivan, *Charisms and Charismatic Renewal*, 32.
20. Yule, "More Pages from a Bohemian Diary," 53.
21. Sullivan, *Charisms and Charismatic Renewal*, 32, cf. 151.
22. Rea, *Wonders Still Abounding*, 8–25. The healing of Sarah McCracken, a child prodigy, is described in Rea, *Witness to Wonders*, 66–69.

It is similar with what is often translated *miracles* (KJV, RSV, NRSV), though the word "miracles" does not appear in the Greek (1 Cor 12:10, 28, 29). Again Paul uses two plural nouns, *energēmata dynameōn*, which Anthony Thiselton translates as "effective deeds of power."[23] This is like Acts 19:11–12, which describes the miracles and exorcisms which God worked through Paul as *dynameis* or "deeds of power."

Why are some healed and some not, in response to our prayers? The issue is a stumbling block to many and the focus of many criticisms. What I find interesting is that those most involved in the healing ministry are the first to admit that they do not know the answer.

Rev. Jim Chambers was an early exponent of the healing ministry in New Zealand. He estimated that some 40 percent are "completely healed," another 40 percent "helped considerably," and the remaining 20 percent show "no signs of healing." He could not say for sure, because so few let him know. Among the reasons why people are not healed he observed a lack of expectation, the lack of a really serious desire to be healed, or being surrounded by people who were not in favor of divine healing. As in Jesus' hometown of Nazareth (Matt 13:58), he found there can be general unbelief among a group of people as a whole. Some are resigned to their sickness or regard it as a cross they have to carry. Others neglect common-sense patterns of healthy living. Ultimately, he admits, why some are healed and others not "still remains a mystery."[24]

Fr. John Rea, reflecting on a lifetime of experience, draws the same conclusion:

> Neither . . . has Jesus Christ healed everyone we have prayed with. Sometimes we have made elaborate preparations beforehand. We have enrolled the support of others . . . and we have fasted. All to no avail as far as we could see. At other times we have reeled off a prayer with little or no thought and no preparation, and the Lord has healed the sick person who often had a serious illness. Some get completely well. Some report notable improvement in health. Others seem to remain unchanged. Some are healed immediately and others over a period of days or weeks or months or years. We do not know why. Nobody knows why. The God of our Lord Jesus Christ remains sovereignly in charge.[25]

---

23. Thiselton, *The Holy Spirit*, 105.
24. Chambers, *Is Any Sick Among You?* 51–53.
25. Rea, *Witness to Wonders*, 5.

As any doctor knows, healing is a combination and interplay of many factors. It is wisest to take a holistic approach. It is also important to view healing in the framework of a realistic eschatology. While the Holy Spirit is the presence of the *eschaton*, the in-breaking of the kingdom of God, we do not yet live in the completion of that reality. New Testament scholarship has reached a consensus that the kingdom of God is both a present and future reality, a view described as "inaugurated eschatology." With the coming of Jesus as the anointed Messiah, the kingdom of God has broken into our imperfect world. But we are not yet in the ultimate fullness of that kingdom. Signs and wonders accompany our testimony and proclamation of Jesus as Savior and Healer. We do see miracles of healing. But not everyone is healed, nor is healing complete, because God's kingdom has not yet fully come. Christian experience lives in this tension between ambivalence and final victory, which keeps us from shallow triumphalism.[26]

## 4. Prophetic Insight

Paul rates the gift of *prophecy* (*prophēteia*) highly, particularly because of its evangelistic potential. He explains that its exercise can bring conviction to a visitor in a Christian gathering. Tongues would at best leave an unbeliever mystified, at worst confirmed in their unbelief. But a prophecy may disclose the secrets of an unbeliever's heart, leading to the conviction of sin or awareness of God's presence (1 Cor 14:24–25).

Arnold Bittlinger links the prophetic gift of discerning the secrets of the heart—closely linked with the word of wisdom—with those specially gifted in spiritual counsel. Seraphim of Sarov (1759–1833), for example, was a Russian Orthodox *starets* who in 1825 emerged from thirty-one years of solitude and prayer with the ability to read the secrets of people's hearts. People, sometimes hundreds a day, flocked to him to receive his counsel. He would often describe their needs before they had even spoken. Jean-Baptiste Vianney (1786–1859), the Catholic priest of Ars, was a Western Christian with a similar ministry. By 1855, he was receiving twenty thousand visitors a year. With very few words he could bring comfort to the troubled, swiftly answer complicated questions of conscience, and give acceptable solutions to complex problems.[27]

The Corinthian Christians appear to have been taking pride in the exercise of *glossolalia*, speaking in tongues. Paul commends prophecy because, unlike *glossolalia*, it combines inspiration and intelligibility. As James

---

26. See my booklet, *The Return of Jesus*, 9–11, 20–21. Thiselton also applies this understanding of the kingdom of God to the ambiguity of hope and disappointment over healing in *The Holy Spirit*, 487–88.

27. Bittlinger, *Gifts and Ministries*, 67–68.

Dunn comments, "prophecy is as much inspired speech, as much a 'speaking with the Spirit,' as much a charisma, as glossolalia; the difference is that glossolalia is unintelligible whereas prophecy is intelligible."[28] Paul lays great stress on intelligibility in Christian gatherings. "I thank God that I speak in tongues more than all of you. But in the church I would rather speak five intelligible words to instruct others than ten thousand words in a tongue" (1 Cor 14:18-19).

Wayne Grudem carefully considers the matter of the authority of prophecy. He argues that no one in the church at Corinth "gave forth words of God," spoke "with a divine authority of actual words," or were thought to speak "with an absolute divine authority" as the Old Testament prophets did.[29] Instead, he characterizes New Testament prophecy—and, by implication, prophecy in Pentecostal and charismatic gatherings today—as the more modest "speaking merely human words to report something God brings to mind."[30]

I would omit the word "merely," which needlessly disparages the phenomenon. But Grudem is right to draw attention to a matter that brings prophecy into disrepute. Assembly of God leader Donald Gee says, "We hear to a point of weariness the phrase, 'I the Lord say unto you.'... It is not essential. The message can be given in less elevated language."[31] It is much better to preface a prophetic intuition more modestly, "I believe the Lord has shown me . . . ," or "I think the Lord is suggesting . . ."[32] Grudem concludes that prophecies today should be viewed "as the prophet's own fairly accurate (but not infallible) report of something he thinks (though not with absolute certainty) has been revealed to him by God."[33]

## 5. Distinguishing Spirits

In Pentecostal and charismatic literature *distinguishing between spirits* (*diakriseis pneumaton*) is usually viewed as "the ability to distinguish between divine, human and demonic powers."[34] Resisting the tendency of scholars to restrict this gift to the testing of prophets and prophecy, Wayne Grudem prefers to define it as "the ability to recognize the influence of the Holy Spirit or of demonic spirits in a person."[35]

---

28. Dunn, *Jesus and the Spirit*, 229.
29. Grudem, *The Gift of Prophecy*, 84-87.
30. Grudem, *The Gift of Prophecy*, 67, 89, 167.
31. Gee, *Spiritual Gifts*, 48.
32. Suggestions quoted by Grudem, *The Gift of Prophecy*, 113, from Yocum, *Prophecy*, 38; and Pain, *Prophecy*, 56.
33. Grudem, *The Gift of Prophecy*, 167.
34. So, for example, Bittlinger, *Gifts and Graces*, 45.
35. Grudem, *The Gift of Prophecy*, 71.

New Testament scholars tend to link discernment of spirits with the exercise of the gift of prophecy, which precedes it in Paul's list. Francis Martin sees discernment of spirits as a "control" on prophecy, just as the gift of interpretation functions as a "control" on tongues. He sees its primary role as "the Spirit-conferred capacity to judge the origin and content of prophecy."[36] Francis Sullivan says, "Prophecy is 'inspired speech', and discerning of spirits has to do with determining by what spirit the speaker is inspired." He limits discerning of spirits to "the grace-given ability to see beneath the phenomenon of inspiration and to judge correctly whether the speaker is really being inspired by the Holy Spirit or not."[37] But there is no reason to limit its scope to prophecy when it also functions as a wider gift of discrimination.

## 6. Tongues and Interpretation

The Greek word *glossolalia* (*en glossais lalein* in the New Testament) is usually translated "speaking in tongues." But as Bittlinger observes, "This translation is unfortunate, for it breeds misunderstanding from the outset."[38] "Tongues" is archaic English for "languages." Confusion arises because today the word is used of the organ of speech. Werner Meyer comments, "Glossolalia is speaking languages. Certainly not, as is so often mistakenly assumed, an inarticulate babbling and rolling of the tongue. The tongue plays no other role in glossolalia than it does in normal speech. The Greek word *glōssa* carries the force here exclusively of 'language.'"[39] So Bittlinger describes the gift of tongues as "praying in the Spirit," the pouring out of the heart to God, and defines it as "the possibility of expressing the inexpressible and praising God in new languages."[40]

Sullivan defines the speaking in tongues that Paul describes in the Corinthian church as "articulate human speech, at least resembling the speaking of an unknown language."[41] Paul uses the word in the plural (1 Cor 14:5), which rules out that he is referring to the speech organ, the tongue (Greek *glōssa*). He also envisages the possibility of saying "ten thousand words in a tongue" (1 Cor 14:19), which means that it is not inarticulate groaning or sighing. Tongues-speaking was unintelligible to both the speaker and to the hearers, which is why Paul lays such stress on the importance of the gift of interpretation (1 Cor 14:13) and gives priority to prophecy as inspired speech that is intelligible (1 Cor 14:5). Paul sees it as a gift that is useful in

---

36. Martin, "Discernment of Spirits," in *DPCM* 246, *NIDPCM* 584.

37. Sullivan, *Charisms and Charismatic Renewal*, 33-34.

38. Bittlinger, *Gifts and Graces*, 97.

39. Meyer, *Der erste Brief an die Korinther* [The First Letter to the Corinthians], 2:194, quoted by Bittlinger, *Gifts and Graces*, 97.

40. Bittlinger, *Gifts and Graces*, 48.

41. Sullivan, *Charisms and Charismatic Renewal*, 127, cf. 123.

private prayer to God (1 Cor 14:2). In a Christian gathering, it is to be used with the accompanying gift of interpretation, when it has the same role as prophecy (1 Cor 14:5), and even then by not more than two or three speakers (1 Cor 14:27).

In New Zealand, I have always found it odd that the indigenous Pentecostal or New Life churches, following the practice of pioneers like Peter Morrow, have mandated a free-for-all session of everyone praying aloud together in tongues. I have never seen in their gatherings anyone practicing the Pauline injunction of tongues plus interpretation (1 Cor 14:6–17, 26–32). They miss the powerful impact that this practice can have.

The New English Bible renders the word *glōssa* "ecstatic utterance" or "tongues of ecstasy," on analogy with the phenomenon in the Greek mystery religions. This imports into the New Testament experience the loss of consciousness that accompanied ecstatic states in the pagan cults.[42] Modern research on tongues shows that, on the contrary, tongues-speaking by Pentecostals and charismatics rarely involves loss of self-control.

Sullivan cites scientific linguistic analyses of tongues-speaking. Such studies show that glossolalia has sophisticated language-like characteristics that differentiate it from contrived speech or mumbo-jumbo. The jury is still out whether genuine foreign languages are involved (*xenoglossia*). But the only evidence of ecstasy or altered mental states was in some instances of speaking in tongues for the first time when a person was baptized in the Holy Spirit. There was no evidence of ecstatic states in the later use of the gift.[43]

Tongues, my late friend John Brook observed laconically, "is not ecstatic utterance. I am quite sure that none of the sober English scholars who translated the New English Bible had ever spoken in tongues."[44]

"Tongues is the least of the gifts," says Brook. "It is like the door to the Church of the Nativity in Bethlehem. It can only be entered by stooping very low. It is often the doorway to the other gifts because it breaks the pride and reserve we often use as a system of defense against God. Tongues is a precious expression of the inner freedom of the children of God. It is an inarticulate prayer of love."[45]

---

42. For criticism of the view that Christian prophecy involves altered states of consciousness, see Grudem, *The Gift of Prophecy*, 124–28. Abraham Heschel similarly rejected the notion of ecstasy as an explanation of the inspiration of the Hebrew prophets (Heschel, *The Prophets*, 2:104–46). The UPCUSA's careful 1970 report used the word "ecstasy" only to indicate that "one may feel emotionally lifted, inspired by God's Spirit, not that one behaves in an irrational or trance-like manner" (UPCUSA, *Work of the Holy Spirit*, 5).

43. Sullivan, *Charisms and Charismatic Renewal*, 132–35, 137–39.

44. Brook, "Charismatic Contribution," 10.

45. Brook, "Charismatic Contribution," 10.

Sullivan notes that singing in the Spirit (1 Cor 14:15) often produces "a strangely beautiful harmony."[46] He likens it to what earlier Christian tradition called *jubilate*, singing without words from a full heart and in harmony when others are present.[47] He compares it to the psalmist "making a joyful noise" to God (Ps 66:1, 95:1-2, NRSV). He quotes Augustine, who says, "to sing in jubilation" means "that you cannot express in words what your heart is singing":

> For whom is such jubilation fitting if not for the ineffable God? For he is ineffable whom one cannot express in words; and if you cannot express him in words, and yet you cannot remain silent either, then what is left but to sing in jubilation, so that your heart may rejoice without words, and your unbounded joy may not be confined by the limits of syllables.[48]

Arnold Bittlinger mentions a tradition that the *Te Deum* came into existence in this manner, as Ambrose and Augustine sang alternate lines together in the Spirit on the night of Augustine's baptism, Easter 387.[49] "Isn't He Great!"—which I consider to be the finest praise song to emerge from the charismatic renewal movement in New Zealand—was composed in similar circumstances by Spreydon Baptist musicians Kirsten Fordyce and Vicki Trustrum. Vicki describes how it came about. "Kirsten kept hearing this melody over and over and one day while I was at her place she played it and sang in tongues. I told her we can pray for the interpretation. The words for 'Isn't He Great!' just flowed." After this, they wrote quite a few songs together in this manner.[50]

In 1 Corinthians, Paul makes three statements clarifying the significance and use of glossolalia. First, he says it is "placed in the church" by God (1 Cor 12:28). It is to be taken seriously, not belittled or dismissed. Cessationists often fasten on a tendentious interpretation of 1 Corinthians 13:8 (KJV), "tongues . . . shall cease," but overlook this positive affirmation of the gift.

Second, it is speaking to God, incomprehensible to humans unless accompanied by the complementary gift of interpretation. "Anyone who speaks in a tongue . . . utters mysteries by the Spirit" (1 Cor 14:2). Such praying in the Spirit is both more specific and more comprehensive than

---

46. Sullivan, *Charisms and Charismatic Renewal*, 146.

47. Sullivan, *Charisms and Charismatic Renewal*, 145-48.

48. From Augustine, *Enarrationes in Psalmos* [Exposition of the Psalms], 32.ii, quoted in Sullivan, *Charisms and Charismatic Renewal*, 147.

49. Mahrenholz et al., *Handbuch zum evangelischen Kirchengesangbuch* [Companion to the Protestant church hymnbook], 220, cited in Bittlinger, *Gifts and Graces*, 112.

50. Vicki Trustrum, email to the author, 13 April 2019.

the prayers we can formulate with the mind, because "the Spirit himself intercedes for us" in ways that words cannot express and "in accordance with the will of God" (Rom 8:26–27).

Third, prayer in tongues "edifies" or "builds up" the personality of the one who exercises the gift (1 Cor 14:4).[51] It is thought to have a psychological benefit to the person praying, as the Spirit of God works in the unconscious, bringing "a non-intellectual means of meditation and release."[52]

Sullivan rightly regards Paul as teaching that tongues "when combined with interpretation is equal to prophecy, and performs the same function."[53] Bittlinger defines *interpretation of tongues* (*hermēneia glossōn*) as "a complementary gift which makes possible the use of tongues in the meeting for worship." The interpretation is not a word for word translation but conveys the essential content or sense of the tongues message.[54]

Why then is tongues not dispensed with and a prophecy given instead? In Sullivan's opinion, speaking in tongues followed by prophecy "is best understood as prophecy in two moments." In a charismatic meeting, "the prior speaking in tongues creates an atmosphere of intense inner listening, of expectancy for a word from the Lord."[55]

> My first realization that the Holy Spirit was prompting me was when I failed to give an interpretation of a tongues message. Jackie Pullinger was speaking at a combined service at Hornby Anglican Church in Christchurch, New Zealand on 7 August 1983. She began her talk in an arresting way, with a message in tongues, then invited someone present to give the interpretation. I sensed something like, "If Jesus Christ is God and died for you, what is . . ." But I couldn't discern what came next. Never having shared an interpretation or prophecy before, I said nothing.
>
> Jackie went on to tell how she came to minister in the squalid, crime-infested, ancient walled city of Hong Kong. She described how she had given up all her possessions except for a valuable oboe, for she was a trained musician. One day, ministering to a female prostitute who had just become a Christian, she was struggling whether to take this woman into her meager home and sacrifice her last bit of privacy. Reluctant to do so, she suggested to the prostitute, "Why don't we pray about it?" So Jackie prayed in tongues for God's guidance. To her astonishment and discomfort, the new convert gave the interpretation: "If Jesus Christ is God and died for you, what's an oboe!" I could have crawled under the seat! I had been given the crunch line of her talk.

---

51. The characteristically Pauline term, *oikodomeo*, means to "benefit, strengthen, establish" as well as to "edify" (AG 561).

52. Hollenweger, *Der erste Korintherbrief* [The First Letter to the Corinthians], 27, quoted by Bittlinger, *Gifts and Graces*, 99. Cf. Kelsey, *Tongue Speaking* (1965).

53. Sullivan, *Charisms and Charismatic Renewal*, 149.

54. Bittlinger, *Gifts and Graces*, 51; Sullivan, *Charisms and Charismatic Renewal*, 149.

55. Sullivan, *Charisms and Charismatic Renewal*, 149.

If I had spoken the interpretation, it would have been an encouragement to her that the Lord was present, underlining her message.

## 7. Permanency or Frequency?

I have already mentioned that Paul never speaks of anyone having a habitual "gift of healing," nor does he describe any individuals as "healers." But he does acknowledge that some individuals are used with greater frequency as instruments of healings. Sullivan sees a parallel with prophecy: "As the vocation of the prophet does not confer the habitual power to prophesy (the prophet must wait for God's word to come to him), neither does the ministry of gifts of healing confer a habitual power to heal people (it is God who heals, when and as he chooses to manifest his power through this person's ministry)."[56]

The only permanent ministries Paul recognizes are apostles, prophets, and teachers, together with evangelists and pastors (Eph 4:11). In 1 Corinthians 12:28–30, after referring to apostles, prophets, and teachers, he reverts to the dynamic terms he has already used in his previous list of charisms, namely *dynameis* (deeds of power) and *charismata iamatōn* (charisms of healing). Sullivan explains: "these terms bring out that Paul's view that each miracle, each healing, is a distinct charism . . . While he speaks of prophets and teachers, he does not speak of 'miracle-workers' or 'healers.'"[57] This means that the occasional exercise of prophecy must be distinguished from the recognized ministry of the prophet. We need to bear this in mind as we consider these ministries.

Paul's list in 1 Corinthians 12:28–30 differentiates between people (apostles, prophets, teachers) and activities (miracles, healings, giving help, governance, speaking in tongues). This, as Bittlinger recognizes, is a link between the gift lists in 1 Corinthians 12:7–11, Romans 12:4–8, and Ephesians 4:11.[58] Of particular interest is Paul's only reference, also in the plural, to *kubernēseis* (1 Cor 12:28) variously rendered "governments" (KJV), "administrators" (RSV), "forms of leadership" (NRSV), or "gifts of guidance" (NIV). This last translation seems especially apposite given its use in the Septuagint of Proverbs 1:5 and 11:14. The position of the term after gifts of healing and giving help, and before those of speaking in tongues, suggest that Paul has in mind a leadership role in the church, involving "the ability to give good counsel" and so provide

---

56. Sullivan, *Charisms and Charismatic Renewal*, 157.

57. Sullivan, *Charisms and Charismatic Renewal*, 36. The RSV views these charisms as permanent ministries: "workers of miracles" and "healers."

58. Bittlinger, *Gifts and Graces*, 66–67.

regular and repeated "guidance" for the community.⁵⁹ Thiselton renders it "gift of strategic thinking" in contrast to the previous gift which he calls "administrative support" (*antilēmpseis*).⁶⁰

## Ministry Gifts

In considering ministry gifts we move from the varieties of charismatic gifts to the different types of ministries needed to build up the Christian community. *Charismata* are dynamic activities of the Holy Spirit. Ministries are the people Christ provides to lead and nurture his body, the church. Paul says of them, "There are different kinds of service (*diakoniai*, 'services, ministries'), but the same Lord" (1 Cor 12:5).

Ministry or leadership gifts are listed in Ephesians 4:11. The risen and ascended Christ, from heaven, provides a variety of leaders to equip his church. "The gifts he gave were that some would be apostles, some prophets, some evangelists, some pastors and teachers" (NRSV). God never intended the church to be a one-person band. A plurality of leadership is God's intention for the church to develop its full potential.

Arnold Bittlinger divides ministries into "ministries for the local congregation" and "ministries for the whole church." In the former category are overseers (*episkopoi*), elders (*presbyteroi*), and those who give practical service (*diakonioi*). It is the latter category that Paul is concerned with in Ephesians 4:11: apostles, prophets, evangelists, pastors, and teachers.⁶¹ As an example of the distinction, he states, "The apostle has freedom of movement; the elder remains in one place."⁶²

The new nondenominational charismatic churches have spawned large and developing networks of relationships and outreach and have made much of the restoration of the fivefold ministries of Ephesians 4:11. As Peter Hocken observes, this "represents a decisive break with a merely congregationalist vision of the local church," which was the norm in independent churches before charismatic renewal gave birth to the revival not only of New Testament gifts but of New Testament ministries. Whereas evangelicals accepted the ministries of evangelist, pastor, and teacher, the new charismatic churches insist on the validity of apostles and prophets as well. They

---

59. "*Kubernēsis*," NIDNTTE 2:767.
60. Thiselton, *The Holy Spirit*, 92–93.
61. Bittlinger, *Gifts and Ministries*, 24.
62. Bittlinger, *Gifts and Ministries*, 41.

recommend that all such translocal ministers should be accountable to the local church where they are based.[63]

## 1. Apostles and Apostleship

Historically, and because of the emergence of the new apostolic networks, there has been a great deal of debate about the nature of *apostles* and apostleship. The New Testament not only identifies them with the twelve disciples specially sent or commissioned by Jesus, but also a number of others called by God and recognized by the churches. Paul, whose letters provide firsthand information, considered himself to be an apostle like the others (1 Cor 9:1–2), save that his call by the risen and ascended Christ was by way of a vision rather than that of an eyewitness (1 Cor 15:8–10).

Hans von Campenhausen explains that, for Paul, apostles "are the foundation-laying preachers of the Gospel, missionaries and church founders possessing the full authority of Christ and belong to a bigger circle in no way confined to the Twelve."[64] Apostles had a distinct calling from Christ, a worldwide mission to make him known and found churches, were recognized in the churches, and distinguished by signs, wonders, and miracles (2 Cor 12:12).

Karl Rengstorf linked the Christian concept of apostleship with the Jewish institution of the *shāliach* (a "sent one" or "deputy"), whose authority represented that of the person or body that commissioned him.[65] Biblical examples are the envoys of David (1 Sam 25:40–41; 2 Sam 10:4, 6) and Saul himself (Acts 9:1–2). The New Testament uses the noun *apostolos* "only in the sense of 'messenger' and particularly as the fixed designation of a definite Christian office."[66] Jesus chose from among his followers twelve "whom he also designated apostles" (Luke 6:14; cf. Mark 3:14). He sent them out and "gave them authority to drive out impure spirits and to heal every disease and sickness" (Matt 10:1; cf. Mark 6:7; Luke 9:1).

Jesus' choice of twelve apostles clearly relates to their future eschatological role "judging the twelve tribes of Israel" (Matt 19:28). But his subsequent sending out of the seventy with a similar authority and commission (Luke 10:1–12) suggests that the Twelve were not an exclusive apostolate. This would appear to be supported by Luke's reference in Acts 8:14 to the "apostles in Jerusalem"—which implies that there were other apostles. "The existence of apostles other than

---

63. Hocken, *Challenges*, 43–45.
64. Campenhausen, "Der urchristliche Apostelbegriff" [The Early Christian Understanding of the Apostolate], 127; quoted in "*Apostellō*," *NIDNTTE* 1:371.
65. Rengstorf, "*Apostolos*," *TDNT* 1:427.
66. "*Apostellō*," *NIDNTTE* 1:367.

those in Jerusalem is confirmed with the naming of 'apostles Barnabas and Paul' in Acts 14:4, 14."[67]

Arnold Bittlinger lists four marks of apostleship as evidenced by the ministry of Paul: calling by God (Gal 1:15–16), setting apart by the congregation (Acts 13:2–3), acknowledgment by the church as a whole (Gal 2:9), and "the marks of a true apostle," including signs, wonders, and miracles (2 Cor 12:12).[68]

Bittlinger argues, "There is no place in the New Testament which implies that the apostolic office was designed only for the first generation of the church's existence."[69] He cites Calvin, often viewed as a cessationist, who in fact defined apostles as "the first builders of the church" and maintained that God "now and again" revives apostles and prophets "as the need of the times demands."[70]

The new apostolic churches define apostolic ministry in terms of the proven ability to found and grow churches. In their understanding, an apostle is one who "designs and lays foundations for new churches."[71] Apostleship is not a title granted in advance, but a reputation acquired through demonstrated performance. One writer on the phenomenon urges historic churches to welcome apostles with a small "a," reserving the big "A" for the original twelve apostles and Paul. By rejecting contemporary apostles, churches risk stifling a "much-needed gift in a time where mission is a central concern of the church in a post-Christian society."[72]

### 2. Prophetic Ministry

Like apostles, there were also *prophets* in the early church: Agabus (Acts 11:27–28; 21:10), Barnabas, Simeon, Lucius, Manaen and Saul (Acts 13:1), Judas and Silas (Acts 15:32), and the four unmarried daughters of Philip (Acts 21:9). Agabus is said to have predicted future events, including famine and Paul's arrest. Though Peter is not called a prophet, he spoke spontaneously of end time events (Acts 3:19–21), showed knowledge of the secrets of the human heart (Acts 5:3; 8:21–23), and perceptively described the role of prophecy (2 Pet 1:19).

---

67. Hewett, "Apostle," *NIDPCM* 319; cf. *DPCM* 14.
68. Bittlinger, *Gifts and Ministries*, 58–61.
69. Bittlinger, *Gifts and Graces*, 68.
70. Calvin, *Institutes*, IV, 3.4, 1056–57.
71. Myer, *Fivefold Ministry*, 6, quoted by Hocken, *Challenges*, 44.
72. McNair Scott, *Apostles Today*, 207–8, quoted by Hocken, *Azusa, Rome, and Zion*, 110–11.

"Although prophecy is a possibility for any Christian," says Earle Ellis, "it is primarily identified with certain leaders who exercise it as a ministry." He defines a prophet as "the Lord's instrument, one among several means by which Jesus leads his church. As one who makes known . . . the meaning of Scripture, exhorts, and strengthens the congregation, and instructs the community by revelations of the future, the Christian prophet manifests in the power of the Spirit the character of his Lord, who is the Prophet of the end-time."[73]

Though prophets had a leadership role, it is doubtful whether the early church formally recognized them as an office or position in the church. Unlike apostles, elders, and deacons (Acts 1:23–26; 6:5–6; 14:23; 1 Tim 4:14; Titus 1:5), there is no record of their ever being commissioned to this role. Indeed, such commissioning would seem to be a contradiction in terms. The prophet, by definition, is a potential critic of other leaders and must be independent of the formal leadership, just as the prophets were independent of the kingship and held accountable the rulers of Israel and Judah. Those who are described as prophets in the New Testament are those who were recognized as exercising a frequent and proven record of prophesying.

### 3. Equipping the Saints

The ministries of *evangelist* (*euanggelistos*), *pastor* (*poiemenos*), and *teacher* (*didaskalos*) are uncontroversial and generally accepted in the church. But their training role has been less recognized. The fivefold ministries given by the risen and ascended Lord are not for them to do all the work themselves, but to "equip" other members of the Christian community for their "works of service" (*ergon diakonias*) (Eph 4:12). Those in Christian ministry are charged with the responsibility of nurturing others.

Bittlinger suggests that in today's world the fivefold ministries are developed "not primarily by individuals" but by specialist ecumenical or interdenominational agencies. He instances the growth of evangelistic and missionary societies in the work of evangelism, retreat and counseling ministries in pastoral care, and seminaries and institutions of learning in the work of teaching. While this is so, the part played by gifted individuals in their formation and success should not be overlooked. In the work of evangelization, for example, the role of Billy Graham in the Billy Graham Evangelistic Association and its offshoot, the Lausanne Committee for World Evangelization, or of Luis Bush in the AD2000 Movement, has been decisive. The role of individuals has also been significant in the emergence of prophetic networks, such as John and Paula

---

73. Ellis, "The Role of the Christian Prophet," 56, quoted in *"Prophetēs," NIDNTTE* 4:172.

Sanford's Elijah House ministry in the United States or the circle represented by Clifford Hill's *Prophecy Today* magazine in the United Kingdom.[74]

A striking impact of the charismatic renewal movement has been the liberating of Christendom from the "one-person ministry." There is still resistance in the more clerical historic churches. But all streams of the Christian church have recovered lost insights about team ministry. Catholic laypeople have taken their rightful place as teachers, worship leaders, and prayer group leaders alongside priests. Anglican clergy have developed leadership teams and sometimes appointed elders. Presbyterian elderships have rediscovered their role of spiritual oversight and praying for the sick. Baptist churches, which used to be led by deacons, have appointed eldership teams alongside pastors. A growing number of Brethren fellowships, following the lead of Te Atatu Bible Chapel in Auckland, have even appointed a pastor-teacher alongside their ruling elders. Other fellowships have discovered the Apostolic Church's historical emphasis on the fivefold ministries of apostles, prophets, evangelists, pastors, and teachers, illustrated by their instructional metaphor of the digits of the hand.[75] Team ministries and leadership teams have flourished. These are signs of the Spirit at work, restoring a neglected corporate leadership pattern to Christ's church and challenging forms of clericalism that block the abundant contribution of lay people.

## Motivational Gifts

Paul observes, "There are different kinds of working (*energēmata*), but in all of them and in everyone it is the same God at work" (1 Cor 12:6). The third class of spiritual gifts is the list of seven *energēmata*, "workings" or "activities," described by Paul in Romans 12:6–8: "prophesying," "serving," "teaching," giving "encouragment," "giving" to the needs of others, "leading," and "showing mercy." Four of the terms in this list are participles rather than nouns—"the one teaching" (*ho didaskōn*), "the one exhorting" (*ho parakalōn*), "the one giving" (*ho metadidous*), and "the one taking the lead" (*ho proistamenos*)—which "seems to suggest activities rather than offices."[76]

Given the importance of Paul's letter to the Romans, Bill Gothard, founder of the Institute in Basic Life Principles (IBLP), felt there had to be some common denominator that linked these particular gifts. What Paul says about surrendering our lives to God as our "reasonable service" (*logikēn latreian*) and so discovering God's "good, pleasing and perfect will" (Rom 12:1–2), suggested the idea of personal motivation. The dynamic term *energēmata* draws attention to the origin of particular activities in the impulses or motivations that give rise to them. Motivational

---

74. See Sanford and Sanford, *The Elijah Task,* and Hill, *Prophecy Past and Present.*

75. The thumb represents the apostle, who holds everything together. The prophet is the forefinger, used for pointing. The evangelist is the central finger, with the longest reach. The pastor is the ring finger, representing love and care. The teacher is the little finger, necessary for balance and completeness.

76. "*Proistēmi*," *NIDNTT* 4:141.

gifts are the unique "energizings" of the Holy Spirit within a believer that give a person the desire and ability to do particular tasks with ease, effectiveness, and a sense of fulfillment and accomplishment.[77]

Bittlinger's definition of a *charism*—a gift "manifested when set free by the Spirit," leading "natural endowments" to "blossom forth"[78]—more appropriately describes the motivational gifts. They illustrate his conviction that "The Holy Spirit never violates an individual, . . . but rather brings the actual gifts and potentialities of a person to full development."[79]

Every Christian has one of the seven primary motivations listed in Romans 12:6–8. Joy and personal fulfillment come from discovering, exercising, and developing the activity or calling for which we are especially gifted. By moving in our motivational gift we "approve" in our own experience what is God's "good, pleasing and perfect will" (Rom 12:2) and discover the "good works, which God prepared in advance for us to do" (Eph 2:10).

The motivational gift of prophecy (*prophēteia*) is best understood as a gift of insight. It is the ability to perceive, quickness of perception, the aptitude to see and assess a situation quickly, clearly, and precisely. The gift of serving (*diakonia*) is the giving of practical assistance to others. It is found in those who love doing things, meeting practical needs, and helping other people. The gift of teaching (*didaskalia*) is the ability to impart knowledge; the motivation to research, verify, and communicate truth. The motivational gift of encouragement or exhortation (*paraclēsis*) is usually found in a sunny, positive person with the ability to encourage or motivate others.

A person with a gift of giving or contributing (*metadotes*) is someone who loves to give time, finance, and energy to benefit others, whose actions often inspire others to give more generously in turn. They can manage assets well and are often frugal in their lifestyle. The person with a motivational gift of leadership—better translated "management" or "facilitation" (*ho proistamenos*)—loves to organize and direct the practical operations of a community. Such a person is often skilled in breaking down a task into manageable parts and in delegation. The person with a gift of showing empathy or mercy (*eleos*) is a genuinely pastoral person, one who instinctively spots the needy, identifies with them, and cares for their spiritual, emotional, and practical needs.

Every Christian views other people and situations through his or her motivational gift. Recognizing one's motivational gift can lead to a joyous sense of self-discovery and personal fulfillment as a person understands how they are "wired," resulting in a release and freedom in their ministry.

---

77. See https://iblp.org/questions/what-are-seven-motivational-gifts.

78. Bittlinger, *Gifts and Graces*, 72.

79. Bittlinger, *Gifts and Graces*, 15.

Recognizing the motivational gifts of others can lead to better mutual understanding, remove friction between people, and bring greater unity and cooperation.

I will never forget the study of motivational gifts which we undertook as a group of elders in my first church, shortly after I was baptized in the Holy Spirit. The church had suffered not one, but two church splits, leaving many people demoralized, hurt, and grieving. We used the little booklet, *Motivational Gifts*, by the Los Angeles pastor Don Pickerill.[80] As we studied the motivational gifts together as an eldership, we began to appreciate for the first time where each of us was coming from. A new sense of mutual insight and appreciation swept the group, resulting in an awakening of love and purpose. It was a transformational experience for our leadership team after a time of great difficulty.

---

80. Pickerill, *Motivational Gifts*.

# 9

# From Glory to Glory

## *The Spirit in Persons*

*The Spirit is the first person of the Godhead we encounter in our relationship with God and the source of all our experience of God. In God's redeeming activity, the Spirit hides his personality and complements the work of the Son, so that the church is constituted as both the body of Christ and the community of the Spirit. The Spirit, poured out in the hearts of believers, communicates the divine nature to human persons. As a foretaste of God's coming kingdom, the Spirit awakens in us a longing for our completion, when God will grant us and all creation a share in the fullness of his divine life and glory.*[1]

### Our Experience of God

IT IS NOT EASY to picture the Holy Spirit, for the Spirit is life and experience of the living God through Jesus Christ.

---

1. Some material in this and the following chapter originated in a lecture on Eastern Orthodoxy and the Holy Spirit, given to the Bible College of New Zealand's Manawatu Regional Learning Centre, Palmerston North, on 28 March 2001.

Indeed, when the divinity of the Holy Spirit was first debated by theologians in the fourth century, it was in the context of Christian experience of salvation in Christ. Both Athanasius in his *Letters to Bishop Serapion Concerning the Holy Spirit* (written in 359–60) and Basil in his treatise *On the Holy Spirit* (written in 375) argued that since our experience of the Spirit brings us fullness of life in Christ, the Spirit cannot be a mere creature, but must be divine, of the same nature as the Father and the Son.[2] These two patristic writings were widely referred to in connection with the Holy Spirit throughout the Byzantine period.

The heart of Christianity is experience of the living God revealed in Christ by means of the Holy Spirit. The Spirit is the "evangelist of the Trinity," what Eastern Orthodox theologian John Meyendorff calls our "first contact" with the Godhead.[3] The Spirit, experienced when we become a Christian and in our Christian living, in our corporate worship and personal devotion, brings Christ to us, who is the fullness of God's self-revelation and life.

It is the Spirit who introduces us to the mysterious divine life of the Trinity. The church fathers never tire of reminding us that all experience of God is "*from* the Father, *through* the Son, *in* the Spirit" (*ek Patros, dia Huiou, en Pneumati*).[4] Conversely, our prayer and worship of God is offered "*in* the Spirit, *through* the Son, *to* the Father." This echoes the trinitarian formula in Paul's letter to the Ephesians: there is "one God and Father of all," who is "over all" as Father, "through all" as the Son, and "in all" as the Spirit (Eph 4:6).

## The Spirit in God's Activity

All God's activity in the world involves the three persons of the Trinity. "The Father does all things through the Word in the Holy Spirit," says Athanasius.[5] This is so whether in the original creation (Gen 1:2), in the incarnation (Luke 1:35), in our regeneration (John 3:5–8), or in the ultimate renewal of humanity and all creation (Rom 8:21–23; Rev 22:17). "The Originator of all things is one," writes Basil. "He creates through the Son and perfects through the Spirit."[6] The Father is the "first cause" (*tēn*

---

2. A point made by John McIntyre in *Shape of Pneumatology*, 92–93, in his discussion of the patristic witness to the Holy Spirit.
3. Meyendorff, *Byzantine Theology*, 168.
4. E.g., Athanasius, *Letters to Serapion*, 1.14, 20, 30, 3.5.
5. Athanasius, *Letters to Serapion*, 1.28, cf. 3.5.
6. Basil, *On the Holy Spirit*, 16.38.

*prokatartikēn aitian*), the Son the "operating cause" (*ten demiourgēn*), the Spirit the "perfecting cause" (*ten teleiōtikēn*).[7]

Everything that God the Father does, says the second-century theologian Irenaeus, he does with his "two hands," the Son and the Spirit. "For, by the hands of the Father, that is, through the Son and the Spirit, man is made into the image and likeness of God."[8] We see this throughout the Scriptures. The "Spirit" and "word" of God are active in creation (Gen 1:2–3). The Father's sending of his Son into the world involves the agency of the Holy Spirit (Luke 1:35). So the Father, Son, and Spirit are each present in the great episodes of Jesus' life. At his baptism, the Spirit descends on him like a dove, and the voice from heaven declares him to be the Son beloved of the Father (Matt 3:16–17). When he is transfigured the Father's voice again affirms him as his Son, and the bright cloud is the enveloping radiance of the Spirit (Matt 17:5). Likewise, the sending of the Spirit on the church involves both the Father and the Son (John 14:16–17, 26; 15:26; Acts 2:33).

Jesus compares the intimacy of his relationship with the Spirit to the closeness of his relationship with the Father. As the Father is "glorified in the Son" (John 14:13), so the Spirit "will glorify" the Son (John 16:14). "All that belongs to the Father is mine," says Jesus. "That is why I said the Spirit will receive from me what he will make known to you" (John 16:15). There is no trace of self-promotion in the Spirit. "He will not speak on his own" (John 16:13). As Jesus seeks to honor the Father, so the Spirit honors the Son. Athanasius and Basil both recognize that the Spirit's relationship to the Son is like the Son's relationship with the Father.[9] "The Son is the image of the Father," says John of Damascus, "and the Spirit is the image of the Son."[10]

The Spirit's function is not to reveal himself, but to reveal the Son (John 15:26), through whom all things were made and who became incarnate in Jesus Christ. The personal being of the Spirit remains anonymous, self–effacingly hidden, even while involved in every divine activity. "In his personal coming the Holy Spirit does not manifest his person," says Vladimir Lossky. "The Holy Spirit, as person, remains unmanifested, hidden, concealing himself in his very appearing."[11] So in the introductory prayer to

---

7. Basil, *On the Holy Spirit*, 16.38, Lossky, *Mystical Theology*, 100.

8. Irenaeus, *Against Heresies*, 5.6.1, cf. 4.20.1, 5.16.1 and 5.28.4. Cf. Theophilus of Antioch, *To Autolycus*, 2.18.

9. Athanasius, *Letters to Serapion*, 1.21, 3.1; Basil, *On the Holy Spirit*, 17.43.

10. John of Damascus, *The Orthodox Faith*, 1.13.

11. Lossky, *Mystical Theology*, 159–60.

his *Hymns of Divine Love*, Symeon the New Theologian addresses the Spirit as the "hidden mystery," the "nameless treasure," the "ineffable reality."[12]

The Spirit does not draw attention to himself, but effaces himself and bears witness to the Son. Just as breath is seldom noticed as it conveys the spoken word, so the Holy Spirit bears witness to Christ and gives glory to Christ, hiding his own personality behind that of the Son. "The Spirit is without a face, and almost without a name," says Yves Congar. "He is the wind who is not seen, but who makes things move."[13] He is the breath who conveys the living Word. He is the fire who imparts the radiance of God. Clark Pinnock suggests that the Spirit enjoys being anonymous and "likes to be viewed as the influence of the risen Lord and not in his own right."[14]

Because of the closeness of these relations, it has become commonplace in theological reflection on the Trinity to say that what the Godhead does outside of itself (*ad extra*) is always the work of all three Persons. *Opera trinitatis ad extra indivisa sunt* ("the outward works of the Trinity are indivisible"). The Catholic theologian Yves Congar articulates this common theological consensus: "There is no activity of the nature or essence of the divinity that exists prior to or independent of the persons. All such activity is performed by those persons according to and through a divinity that is common to all three, not only because they are consubstantial, but also because they are inside one another." Because of this mutual indwelling, "no action can be attributed to the Holy Spirit independently of the Father and the Son."[15]

The following features of God's revelation, though, are at variance with this traditional formulation, and suggest that the three persons of the Trinity do in reality have distinctive roles:

1. The Father "gave" his only-begotten Son (John 3:16), but is not himself "given."

2. Neither the Father nor the Spirit, but only the Son becomes incarnate as a human being, in our time and history, being born in the days of Caesar Augustus and crucified under Pontius Pilate.

3. Neither the Father nor the Spirit, but only the Son, bears the dissolution and death that are the outcome of our sin and fallen condition.

---

12. Symeon, *Divine Eros*, 33. For the full prayer, see appendix 3, below.
13. Congar, *I Believe in the Holy Spirit*, 3:144.
14. Pinnock, *Flame of Love*, 36.
15. Congar, *I Believe in the Holy Spirit*, 2:85, citing extensive sources (95, note 24). Theologians call this mutual indwelling or coinherence of the persons of the Trinity their *perichōrēsis* (Greek) or *circumincession* (Latin).

4. The Father "sends" the Spirit (John 14:26), but is not himself "sent."

5. Neither the Father nor the Son, but only the Spirit is outpoured at Pentecost (indeed, the Spirit is outpoured only after Jesus was "exalted to the right hand of God," Acts 2:33).

6. Neither the Father nor the Son, but only the Spirit indwells the believer (for Jesus is now ascended, seated at the Father's "right hand," Ephesians 1:20).[16]

7. Indwelling the believer, the Spirit does not "speak on his own," hides his person, and "makes known" the person of the Son (John 16:13-15).

8. Indwelling the believer, the Spirit is the agent of our new birth (John 3:5-8), growth in holiness (Rom 8:4-13; Gal 5:16-26), and transformation into the divine likeness (2 Cor 3:18).

9. The Spirit, on behalf of the Son, communicates divine grace, eternal life, supernatural power, and spiritual gifts (*charismata*) to human persons.

10. The Spirit of the Father, whose power raised the Son from the dead (Rom 1:3-4, 8:11), brings the future into history, awakening in our hearts a longing for our liberation from the present frustration of creation, to share in the glorious freedom of the children of God (Rom 8:11, 16-27).

11. In the eschatological consummation, the Son will yield up the kingdom to God the Father, so that God may be "all in all" (1 Cor 15:24-28).

From these peculiarities in the historical drama of redemption, we can see that the Bible testifies to a dynamic relationship between the three persons of the Trinity. Each plays a particular and distinctive role in salvation and redemptive history.

I had compiled the majority of items in this list before I discovered that the doyen of contemporary Greek Orthodox theologians, one of my teachers in Edinburgh, Dr. John D. Zizioulas,

---

16. Because Jesus is now ascended, David Pawson criticizes the commonly accepted notion in evangelistic counseling that conversion is "receiving Jesus into your heart" (*The Normal Christian Birth*, 60-62). He admits, though, the trinitarian paradox that when the Spirit came into the disciples at Pentecost, "the Father and the Son also took up residence within them at the same time, while remaining outside them as well" (326). The widespread use of "receiving Jesus" in Christian initiation obscures the need for new Christians to "receive the Spirit," depriving them of a fundamental element of Christian experience. However, Billy Graham, whose evangelism has popularized such language, is careful to state in his book, *The Holy Spirit*, 36, that "the Holy Spirit is the person of the Trinity who actually dwells in us."

later Metropolitan of Pergamon, also draws attention to the distinctive contribution of each of the divine persons to the divine economy. He elaborates on several of these points, particularly the second one, that "only the Son becomes incarnate." As he explains, "Both the Father and the Spirit are involved in history, but only the Son *becomes* history." By contrast, "The Spirit is the *beyond* history, and when he acts in history he does so in order to bring into history the last days, the *eschaton*."[17] The Spirit introduces into time and history what is beyond time and history, the very power that raised Christ from the dead. The Spirit is the power that transformed Christ into an eschatological being, the "last Adam," "the heavenly man," the precursor of our glorified state (1 Cor 15:45–49).

The German Catholic theologian, Karl Rahner, also recognized that only the Son became incarnate. "Here something occurs 'outside' the intra-divine life in the world itself, something which is not a mere effect . . . of the triune God acting as one in the world, but something which belongs to the Logos alone."[18] But neither he nor Zizioulas considers the parallel situation of the distinctive operations of the Spirit (my points 4–9): the Spirit's informing, inhabiting, sanctifying, empowering, and transforming the believer.

## The Spirit in Human Persons

The German Catholic theologian Matthias Scheeben has made a comparison between the physical union of the Son of God with Jesus' humanity, and the Holy Spirit's indwelling of our humanity as Christians:

> We have been made similar to the Son of God, not only because we have been conformed to him, but because we also possess the same Spirit personally in us. . . . That is why the apostle was able to call the Holy Spirit "the spirit of sonship, in whom we cry 'Abba! Father!'" (Rom 8:15), that is to say, the Spirit brings about our adoption as sons [as God's children].

This similarity led Scheeben to describe the church as "a kind of incarnation of the Holy Spirit."[19]

Suggestive as it is, the defect in this line of thinking is that the Spirit does not, in reality, become incarnate in human beings. As John McIntyre observes, "the Holy Spirit cannot 'be seen and heard, touched and handled' as Jesus was; he performs a different role in the *ordo salutis*, the order of

---

17. Zizioulas, *Being as Communion*, 129–30, citing McIntyre, "The Holy Spirit in Greek Patristic Thought," 353–75, an article reproduced in modified form in McIntyre, *Shape of Pneumatology*, chapter 4. For points 2, 3, and 10, see also Zizioulas, *Lectures in Christian Dogmatics*, 148.

18. Rahner, *The Trinity*, 23.

19. Scheeben, *The Mysteries of Christianity*, 166, quoted by Congar, *I Believe in the Holy Spirit*, 2:88, my clarification in square brackets.

salvation, from Jesus."[20] The Russian Orthodox theologian Vladimir Lossky points out that there is a profound difference between the way God reveals himself through the Son and in the Holy Spirit. "Pentecost is not a 'continuation' of the incarnation. It is its sequel, its result.... In his personal coming the Holy Spirit does not manifest his person.... The Holy Spirit, as person, remains unmanifested, hidden, concealing himself in his very appearing."[21]

The Son of God became incarnate as a specific human person, the Jewish man Jesus of Nazareth (John 1:14; 1 John 1:1–3). "The incarnate Word has a face."[22] But the Holy Spirit comes to us without a face, effacing his individuality, anonymously enhancing the uniqueness of a multiplicity of human persons. This is graphically signified by the event of Pentecost when the Spirit came as a flame that divided into separate tongues of fire. The divine radiance rested on each of the apostles and their colleagues separately and personally (Acts 2:3).

In the incarnation of the Son, when the second person of the Godhead became a human being, a single divine person was united with human nature, the generic nature of every human being. But in the indwelling of the Spirit, the third person of the Godhead, the converse happens. The divine nature is conveyed to a plurality of human persons. In the incarnation, we meet a single person, the Son of God, in whom our human nature is redeemed. In the indwelling of the Spirit, our personal uniqueness or individuality is enhanced. The Spirit effaces his personality to communicate the gifts and graces of the divine nature to a multiplicity of human persons.

"The work of Christ concerns human nature," Lossky explains. "The work of the Holy Spirit, on the other hand, concerns persons, being applied to each one singly.... The one lends his *hypostasis* [person] to the nature, the other gives his divinity to the persons. Thus, the work of Christ unifies; the work of the Holy Spirit diversifies."[23] Hiding his own personality, the Holy Spirit indwells human persons, affirms their uniqueness, and inspires their personal richness and diversity.

The German Catholic theologian Heribert Mühlen has suggested a different schema to that of Lossky, without showing any awareness of him or interacting with him. Mühlen notes

20. McIntyre, *Shape of Pneumatology*, 19, alluding to 1 John 1:1.
21. Lossky, *Mystical Theology*, 159–60.
22. Congar, *I Believe in the Holy Spirit*, 3:5.
23. Lossky, *Mystical Theology*, 166–67. The Greek word *hypostasis* (plural *hypostases*) originally meant "objective reality" or "substantial reality," as opposed to mere appearance or illusion. But in formulations of the doctrine of the Trinity from the middle of the fourth century on, the word came to be contrasted with *ousia* and used to mean a "person" (*ODCC2*, 685) or "individual reality" (*ODCC3*, 817).

that God is three persons in one nature, and Christ is two natures in one person. He, therefore, suggests that the church, as the mystery of the Holy Spirit's indwelling of Christ and Christians, is the one person of the Spirit in many persons, "one mystical person in many persons."[24] By contrast, Lossky's schema could be represented as God being three persons in one nature, Christ two natures in one person, and the church many human persons infused by the one divine nature of the Holy Spirit.

Mühlen agrees that the church cannot be regarded as an extension of the incarnation. The incarnation is a once-for-all event, and there is no hypostatic union between Christ and his body, the church. Instead, he suggests that the church is the continuation of Christ's anointing by the Holy Spirit; that what unites Christians to one another and to Christ is their common anointing with the Spirit.[25] The Pentecostal-charismatic theology that I am advocating here would rule this out, because the equivalent for Christians of Christ's anointing with the Spirit is not baptism, regeneration, or new birth, but the specific experience of being baptized in or empowered by the Holy Spirit.

"The personal being of the Spirit remains mysteriously hidden, even if he is active at every great step of divine activity," says John Meyendorff. "The Spirit does not reveal his person, as the Son does in Jesus . . . ; he communicates his uncreated grace to each human person, to each member of the body of Christ."[26]

Lossky describes the self-effacement of the Spirit before human persons, on analogy with Christ's self-emptying (Phil 2:7), as "the *kenōsis* of the Holy Spirit's coming into the world."[27] Like water, the Spirit flows to the lowest level and penetrates human hearts. "The Spirit of love effaces himself in order to bless others," says Pinnock. "He is humble and dwells in the hearts of the poor in spirit."[28]

This effacement extends to the manner of the Spirit's indwelling. The sovereign Spirit mysteriously unites himself with us without overriding our personalities, infusing within us the inexpressible wonder of the divine life. As Symeon the New Theologian puts it in the introduction to his *Hymns of Divine Love*, "I thank you because you have become one spirit with me,

---

24. Mühlen, *Der Heilige Geist als Person* [The Holy Spirit as Person], 9.01–30; *Una Mystica Persona* [One Mystical Person], 9.01–37, as reported by Kilian, "The Holy Spirit in Christ and in Christians," 100, 112.

25. Mühlen, *Der Heilige Geist als Person*, 9.01–11.03; *Una Mystica Persona*, 7.01–9.115; Kilian, "The Holy Spirit in Christ and in Christians," 102.

26. Meyendorff, *Byzantine Theology*, 168, 173. At Pentecost, Meyendorff points out, the apostles received the divine gifts or "energies" of the Spirit, but unlike when the Son became incarnate, "there was no new hypostatic union between the Spirit and humanity" (173).

27. Lossky, *Mystical Theology*, 168.

28. Pinnock, *Flame of Love*, 40. If there is truth in the Spirit's "preferential option" for the poor, this is its theological justification.

unmixing, unmoved [without confusion, without change], immutable God over all things, and because you yourself have become the all in all for me, utterly inexpressible food . . . endlessly overflowing the lips of my soul, and gushing out in the fountain of my heart."[29]

## The Spirit and the Christian Community

With the coming of the Holy Spirit, a new reality comes into the world, the church, an entity with a mysterious and ineffable dual nature. The church is both the body of Christ (*sōma Christou*, 1 Cor 12:12; Col 1:18) and the community of the Spirit (*koinōnia Pneumatōn*, Acts 2:42; Phil 2:1), one nature in the divine person of Christ, many persons in the divine nature of the Holy Spirit. As the body of Christ, the church unites many human persons in one organism, a single redeemed nature. As the community of the Spirit, the church expresses the divine life in a rich diversity of personal gifts.

The church presents us with a paradox. On the one hand, it is *instituted* by Christ (Matt 16:18), and as a historical reality comes to us as a *fait accompli*, inviting our membership and participation. But on the other hand, the church is *constituted* by the Spirit: "something that involves us in its very being, something we accept freely, because we take part in its very emergence."[30] The church, Lossky points out, is "founded on a twofold divine economy: the work of Christ and the work of the Holy Spirit, the two persons of the Trinity sent into the world. . . . The church is *body* in so far as Christ is her head; she is *fullness* in so far as the Holy Spirit quickens her and fills her with divinity."[31]

| Table 3 ||
|---|---|
| Two Aspects of the Church ||
| The mission of the Son | The mission of the Spirit |
| God "with us" (Matt 1:23) | God "in us" (John 14:17) |
| The divine person of the Son embodied in human nature | The divine nature of the Spirit communicated to human persons |
| Human nature redeemed by the divine person of the Son | Human persons renewed by the divine nature of the Spirit |
| The church as instituted by Christ | The church as constituted by the Spirit |

29. Symeon, *Divine Eros*, 33–34, traditional rendering in square brackets. Cf. 1 Cor 6:17, "Whoever is united with the Lord is one with him in spirit."

30. Zizioulas, *Being as Communion*, 140.

31. Lossky, *Mystical Theology*, 156–57.

| The church's christological basis | The church's pneumatological basis |
|---|---|
| The body of Christ (*sōma Christou*) | The community of the Spirit (*koinōnia Pneumatōn*) |
| Our abiding in Christ (John 15:5) | The Spirit's dwelling in us (Rom 8:9) |
| "Built on the foundation of the apostles and prophets, with Christ Jesus himself as the chief cornerstone" (Eph 2:20) | "Being built together to become a dwelling in which God lives by his Spirit" (Eph 2:22) |
| "The pillar and foundation of the truth" (1 Tim 3:15b) | "The church of the living God" (1 Tim 3:15a) |
| The church's stability and historical continuity | The church's dynamism and capacity for renewal |
| The church's teaching role | The church's prophetic function |
| The church as an authoritative institution | The church as a charismatic community |
| The church as a social organization | The church as a society of persons |
| Unity of purpose | Diversity of persons |
| Unity as a given: "There is one body . . . , one hope . . . , one Lord, one faith, one baptism, one God and Father of all" (Eph 4:4) | Unity as a task: "Make every effort to keep the unity of the Spirit through the bond of peace" (Eph 4:3) |
| The church as apostolic | The church as eschatological |
| *Anamnēsis*: remembrance of the past | *Arrabōn*: foretaste of the future |

"This is the unfathomable mystery of the church," Lossky continues, "the work of Christ and of the Holy Spirit; one in Christ, multiple through the Spirit, *a single human nature* in the *hypostasis* [person] of Christ, *many human hypostases* [persons] in the grace of the Holy Spirit."[32] Congar makes a similar observation: "a personal principle and a principle of unity are united in the church. . . . brought into harmony by the Holy Spirit."[33]

The one Spirit is the author of our rich personal diversity. Paul says of the variety of charisms, "All these are the work of the one and the same Spirit, and he distributes them to each one, just as he determines" (1 Cor 12:11).

Cyril of Alexandria compares the Holy Spirit's influence to rainwater, which falls from heaven and nourishes the wide variety of plants and flowers. "One and the same rain comes down on all the world, yet it becomes

---

32. Lossky, *Mystical Theology*, 183, my square brackets.
33. Congar, *I Believe in the Holy Spirit*, 2:16.

white in the lily, red in the rose, purple in the violets and the hyacinths, different and many-coloured in manifold species. Thus it is one in the palm tree and another in the vine, and all in all things, though it is uniform and does not vary in itself. For the rain does not change, . . . but adapts itself to the thing receiving it and becomes what is suitable to each."[34]

Effacing his person behind that of human persons, the Spirit's presence is a marvelous divine influence that enhances our personal freedom and creativity. "Persons are the great wealth of the church," exclaims Congar. "Each one is an original and autonomous principle of sensitivity, experience, relationships and initiatives. What an infinite variety of possibilities is contained in each individual!"[35] What a rich source of creative energy is released for the church's mission in the world when we honor and invoke the inspiration of the Holy Spirit!

## The Spirit and the Christian Life

Through the coming of the Holy Spirit, we are brought into a living communion with God. Whereas the incarnation of the Son is the embodiment of a divine person in human nature, the indwelling of the Spirit involves the impartation of the divine nature to human persons.

It is through the indwelling of the Spirit that we are regenerated or "born anew" (John 3:3-8; 1 Pet 1:3): that we become "children of God" (John 1:12-13; 1 John 3:1-2), are given a share of eternal life (John 3:15-16; 6:54; 10:28; 17:2-3; Rom 6:23; 1 John 2:25; 5:11), and enabled to "participate in the divine nature" (2 Pet 1:4). It is an extraordinary privilege, an incredible elevation of our status, that we as mere creatures should be raised to the dignity of God's children. Hence Paul calls the Spirit the "Spirit of adoption," through whom we enter God's family, cry "Abba, Father," and become heirs of God's glory (Rom 8:15-17).

The Spirit brings us into a living communion with God himself. God's love is "poured out into our hearts through the Holy Spirit, who has been given to us" (Rom 5:5). Living in us the Spirit imparts God's life, invigorates us with God's "uncreated energies," endues us with divine wisdom, works in us the fruit of God's holiness, and empowers us with the efficacy of God's gifts.

God's grace, Lossky points out, is "no longer as in the Old Testament an effect produced in the soul by the divine will acting *externally* upon the

---

34. Cyril of Alexandria, *Catechesis*, 14.12.

35. Congar, *I Believe in the Holy Spirit*, 2:16, where Congar acknowledges the Catholic Church's historic "distrust of expressions of the personal principle."

person. Now it is the divine life that is opened up *within us* in the Holy Spirit. For he mysteriously identifies himself with human persons, whilst remaining incommunicable. He substitutes himself, so to speak, for ourselves; for it is he who cries in our hearts 'Abba, Father!' as St. Paul puts it. We should say, rather, that the Holy Spirit effaces himself, as person, before the created persons to whom he appropriates grace."[36]

The Eastern Orthodox Church understands God's grace to be the impartation of the divine nature (2 Pet 1:4). "That which is common to the Father and the Son is the divinity which the Holy Spirit communicates to people within the church, in making them 'partakers of the divine nature,' in conferring the fire of deity, uncreated grace, upon those who become members of the body of Christ."[37]

Basil compares the perfecting work of the Spirit to sunlight, which, when it falls on a transparent substance, causes that substance to become brilliant and radiate light in turn. "From this comes knowledge of the future, understanding of mysteries, apprehension of hidden things, distribution of wonderful gifts, heavenly citizenship, a place in the choir of angels, endless joy in the presence of God, becoming like God, and, the highest of all desires, becoming God."[38]

The church fathers use such analogies as breath, light, and fire to illustrate how divine grace can pervade and transform human persons without violating their human nature. The most common is that of fire. Fire warms iron so that it acquires properties that transcend its essential nature. A heated knife can burn as well as cut, and heated metal can be bent and shaped. In the same way, the radiance of the divine energies confers supernatural abilities and a capacity for self-transformation not innate to our unaided human nature.

Protestant and evangelical theologians, on the other hand, place more emphasis on sanctification and the personal aspect of the Spirit's indwelling. It is possible to grieve the Holy Spirit by wrong attitudes and wrong relationships with other people (Eph 4:1–3, 30–32; 5:18—6:9).[39] Our bodies are temples of the Holy Spirit, which becomes a motivation to holy living, particularly in sexual relations (1 Cor 6:18–20; 1 Thess 4:3–8). The Spirit is opposed to "the flesh" (*sarx*), our fallen, sinful human nature (Gal 5:17),

---

36. Lossky, *Mystical Theology*, 172, my italics.
37. Lossky, *Mystical Theology*, 162.
38. Basil, *On the Holy Spirit*, 9.23.
39. See especially Lloyd-Jones, *Life in the Spirit*.

and it is the indwelling of the Spirit that gives us the grace to overcome "the desires of the flesh" (Gal 5:16; Rom 8:5-6).[40]

This sanctifying aspect of the work of the Spirit is too little emphasized today, yet the pervasive influence of a media-saturated and sexualized culture makes it more critical than ever. The Holy Spirit desires embodiment in our lives. The post-Reformation Protestant theologians stressed that sanctification "is not just a moral but a physical effect of the Holy Spirit," by which God infuses into a Christian the motivation to strive for holiness and to live a life pleasing to God. The "direct inworking" of the Spirit enlightens our understanding, transforms our desires, claims our bodily life (Rom 6:12-13; 12:1), motivates our actions, and issues in a life of good works that God has prepared beforehand for us to do (Eph 2:10).[41]

## The Spirit as a Foretaste of Glory

The Spirit is given to human beings not only to save us from the grip of sin and death (Rom 8:1-13; Gal 5:16-26), but to make us children of God, give us a share in the divine nature, impart to us eternal life, and transform us into the divine likeness. The downward movement of redemption from God to human beings accomplished in the incarnation is not an end in itself. It is meant to be completed in the upward movement of redemption from human beings to God, with its goal in our glorification. This follows the path of what Reformed theology used to describe as Christ's humiliation and exaltation. Just as the Spirit and the Son cooperated in the downward movement of the incarnation, so the Son and the Spirit both play a part in the upward movement of our glorification (see Figure 1).

The resurrection and ascension of Jesus—his exaltation to "the right hand of God"—means that our human nature united with the person of the Son of God has been imbued with immortality and brought into God's immediate presence (cf. Col 3:1-4). The Spirit, poured out by the ascended Son from the Father, now conveys the divine nature to human persons. The risen and ascended Christ is the forerunner or first instance of redeemed humanity (1 Cor 15:20-23).

So when Paul says that the Spirit is given to us as "a deposit guaranteeing our inheritance" (Eph 1:14) he is saying that the Spirit poured out in the hearts of believers is a pledge of this new creation, a foretaste or first

---

40. Cranfield, *Romans*, 1:379, translates *sarx hamartias*, "sinful flesh" (Rom 8:3), as "fallen human nature."

41. For a summary of these neglected aspects of sanctification, see Heppe, *Reformed Dogmatics*, 565, 568, 579.

experience of our future redeemed state. The Semitic loanword *arrabōn* that he uses here to describe the Holy Spirit, is a "first installment," "deposit" or "down payment," the "payment of part of a purchase price in advance, . . . which secures a legal claim to the article in question, or makes a contract valid."[42] The Spirit, poured into our hearts from God himself, is the divine guarantor of our future redemption.

Paul describes the goal of the Spirit's work in our lives as our "glorification," when we will shine with the splendor, holiness, and refulgence of God himself. The Spirit who makes us "children of God" and "testifies with our spirit that we are God's children," will, in turn, give us a "share in his [Christ's] glory" (Rom 8:14–17). This participation in God's glory will ultimately extend from humans to the entire subhuman realm, for "creation itself" will one day "be liberated from its bondage to decay and brought into the freedom and glory of the children of God" (Rom 8:21). Paul describes the Spirit dwelling in us as the "firstfruits" of this coming redemption (Rom 8:23). Just as the firstfruits anticipate the full and completed harvest, so too the Holy Spirit in us is both the present enjoyment of salvation and the pledge of its ultimate consummation.

The goal of human life is the vision of God in his resplendent glory. "We shall be like him, for we shall see him as he is" (1 John 3:2). Paul speaks of us "being changed into his [God's] likeness from one degree of glory to another" by the agency of the Spirit (2 Cor 3:18, RSV). John describes our being made "children of God" (John 1:12; 1 John 3:1–2). Peter speaks of Christians as "participants in the divine nature" (2 Pet 1:4). By nature, we are creatures and not God, but God by his grace, desires to grant us a share in the abundance and immortality of his own divine life. This is our supreme joy, felicity, and ultimate fulfillment. As we delight ourselves in the Lord, he gives us the desires of our heart (Ps 37:4). In God's presence is "fullness of joy" (Ps 16:11, NRSV).

Eastern Orthodox theologians use the term *theōsis* to refer to the ultimate aim and purpose of human life, where the West uses both "sanctification" and "glorification." Georges Florovsky admits that the term, meaning "deification" or "divinization," is "rather offensive" to the modern ear.[43] But it is not used in a pantheistic sense. It does not imply any impairment of our humanity or God's divinity. Just as the Son of God was born of Mary and became incarnate as a human being without ceasing to be divine, so too we are called to be born anew of the Spirit and become children of God, without ceasing to be fully human.

All the fathers of the Eastern Church understand *theōsis* on the basis of this parallelism with the incarnation. "The Son of God became a human being so that human beings might

---

42. "*Arrabōn*," BDAG 134.
43. Florovsky, "Tradition of the Fathers," 114.

become children of God," is the formula coined by Irenaeus, repeated by Clement of Alexandria and Athanasius, and passed on by Gregory of Nyssa and Maximus the Confessor into the Byzantine theological tradition.[44]

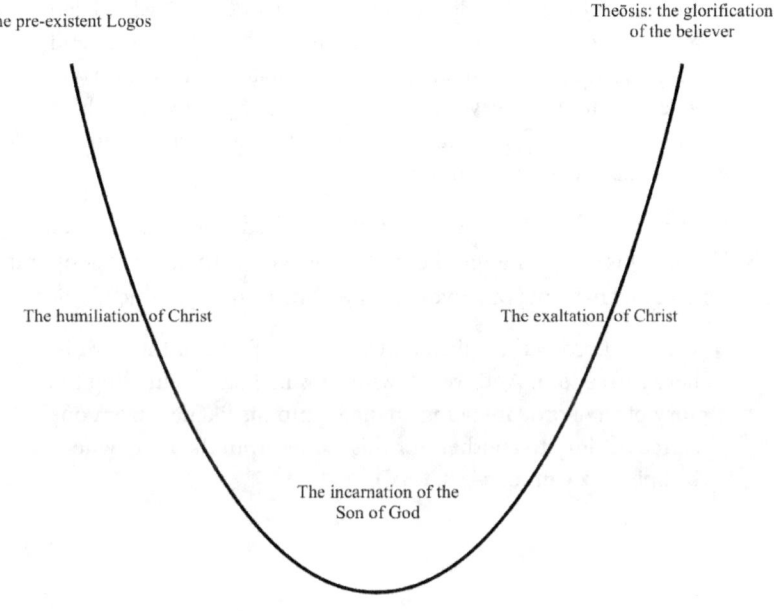

Figure 1. The Parabola of Redemption

The manward movement of God's condescension in the incarnation is only the first part of redemption; its purpose is to awaken in us the Godward movement of our glorification. The Holy Spirit and the life of prayer are given so that we may share in the life of God and the divine likeness be reproduced in us. Just as the Spirit is the one who brings order to the original creation, so the Spirit is the one who fulfills creation in God's new creation, the firstfruits of which are already realized in the resurrection and glorification of Jesus Christ (1 Cor 15:20–28, 42–57).

Yves Congar describes this perfecting activity of the Spirit:

44. Irenaeus, *Against Heresies*, 5, preface, 3.19.1; Clement of Alexandria, *Exhortation to the Greeks*, 1; Athanasius, *On the Incarnation*, 54; Gregory of Nyssa, *Catechetical Oration*, 25. For Maximus the Confessor, see Thunberg, *Microcosm and Mediator*, 454–59, and Pelikan, *Christian Tradition*, 2:10–12. See also Lossky, "Redemption and Deification," 97–110, for the contrast with the more juridical Western, Anselmic, understanding of redemption.

> The Spirit, who is both one and transcendent, is able to penetrate all things without violating or doing violence to them. . . . The Spirit is unique and present everywhere, transcendent and inside all things, subtle and sovereign, able to respect freedom and to inspire it. That Spirit can further God's plan, which can be expressed in the words "communion," "many in one" and "uniplurality." At the end, there will be a state in which God will be "everything to everyone" (1 Cor 15:28), in other words, there will be one life animating many without doing violence to the inner experience of anyone.[45]

Our personal transformation is not a finished work but a work in progress. The Spirit is God's change agent, the one who with our free cooperation progressively transforms our lives and persons into the divine likeness:

> Now the Lord is the Spirit, and where the Spirit of the Lord is, there is freedom. And we all, with unveiled face, beholding the glory of the Lord, are being changed into his likeness from one degree of glory to another; for this comes from the Lord, who is the Spirit. (2 Cor 3:17–18, RSV)

---

45. Congar, *I Believe in the Holy Spirit*, 2:17.

# 10

## The Spirit in the Triune God

*From our experience of the Spirit, we turn to what can be known of the Spirit in the Godhead. Unlike the Son, the Spirit is not begotten but "proceeds" from the Father. The manner of this procession is the subject of the longest dispute and greatest schism in Christian history, between the Eastern Orthodox and Roman Catholic churches. Far from being an esoteric case of doctrinal hair-splitting, it has significant repercussions for how we understand the Trinity, the church, the Christian life, and indeed the Holy Spirit. The worldwide growth of the Pentecostal-charismatic movement draws attention to the dynamism of the Spirit, which suggests that the Spirit is a recognizable person, parallel to the distinctive personalities of the Father and the Son.*

So CLOSE ARE THE relations between the Spirit and the Son in God's revelation that many theologians, particularly in the West, have wondered whether this mirrors their relationship in the Godhead. This raises profound questions about the inner-trinitarian relations of the three persons of the Godhead that have preoccupied theologians and given rise to the most long-lasting dispute in the history of theology.

Theologians distinguish between the realm of God as he is in himself (*ad intra*), and God's relations with the created universe external to himself (*ad extra*); between the inner-trinitarian relations of the persons within the Godhead (the immanent Trinity), and the actions of the Godhead in creation and redemption (the economic Trinity).

In two texts, Jesus describes the relation of the Holy Spirit to the Father. In the first, Jesus is clearly referring to the Father's sending of the Spirit into the world, *ad extra*, external to himself: "The Paraclete, the Holy Spirit, *whom the Father will send in my name*, will teach you all things and will remind you of everything I have said to you" (John 14:26). In the second, Jesus not only describes the sending of the Spirit into the world, *ad extra*, but also the origin of the Spirit in the Godhead, *ad intra*: "When the Paraclete comes, whom I shall send to you from the Father, even the Spirit of truth, *who proceeds from the Father*, he will bear witness to me" (John 15:26, RSV).

## Begetting and Making

The Greek word used here, *ekporeuomai*, describes the Spirit as "proceeding" from the Father. "Procession" (Greek *ekporeusis*, Latin *processio*) is how theologians describe the manner of the Spirit's origin from God the Father. This is to distinguish the Spirit's origin from that of the Son, who is described as being "begotten" or the "only-begotten" (*monogenous*) of the Father (John 1:14, 18; 3:16, 18; 1 John 4:9). To "beget" is to bring into existence a being with the same nature as oneself. To "make" or "create" is to bring into existence something with a different nature than oneself.

> C. S. Lewis draws this basic distinction in his popular exposition of Christian belief, *Mere Christianity*. "We don't use the words *begetting* or *begotten* much in modern English, but everyone still knows what they mean. To beget is to become the father of: to create is to make.... When you beget, you beget something of the same kind as yourself.... But when you make, you make something of a different kind from yourself." Even if a man makes a statue like himself, "it is not a real man; it only looks like one.... A man begets a child, but he only makes a statue. God begets Christ, but he only makes men."[1]
>
> In distinguishing *begetting* from *making* Lewis follows the thought of the early Greek theologians, summarized, for example, by John of Damascus. "We hold that it is from him, that is, from the Father's nature, that the Son is generated.... For generation means that the begetter produces out of his own essence offspring similar in essence. But creation and making mean that the Creator and Maker produces from that which is external, and not of his own essence, a creation of absolutely dissimilar nature."[2]

---

1. Lewis, *Mere Christianity*, 134, 136.
2. John of Damascus, *The Orthodox Faith*, 1.8, quoted by Florovsky, "The Idea of

The distinction between *begetting* and *making*, *generation* and *creation*, is a crucial one because it distinguishes the Judeo-Christian outlook from pantheistic and monistic religious and philosophical worldviews. If we confuse begetting and making we obliterate the distinction between God and the universe. Eastern religions consider the universe to be the same nature as God, which is to view the universe as divine, and God as neither transcendent nor personal. The eternal generation of the Son and the eternal procession of the Spirit occur *within* the divine nature or essence of God, whereas the work of creation is a free act of God's will that brings into existence something entirely different in nature than himself. God begets his beloved Son. God makes his majestic universe.

## The Spirit's Procession

The Holy Spirit, as the third person of the Trinity, also has its origin eternally from the Father. But the Spirit is not begotten. *Procession* or *spiration* is not begetting. The Spirit is not the son of the Son or the grandson of the Father. Procession means the Spirit originates in a different manner than the Son, a manner that ensures its full participation in the divine nature of the Father, but also its distinctive personhood as the Spirit.

The Eastern Orthodox Church affirms that the Spirit proceeds from the Father alone, or sometimes (recognizing the close relationship of the Spirit to Christ spoken of in the Paraclete sayings in John's Gospel), proceeds from the Father *through the Son*. But in the Western or Catholic Church, an addition was made to the Nicene Creed without the consent of the Eastern Church, that the Spirit "proceeds from the Father *and the Son*" (Latin *Filioque*). This is the famous "*Filioque*" clause, which has caused more conflict in church history than any other theological dispute.

The *Filioque* was originally a local addition to the creed, made first in Spain at the Third Council of Toledo in 589, perhaps to safeguard the faith against Arianism. Thence it spread throughout churches in the West, particularly with Emperor Charlemagne's support in the ninth century. At first papal sanction was refused. Pope Leo III in 808, while approving the doctrine, opposed its insertion into the creed. But its acceptance by the eleventh-century popes provoked strong dissent in the Eastern Church. In 1054, the year of the schism between Rome and Constantinople, the Pope's anathema made the accusation that, far from being a Western innovation, it had been the Eastern Orthodox who had removed the *Filioque* from the creed! Its introduction is considered by the Orthodox Church to be the main reason for the division between Eastern and Western Christendom.[3]

---

Creation," 58–59.

3. "Whether we like it or not," says Vladimir Lossky, "the question of the procession of the Holy Spirit has been the sole dogmatic grounds for the separation of East and West" ("The Procession of the Holy Spirit," 71). Yves Congar presents a representative Western view in his account of the *Filioque* (*I Believe in the Holy Spirit*, 3:xv–xvi, 49–78, 81–89, 128–32, 174–214), though admits that he personally favors removing the *Filioque* from the creed, "as a gesture of humility and brotherhood on the part of

John Zizioulas suggests that one of the factors that contributed to the West's introduction of the *Filioque* was the use of the same Latin verb to describe the proceeding of the Spirit from the Father in the Godhead and the sending of the Spirit by Jesus in the economy of salvation. "The Greek-speaking East had used 'proceeding from' (*ekporeuetai*) only within the immanent and eternal Trinity.... But from the fourth century the Greek *ekporeuetai* (proceeding from) and *pempetai* (sent by) were translated into Latin simply as '*procedere*.'"[4] This compounded the confusion whether one was speaking of the eternal origin of the Spirit in the Godhead or the temporal sending of the Spirit in the history of salvation.

In the realm of God's external operations *ad extra*, it is certainly correct to stress the Spirit's close relationship to the Son, as the Son is to the Father. "All that belongs to the Father is mine," says Jesus. "That is why I said the Spirit will receive from me what he will make known to you" (John 16:15). Both Eastern and Western Churches agree on this. But Hilary of Poitiers, quoting this text while in exile in the East, ponders whether it applies within the Godhead as well:

> He who is sent by the Son and proceeds from the Father, receives from the Son. And I wonder whether receiving from the Son and proceeding from the Father are the same. If we believe that there is a difference between receiving from the Son and proceeding from the Father, it is nonetheless certain that receiving from the Son and receiving from the Father are the same.[5]

Thinking along these lines, the Eastern theologian Maximus the Confessor, in his *Questions to Thalassius*, 63, and in his *Letter to Marinus*, spoke of the Spirit proceeding "from the Father through the Son" (*di Huiou* or *dia tou Huiou*). From their respective sides of the debate both Congar[6] and Zizioulas[7] suggest that this could be a possible way to find agreement between the Catholic and Orthodox Churches. The Romanian Orthodox theologian Dumitru Staniloae, though, prefers to say that the Spirit "proceeds from the Father and shines forth through the Son."[8]

My own view is that something along the lines of Staniloae's suggestion could accommodate the strong conviction among evangelical Protestants, based on the Paraclete sayings in John's Gospel, that the Spirit bears witness to Christ and has a christological orientation. I suggest

---

the Roman Catholic Church" (206, cf. 214). See Siecienski, *The Filioque*, for a recent account of this greatest rift in Christendom.

4. Zizioulas, *Lectures in Christian Dogmatics*, 78.

5. Hilary of Poitiers, *On the Trinity*, 8.20, quoted by Congar, *I Believe in the Holy Spirit*, 3:200.

6. Congar, *I Believe in the Holy Spirit*, 3:187, 201.

7. Zizioulas, *Lectures in Christian Dogmatics*, 82.

8. Staniloae, "The Holy Spirit," 5.

that the Nicene Creed could be reworded with the addition of two clarifications, "who proceeds *eternally* from the Father and *is sent in time by* the Son."[9] This echoes John 15:26 and would be acceptable to Eastern Christians in affirming the sole monarchy of the Father in the Godhead, and to Western Christians in affirming the christological alignment of the Spirit in the economy of salvation.

According to the Eastern Church, the Spirit proceeds "from the Father alone" (*ek mono tou Patros*): the Father is the sole source of the Godhead, the one principle of origin and unity in the Trinity. The Orthodox claim that, far from being a trivial matter, acceptance of the *Filioque* by the Western Church seriously distorts our understanding of the nature of God and the nature of the church.[10]

## God is Truly Personal

The Eastern Church, like the Bible and the baptismal formula, "in the name of the Father and of the Son and of the Holy Spirit" (Matt 28:19), begins with the persons and moves to the shared nature of the Godhead, viewing the Father as the sole principle (*monarchē*), source (*archē*), or "cause" (*aitia*) of the other two persons, the Son and the Spirit, and thus the "fount and origin of the divine nature." The Eastern Church believes that its emphasis on the sole monarchy of the Father—the view that the other two persons of the Godhead derive from the Father alone—safeguards the unity and personal nature of the Godhead. It is from the person of the Father that the other two persons have their origin and unity. The divine essence, the principle of oneness in God, is personal. As John Zizioulas puts it, "the ontological 'principle' of God is the Father. . . . The being of God is identified with the person."[11]

The Western Church, by contrast, makes the essence and unity of God something abstract and impersonal. It becomes a fourth element which underlies the three persons, as in the common Western trinitarian formula, "three persons in one essence." In the Western view, the ontological principle or being of God is the divine substance rather than the person of the Father. So the West tends to be more rationalistic and speculative in its

---

9. Cf. Nissiotis, "The Doctrine of the Trinity," 42.

10. The views I expound here go back to discussions with Dr. John Zizioulas in 1970–71, during my postgraduate study at New College, Edinburgh. He pinned my last defences of the *Filioque* against the ropes with his probing Socratic questioning. I have been a convinced supporter the Eastern Orthodox view ever since, and remain silent when the *Filioque* clause is recited in the Nicene Creed.

11. Zizioulas, *Being as Communion*, 41.

understanding of the Trinity. It follows Augustine in seeing the Holy Spirit as the "bond of love" (*vinculum caritatis* or *vinculum amoris*) between the Father and the Son, proceeding from both and joining them in unity.[12]

The disagreement over the *Filioque* might seem to be making a mountain out of a molehill, but it has far-reaching consequences:

1. The Eastern view ensures that the relationship between the three persons of the Godhead is a fully personal one. Each person is in a personal relationship with the other two persons.

2. The Western view, by interposing the Spirit as the relationship of love between the Father and the Son, compromises either the personality of the Spirit or the personal nature of their relationship. If the relationship between Father and Son is treated as personal, the Spirit is reduced to a relationship and the Trinity to a Duality. On the other hand, if the Spirit is treated as personal, the relationship of Father and Son ceases to be a personal relationship and instead becomes a mediated one.

3. The Eastern view preserves the sole monarchy of the Father, treating the Father as the source of both the persons and the nature of the Godhead and the source of unity in the Trinity. The Western view, typically, invokes the common nature of the three persons as the source of unity in the Godhead, making for a "Quaternity" of three persons and a divine essence rather than a Trinity.

Lossky explains: "The Greeks saw in the formula of the procession of the Holy Spirit from the Father and the Son a tendency to stress the unity of nature at the expense of the real distinction between the persons. The relationships of origin which do not bring the Son and the Spirit back directly to the unique source, to the Father—the one as begotten, the other as proceeding—become a system of relationships within one essence.... The hypostatic characteristics (paternity, generation, procession), find themselves more or less swallowed up in the nature or essence which... becomes the principle of unity within the Trinity."[13]

While I greatly respect the work that the New Zealand theologian Myk Habets has done to promote contemporary ecumenical discussion of the *Filioque*, I feel that his attempt at a rapprochement tends to illustrate Lossky's concern. Habets wants to resolve the controversy by moving beyond the sole monarchy of the Father to a view in which each of the divine persons contributes relationally to the others. He says, "The Father is the source of both the Son and the Spirit; the Son through his eternal generation, the Spirit by his eternal spiration." So far, so good. But he adds, "neither Son nor Spirit are passive in such begetting and spirating, *and the Father*

---

12. Augustine, *On the Trinity*, 6.7, 15.17–19.
13. Lossky, *Mystical Theology*, 57.

*himself receives from the Son as much as he gives.*"[14] He then proceeds to generalize the monarchy of the Father, attributing the power of generation and spiration to the being of the Godhead and so swallowing up the distinctive characteristics of the persons in the unity of the divine nature.

"The Greek Fathers always maintained that the principle of unity in the Trinity is the person of the Father," says Vladimir Lossky. "This is why the East has always opposed the formula of *Filioque* which seems to impair the monarchy of the Father: either one is forced to destroy the unity by acknowledging two principles of Godhead, or one must ground the unity primarily on the common nature, which thus overshadows the persons and transforms them into relations within the unity of the essence."[15]

The characteristic Western approach to the doctrine of the Trinity has therefore tended to be theoretical, philosophical, and rationalistic, whereas the approach of the East is more relational, worshipful, and contemplative.[16]

## God Is Really Transcendent

The rationalistic implications of the Western view of the Trinity can be most clearly seen in the theology of Karl Barth, perhaps the greatest Protestant theologian of the twentieth century, certainly the most prolific. Though he sees the Trinity as the foundation of Christian theology, he expounds this as God's threefold reiteration of himself rather than as God being a society of persons. Indeed, he is critical of the very notion of divine "persons," preferring instead to use the term "mode of being" (*Seinsweisen*).[17]

Over against the anthropocentric starting-point of liberal theology, Barth maintains that the Trinity is the basis of God's revelation. He argues, "statements about the divine modes of being antecedently in themselves

---

14. Habets, *Ecumenical Perspectives*, 227–28. I italicize what is questionable about this statement, for whatever their mutual relations, neither the Son nor the Spirit contribute to their *origin* what the Father does.

15. Lossky, *Mystical Theology*, 58. In 1996, the Roman Catholic Church finally issued a statement recognizing the sole monarchy of the Father: "The Father alone is the principle without principle (*archē anarchos*) of the two other persons of the Trinity, the sole source of the Son and of the Holy Spirit . . ." ("The Greek and Latin Traditions," 39, quoted by Siecienski, *The Filioque*, 210). The Anglican Communion, in the Lambeth Conference of 1978, had already agreed to remove the *Filioque* from the Creed.

16. This can be seen even in Karl Rahner's *The Trinity*, a modern Western theologian's commendable but highly abstruse attempt to go behind Augustine and Thomas Aquinas and restore the patristic Greek emphasis to the Catholic doctrine of the Trinity.

17. Barth, *CD*, I, 1, 348–68. Karl Rahner prefers the phrase "distinct manner of subsisting" (Rahner, *The Trinity*, 109–13).

cannot be different in content from those that are to be made about their reality in revelation."[18]

This requirement means that we must make our understanding of the immanent Trinity—what God is in himself—conform with our understanding of the economic Trinity—what God does in his activities in the world. So, if the Holy Spirit who acts in our lives is the Spirit of the Father and the Son, as Jesus said he is (John 14:26; 15:26; 16:15), he can be no other than the Spirit of the Father *and the Son* in the internal relations of the Godhead, in the immanent Trinity. In denying the procession of the Spirit from the Son, Barth says, "The Eastern doctrine ... goes beyond revelation to achieve a very different picture of God 'antecedently in himself.'"[19]

This seems to be a convincing defense of the *Filioque* until we examine how Barth expounds it. For Barth defines the Holy Spirit, in the manner of Augustine, as the "togetherness or communion of the Father and the Son," "the common element" or "the fellowship" of the Father and the Son.[20] The Father loves the Son and the Son the Father, and the love or communion that exists between them and unites them is the Holy Spirit. Barth maintains that this "communion between the Father and the Son" in the inner, divine life of the Trinity is the basis of the relationship between God and human beings, established by God's self-revelation through the Spirit. If this relationship did not exist in the inner life of the Trinity prior to God's revelation, Barth claims that the communion of the Spirit between God and human beings would lack an objective basis.[21]

Three objections can be brought against Barth's position. The first, a *reductio ad absurdum* of his view, is mentioned by George Hendry: "Defenders of the double procession of the Spirit ought in consistency to maintain the double generation of the Son."[22] For the Nicene Creed mentions the role of the Holy Spirit in the external mission of the Son ("by the power of the Holy Spirit he became incarnate"). To be consistent, should not a *Spirituque* be added to the second article of the Creed: "eternally begotten of the Father *and the Spirit*"? If one is valid, why not the other? But Barth follows Western theology in resisting the inference that the Spirit has a role in the eternal generation of the Son, and rightly so.[23]

---

18. Barth, *CD*, I, 1, 479, cf. 332–33, 466.
19. Barth, *CD*, I, 1, 480.
20. Barth, *CD*, I, 1, 469–70.
21. Barth, *CD*, I, 1, 480–81.
22. Hendry, *The Holy Spirit*, 44.
23. Barth, *CD*, I, 1, 485–86.

The second objection relates to what we have already seen in the deficiencies of Augustine's view of the Holy Spirit as the love that joins the Father and the Son in the unity of the Godhead. How can a bond that unites two divine persons itself be a distinct person like the other two? Either, as a bond, it denotes a relationship, not a person. Or, as a person, the Spirit ceases to be a bond and becomes a mediator between the other persons, rendering their relationship a mediated and less than fully personal one. Indeed, Barth explicitly states that the Holy Spirit "could not possibly be regarded" as a person like the Father and the Son.[24]

The third objection relates to Barth's insistence on grounding God's revelation *ad extra* in the inner-trinitarian relationships of the Godhead. This is to rationalize the Godhead by projecting back into his eternal being what belongs properly to the economy of revelation. Contrary to Barth's original intention at the outset of his theological project, which was to magnify God's transcendence and "the Godness of God,"[25] this is to project the realm of creation back into the being of God. Barth even speaks elsewhere of "temporality" in God.[26] This confirms the fears of Eastern theologians, who argue that the *Filioque* leads to a denial of the transcendence and mystery of God.

The modern Catholic theologian Karl Rahner holds a similar view to Barth. In a famous axiom, he asserts that "The 'economic' Trinity is the 'immanent' Trinity and the 'immanent' Trinity is the 'economic' Trinity."[27] It is true that God in his self-communication is consistent in his identity and character. But as a general principle, Rahner's axiom is questionable. As Athanasius argued against the Arians, even if God had never created the world, the Son would still have been eternally with the Father.[28] By implication, even if there were no creation, the triune God would still have been the triune God. Indeed, Rahner modifies his position along the lines of what I am arguing here when he subsequently admits that God's "threefold, free, and gratuitous relation to us *is* not merely a copy or an analogy of the inner Trinity."[29] As Clark Pinnock points out, endorsing the *apophatic* theology of the Eastern Church, "the economic Trinity does not exhaust the immanent Trinity, since the divine mystery overflows revelation and is unattainable by the creature."[30]

24. Barth, *CD*, I, 1, 469.

25. Busch, *Karl Barth*, 119.

26. Barth speaks of "the temporality of eternity," and says that "eternity . . . is itself temporal, and would be so even if no time existed apart from it" (*CD*, II, 1, 619–20). God "is supremely temporal" (*CD*, III, 2, 437).

27. Rahner, *The Trinity*, 22. "The economic Trinity *is* the immanent Trinity and vice versa" (Rahner, *Theological Investigations*, 18, 114).

28. Athanasius, *Orations against the Arians*, 2.31.

29. Rahner, *The Trinity*, 35.

30. Pinnock, *Flame of Love*, 32.

The inadmissibility of Barth and Rahner's insistence on the identity of the economic and immanent Trinity can be shown with reference to Jesus' knowledge and self-consciousness.[31] Jesus' human knowledge was clearly different from the omniscience of the preexistent divine Logos. Though he was noted for his wisdom, he grew in knowledge like any human being (Luke 2:40). His limited and developing knowledge as the incarnate Son of God shows that God's self-revelation is not simply a copy of God's inner-trinitarian life. His "economic" knowledge, so to speak, differed from his "immanent" knowledge in the Godhead.

Theologians properly distinguish the birth of Jesus as a human being from the eternal generation of the Son. By analogy, therefore, when considering the third person of the Trinity, the difference between the temporal sending of the Spirit in the economy of redemption and the eternal procession of the Spirit in the Godhead should be acknowledged as well. They are different and not to be confused.

## The Church Is Truly Spiritual

The Orthodox say that the *Filioque* clause, by subordinating the Spirit to the Son, accounts for the subordination of the Spirit to the institution of the church in Roman Catholicism and the widespread neglect of the Spirit in Western theology before the charismatic renewal of modern times. Typically, most Western theologians discuss the Spirit as the one who reveals Christ or who is at best the activity of the risen Christ, rather than the unique divine person who imparts to Christians a share in the divine life and an experience of the charismatic gifts.

The Hispanic Pentecostal theologian Eldin Villafañe observes, "There is a tendency to a '*practical* subordination, if not an ontological subordination' in the Western Church's understanding of the Spirit."[32] He thinks it is significant that Jesus promises "*another* Paraclete" than himself (John 14:16). The Spirit is different from, not identical with, the person of Jesus. John McIntyre also emphasizes that the Spirit "plays a different role in the economy of salvation from that played by Jesus."[33] He questions whether the Holy Spirit can be viewed as "the extension of the incarnation"[34] and asks whether we need to "recognize the personality of the Spirit and the autonomy and freedom which go with it."[35] He accepts that this commits him to "a social theory of the Trinity" like that of the Eastern Church.[36]

---

31. I first began to reflect on this in a postgraduate seminar on "The Knowledge and Self-Consciousness of Christ" at New College, Edinburgh in 1970, which included such distinguished participants as Rudolf Ehrlich, James Torrance, Roland Walls, and Kenneth Woollcombe, soon to be bishop of Oxford.

32. Villafañe, *The Liberating Spirit*, 183.

33. McIntyre, *Shape of Pneumatology*, 71.

34. McIntyre, *Shape of Pneumatology*, 205.

35. McIntyre, *Shape of Pneumatology*, 206.

36. McIntyre, *Shape of Pneumatology*, 208.

Eastern Orthodox theologians view the church as a living community indwelt by the fullness of the Spirit. They believe this dynamism is safeguarded by their refusal to subordinate the Spirit to the Son in the Godhead, or the Spirit to the institution of the church in society. In the Orthodox view, both Spirit and Son derive from the Father, so the Spirit is equal in majesty to the Son and as significant in the life of the church as the Son.

Orthodox do not view the church merely an earthly institution left on earth by Christ to perpetuate his presence. Rather, they see it as the "community of the Spirit," "heaven on earth," a divine society animated by the abundant life of the Holy Spirit. They hold that tradition is "the life of the Holy Spirit in the church,"[37] "a continuity of the abiding presence of the Holy Spirit in the church."[38] Orthodoxy seeks to preserve a personal or relational understanding of the church and has historically resisted becoming the institution of secular power that the papacy became in the West. It may be wondered, though, whether the life of the Orthodox churches today sufficiently reflects the vitality of the Spirit that their theology professes. "For all too many Orthodox . . . ," says Kallistos Ware, "their church is the link with the mother-country rather than with God. . . . They are Orthodox because they are Greeks, Russians or Serbs, not because they have made any deep and conscious act of personal commitment to God."[39]

The teaching office of the pope as bishop of Rome was always central in the disagreement between the Eastern and Western Churches over the *Filioque*. The Eastern Orthodox saw the insertion of the *Filioque* into the Creed as a usurping by the pope of the authority of an ecumenical council to determine the doctrine of the church. Catholic theology, though, has seen it as a proper exercise of papal authority to clarify and proclaim the church's faith.

Vladimir Soloviev, the "Russian Newman," argued that the church needs the teaching office of the papacy to ensure its universality and prevent it from lapsing into heresy and cultural accommodation. This was the thesis of his famous work *Russia and the Universal Church* (1889). The weakness of the Eastern Church has been its captivity to nationalism and local culture—a tendency still evident in Putin's Russia. The blight of the Western Church, though, has been its authoritarian tendency and at times brutal suppression of dissent.

---

37. Lossky, "Tradition and Traditions," 152
38. Florovsky, "Tradition of the Fathers," 106.
39. Ware, "Orthodoxy and the Charismatic Movement," 185.

These issues need to be faced with humility in the construction of a truly charismatic and ecumenical theology of the Holy Spirit in our day. The Pentecostal-charismatic renewal movement represents a rediscovery in the church of the dynamism and freedom of the Holy Spirit. Clark Pinnock considers it "the most important event in modern Christianity."[40] Its contribution is vital not only for the church's renewal, but for the recovery of lost insights concerning its fullness and reunification. The activity of the Holy Spirit complements the understanding of the church as the pillar and guardian of the truth (1 Tim 3:15), which on its own can lead to authoritarian and persecuting tendencies. It guarantees the diversity in unity of the church as a fellowship of free and autonomous persons. "Where the Spirit of the Lord is, there is freedom" (2 Cor 3:17).

## The Spirit Is Fully Personal

The worldwide growth of the Pentecostal-charismatic movement in our time draws attention to the dynamism of the Holy Spirit, invigorating Christians, renewing churches, and initiating new forms of mission. This vitality is raising new insights into the very nature of the Spirit, aspects concealed in inherited forms of church life, and insufficiently articulated in traditional theological thinking about the Spirit.

The historical neglect of the Holy Spirit in theological formulation is evident in the brevity of the Third Article of the church's creed compared with the Second Article.[41] This reflects the christological preoccupation of theologians and church councils in the Byzantine era. But the impact of charismatic renewal suggests that it is now opportune for this lack to be remedied. Any revision of the Nicene Creed must, of course, be the decision of the relevant church authorities. But an initiative must begin somewhere. At the very least, the creed should be broadened to include the Spirit's role in commissioning Jesus as Messiah, as attested by John the Baptist—to parallel the reference to his suffering under Pontius Pilate. Its revision should also include the Holy Spirit's constituting of the church on the day of Pentecost.

As a start, here is a draft that I have composed of a possible enhancement of the Third Article of the Nicene Creed, with additions in italics, to take account of matters raised by the renewal movement and contemporary theology, and as a contribution to Christian unity:

40. Pinnock, *Flame of Love*, 18, cf. 240.

41. Kilian McDonnell has some fine insights into the origin of the statements about the Holy Spirit in the Nicene-Constantinopolitan Creed, but has nothing to say about their possible enhancement (McDonnell, *The Other Hand of God*, 155–58).

> We believe in the Holy Spirit, the Lord, the giver of life,
> who proceeds *eternally* from the Father and *is sent in time by* the Son,
> who with the Father and the Son is worshiped and glorified,
> who has spoken through the prophets,
> *who overshadowed the Virgin Mary,*
> *and anointed Jesus of Nazareth with power as Messiah*
> *as attested by John the Baptist.*
> We believe in one holy catholic and apostolic church,
> *founded on the day of Pentecost*
> *as the body of Christ and community of the Spirit.*
> We acknowledge one baptism for the forgiveness of sins,
> *and the Spirit's many charisms for effective service.*
> We look for the resurrection of the dead,
> and the life of the world to come. Amen.[42]

The suggested modification to the *Filioque* clause is based on John 15:26. It embraces both the Spirit's origin in the Godhead and role in the economy, and could satisfy the concerns of both Eastern and Western Christians. Other modifications enshrine the Spirit's role in Jesus' installation as Messiah, the place of Pentecost in the founding of the church, and the Spirit's empowerment for effective service.

These proposals will doubtless stimulate vigorous discussion and perhaps some tut-tutting. But the contemporary renewal movement also raises matters about the Holy Spirit that are wider than the church's historic creeds. John McIntyre has highlighted seven ways in which the Holy Spirit may be observed to be active today:

1. The Holy Spirit relates in an utterly loving, humbling, and disturbing way to every detail of each person's existence.

2. The Holy Spirit is involved in the details of human volition, action, thought, and feeling, without violating people's personal integrity. "When he works miracles, he does so not as an alien irrupting into an order which forms a totally enclosed system and breaking laws that hold therein; but in accordance with fundamental principles of the universe which he has himself created."[43]

---

42. English translation of the Nicene Creed adapted © 1998, English Language Liturgical Consultation (ELLC), used by permission, http://www.englishtexts.org.

43. From the Eastern Orthodox perspective, Dumitru Staniloae also emphasizes that the Spirit, "without destroying the laws of nature, inspires effects which do not spring from nature" (Staniloae, "The Holy Spirit," 9).

3. The Holy Spirit identifies with human beings in their condition or situation, including the poor in their distress and sinners in their need.

4. The Holy Spirit joins people to one another in fellowship and communion.

5. The Holy Spirit prepares the hearts of people beforehand to respond freely to God's saving love and purpose.

6. The Holy Spirit not only puts people in a right relationship with one another but also with the whole world of nature in which human beings are rooted.

7. The Spirit makes appropriate the attribution of the categories of personality and spirit to God himself.[44]

To these, I would add the following further features:

8. The Spirit is renewing local churches to be attractive missional communities in an increasingly secular culture. Anticipating the demise of Christendom, the Holy Spirit has been reinvigorating the global church to address the challenges of the new mission situation in which it finds itself.

9. The Spirit is rejuvenating Christian worship and community life to be more engaged with local culture. Just as the Spirit was the agent of the incarnation, the "humanization" of the Son of God, so the Spirit is the agent of enculturation, the "indigenization" of the church, creating appropriate forms of church life for effective engagement with its local culture.[45] This is especially apparent in the emergence of the Messianic Jewish and Islamic Christian movements but is also evident in indigenous Pentecostal and charismatic developments around the world. This phenomenon is, in part, a Spirit-led "protest against a homogenizing globalization."[46]

10. The Spirit, as the Spirit of the *eschaton*, the eschatological future, is preparing the global church to meet its future challenges. These include not just the church's emergence from the inherited form of Christendom, or the transition from print to digital culture, but above all the challenge of a pluralistic and even persecuting society, as we

---

44. McIntyre, *Shape of Pneumatology*, 174, 177, 181–82, 183, 185, 190, and 193 respectively.

45. In contrast to anemic and "bloodless" forms of spirituality, my Edinburgh teacher Roland Walls used to emphasize that "wherever the Holy Spirit is, there is always embodiment" (Ferguson and Chater, *Mole under the Fence*, 141).

46. Hocken, *Challenges*, 128.

enter the perilous times predicted by Jesus and the prophets for the latter days.

These ten features of the Holy Spirit's activity in the Pentecostal-charismatic movement of our time are what theology would describe as operations *ad extra*. But their dynamism and particularity suggest characteristics of the Spirit's distinctive personality *ad intra*. This has led John McIntyre to speak of an "autonomous Spirit" who acts in a wider way than as an extension of the incarnation or a continuation of the ministry of Jesus. He believes that we should regard the Holy Spirit as a "'personality' in the full modern psychological sense of a substantival and autonomous being."[47] Certainly, these phenomena call into question the Augustinian understanding of the Spirit as an impersonal bond or relationship between the Father and the Son.

We can discern in these developments that the Spirit has a recognizable personality, parallel to the distinctive personalities of the Father and the Son. The Father is the initiator and creator, *ad intra* as the originator of the other two persons, *ad extra* as the originator of creation. The only-beloved Son of the Father is the mediator and redeemer, the one in whom all creation coheres and in whom humanity is reconciled (Col 1:15–20). The God-breathed Spirit is the indweller, liberator, and perfecter, the one who self-effacingly indwells the children of God without violating their integrity and moves all things to their perfection (Rom 8:21–23; 2 Cor 3:18).

---

47. McIntyre, *Shape of Pneumatology*, 208.

# 11

# Persons, Nature, and the Role of the Spirit

*The concept of the person is a unique Christian contribution to human thought. It originated in the christological and trinitarian controversies in the Byzantine Church. Modern Eastern Orthodox theologians, continuing this discussion, focus on the unique roles which the Son and the Spirit play in God's economy of salvation. In particular, Vladimir Lossky has developed a fascinating schema of person and nature, which associates the unity of human nature with Christ and the multiplicity of human persons with the Spirit. I examine John Zizioulas's criticism of this schema but remain convinced of its validity. Lossky shows that the Holy Spirit has a distinctive personalizing role in the divine economy within the uniting of all things in Christ.*

## Persons and Personhood

THE CONCEPT OF THE person is a radical Christian innovation in the history of ideas. Vladimir Lossky rightly identified that it "comes to us from

Christian theology."¹ John Zizioulas says that it is "the product of patristic thought."² The mystery of personhood was first intuited and grappled with in the christological and trinitarian controversies in the early Byzantine Church. The notion of person emerged in the debates about the assumption of human nature by the person of the Son of God in the incarnation. It was clarified in later disputes about the relation of the three persons in the unity of the Trinity. The mystery and implications of personhood continue to be debated today, particularly by Eastern Orthodox theologians, the heirs of this tradition.

Intimations of personhood first appear in the ancient Greek tragedies, in association with the Greek term *prosōpon*, the mask worn by actors. I used to think this was an inappropriate way to denote persons and personhood because I associated it with acting a role and with hiding the identity of the actor. But I have come to realize how appropriate it is to denote a "character"—the cluster of distinctive qualities that uniquely constitute a person. Far from being a disguise to conceal a person's identity, a *prosōpon* was a dramatic medium to identify a person and convey to an audience the life issues and emotions of that person. This is how we understand the parallel Latin word *persona*, which denotes a person's character or personality as presented to or perceived by others.

The church fathers, though, from Athanasius on, chose to use the term *hypostasis* ("substantial nature, essence, actual being, reality") for the persons of the Trinity, to give the concept of person an ontological grounding that the term *prosōpon* lacked. As Zizioulas puts it, "from an adjunct to a being (a kind of mask) the person becomes the being itself."³ *Hypostasis* came to describe the unique, hidden depths and identity of a person, *prosōpon* the "face," which reveals the person to others. We see the former in Hebrews 1:3: "The Son of God is *character tes hypostaseos autou* [an exact representation of (God's) *real being*]."⁴ The latter is in 1 Corinthians 13:12: "Now we see only a reflection as in a mirror; then we shall see face to face (*prosōpon pros prosōpon*). Now I know in part; then I shall know fully, even as I am fully known."

Person, personhood, and personality elude all rational definitions. A person is a unique and irreplaceable world of experience and creativity. The mystery of our inner life is most profoundly revealed in our creative activity. "Personality can only be grasped in this life by a direct intuition," says Lossky; "it can only be expressed in a work of art. When we say 'this is by Mozart,' or 'this is by Rembrandt,' we are in both cases dealing with a personal world which has no equivalent anywhere."⁵

1. Lossky, *Mystical Theology*, 53.
2. Zizioulas, *Being as Communion*, 27. Its origin and development, overlooked in the history of philosophy, is discussed by Zizioulas in *Being as Communion*, 27–41.
3. Zizioulas, *Being as Communion*, 39.
4. "*Hypostasis*," BDAG 1040.
5. Lossky, *Mystical Theology*, 53.

Persons exist in relation to other persons. The capacity for relationship is a defining characteristic of persons. But John Zizioulas goes too far when he says, "A person is identifiable *only* within a relationship with another person. There is no person outside a relationship with other persons, so one person is no person at all."[6] Persons are not definable solely by the relations in which they stand with other persons. Each and every person is unique. A person is a unique center of consciousness and experience, identity and intentionality, character and creativity, irrespective of his or her relations with other persons. The apostle Paul understood this: "For who knows a person's thoughts except their own spirit within them?" (1 Cor 2:11).[7]

John Zizioulas is rightly concerned to reject the individualistic understanding of the person that has come to characterize modern Western culture. He traces this to Boethius's early scholastic definition of the person as *naturae rationabilis individua substantia* (an "individual substance of a rational nature").[8] The scholastic heritage of rational individuality has combined with the modern psychological understanding of consciousness to produce the contemporary individualistic concept of the person.

Zizioulas develops his understanding of personhood in his discussion of the persons of the Trinity. "When we talk about a person, we can do so only by referring to other beings, even though each person is distinct so that what is particular to this person is found in no other. Every person is unique, unprecedented and irreplaceable, even though he [or she] exists only through relation with others. The person is the identity born of a relationship, and exists only in communion with other persons. There cannot be a person without relationship to other persons, so if all the relationships which constitute a person disappear, so does that person."[9]

Zizioulas acknowledges that there is a conflict between the notions of uniqueness and relationship. "At first glance, the concept of the 'particular' appears to conflict with that of relationship. If we define a person by a relationship, how can we say that the person is entirely unique and particular? And yet, its particularity springs from a relationship for the relationship creates a 'particularity' which is non-communicable, and without being in communion, this 'singularity' cannot exist."[10]

Relationship is undoubtedly an identifying mark of personhood. But it cannot be said to constitute the person. Edinburgh theologian John McIntyre says that he learned from the Scottish-Australian philosopher John Anderson—no friend of Christianity but in this respect correct—that "an entity is not definable solely in terms of the relations in which it stands to

---

6. Zizioulas, *Lectures in Christian Dogmatics*, 25, my italics.

7. I write this with some poignancy, as my beloved wife of fifty-two years slowly loses her memory, self-awareness, sparkle, and ability to communicate.

8. Boethius, *Contra Eutychen et Nestorium* [Against Eutyches and Nestorius], 3, quoted by Zizioulas, "Human Capacity and Human Incapacity," 405.

9. Zizioulas, *Lectures in Christian Dogmatics*, 57. This and all subsequent clarifications in square brackets are mine.

10. Zizioulas, *Lectures in Christian Dogmatics*, 58.

other entities."[11] McIntyre showed how this undermines Augustine's account of the persons of the Trinity, each of whom he defines in terms of their relations with the other two persons. But it also calls in question Zizioulas's exclusively relational view of persons and denial of essentialism. Persons *are* in relationship with other persons. But they are not defined *solely* by their relations. Each person is a unique center of thought, consciousness, character, intentionality, activity, and creativity—and sometimes besetting flaws and weaknesses—factors that are not reducible to their relations with other persons.

Zizioulas gives a truer account of the mystery of personhood in a footnote to his original article on the subject. "*Stasis* (being 'as it stands', as it is 'in itself') is realised in personhood both as *ek-stasis* (communion, relatedness) and as *hypo-stasis* (particularity, uniqueness)."[12] It is this blend of uniqueness and relatedness that captures exactly the paradoxical reality of persons and personhood.

The communicable and incommunicable aspects of the person

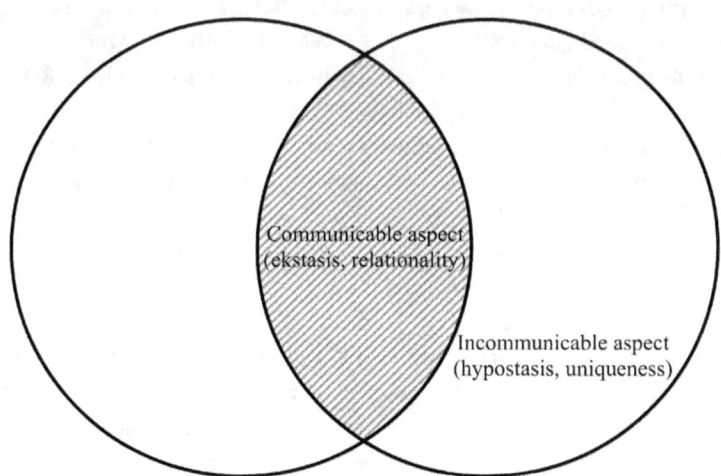

The concept of the person includes two contrasting features: uniqueness and relationality. On the one hand is the irreplaceable particularity of each person, on the other a person's capacity for self-disclosure, relationship, and inter-personal communion.

**Figure 2. The Paradox of Personhood**

Personhood is a mystery that constitutes a paradox for rational thought. On the one hand, it entails a uniqueness and a particularity that is

---

11. McIntyre, *Shape of Pneumatology*, 117.
12. Zizioulas, "Human Capacity and Human Incapacity," 425.

incommunicable. On the other hand, it involves a capacity for self-transcendence, relationship, and interpersonal communion that involves self-disclosure and communication. It is this blend of what is communicable and what is incommunicable that explains how two persons, without forfeiting their otherness and uniqueness, can love one another and, in marriage, become one with one another. Supremely, in the Godhead, this identifies how it is that three persons can be one God through their personal communion and coinherence (*perichoresis*), without compromising monotheism.

I would also give more emphasis than Zizioulas does to the reality that our personhood and personal existence not only transcends nature but is also rooted in nature, as suggested by Pauline theology. For Paul, salvation in Christ involves not just the liberation of our person, but the overcoming of the corruption of death and the redemption of the fallen nature in which we are bound up (Rom 8:21; 1 Cor 15:42–49). For Paul, too, the Christian life consists in a vital struggle, involving each of us as persons with the aid of the Spirit, to overcome the passions of the flesh, the fallen nature in which we are enmeshed (Rom 8:13; Gal 5:16). We will not be fully redeemed until the whole creation is liberated from its "bondage to decay" (Rom 8:21–23).

Because we as persons are both rooted in nature and transcend nature, personhood contains a whole world—one could even say, *the* whole world—in itself. Lossky points out that a human being has a "double character": "As an individual nature, he is part of a whole, one of the elements which make up the universe; but as a person, he is in no sense a part: he contains all in himself. The nature is the content of the person, the person the existence of the nature."[13]

So our unique world as persons includes what is universal in human experience in ourselves. "Every person is unique, unprecedented and irreplaceable."[14] Zizioulas illustrates this with reference to deaths in war. An army announces its casualties as mere statistics: Ten were killed in this firefight. But for the wife or mother of one of those ten soldiers, that man was a unique person, and a whole world of experience has died with him. "The man who has gone now is not one of ten, but one of one, the one and only. He represents life as a whole, so all life has gone with him. . . . The more we regard someone as a person, the more we regard them as representative of humanity as a whole. So we can see from our own existence how we could regard all humanity through the life of a single person, as though all the many persons of the human race were also just a single being."[15]

---

13. Lossky, *Mystical Theology*, 123.
14. Zizioulas, *Lectures in Christian Dogmatics*, 57.
15. Zizioulas, *Lectures in Christian Dogmatics*, 63.

## Humanity Personalized

These insights into the reality of personhood allow us to understand the meaning of the theological term *enhypostatos* (literally "in-personal," "being or existing in a person").[16] The term was devised by Leontius of Byzantium, a sixth-century theologian, to clarify the church's understanding of the assumption of human nature by the Son of God. It was developed by Maximus the Confessor in the seventh century and John of Damascus in the eighth. According to Leontius, all nature is found in a person, a *hypostasis*. Nature—and by extension, universal human experience—is not encountered as something abstract or generic, but is concretely personalized or experienced *in a person* (*enhypostatos*). Christ's humanity had its personal subsistence in the person of the *Logos*. But embodying human nature *in his person*, Jesus Christ, the Son of God, experienced human life on behalf of all and was able to offer his life on behalf of all.

Lossky applies this understanding to Christ as the head of his body, the church, which he is gathering from throughout the world. "If human nature finds itself reunited in the *hypostasis* of Christ, if it is an '*enhypostasised*' nature—one existing in an *hypostasis*—the human persons who form the *hypostases* of this unified nature are not suppressed. They are not mingled or one with the divine person of Christ. For one *hypostasis* cannot be identified with another *hypostasis* without ceasing to exist as a personal being: that would mean the annihilation of persons in the unique Christ, an impersonal deification." So, he concludes, "The church, the new body of humanity, while it is one nature in Christ, yet includes many human *hypostases*."[17]

Reflecting on this mystery, Lossky arrives at his creative synthesis of the distinctive and complementary ministries of the Son and the Spirit. The Son becomes incarnate as a human being, uniting human nature to his divine person. But unlike the Son, the Spirit does not become incarnate. Rather, the Spirit communicates the divine nature to the diversity of human persons. Thus, says Lossky, "The work of Christ concerns human nature which he recapitulates in his *hypostasis*. The work of the Holy Spirit, on the other hand, concerns persons, being applied to each one singly. Within the church the Holy Spirit imparts to human *hypostases* the fullness of deity after a manner which is unique, 'personal,' appropriate to every [human being] as a person created in the image of God."[18] In this way, the Father

---

16. "Being, existing in an *hypostasis* or person," *PGL*, 486.
17. Lossky, *Mystical Theology*, 165–66, my italics.
18. Lossky, *Mystical Theology*, 166, my italics.

accomplishes our redemption by means of the complementary action of his Son and Spirit.

## The One and the Many

John Zizioulas disagrees with Lossky over this schema of person and nature, which associates the unity of human nature with Christ and the multiplicity of human persons with the Spirit. Their point of difference, if I understand it correctly, focuses on the issue of whether Christ unites us by his assumption of human nature, or by way of his person. Are the many united in Christ's *nature*, or by Christ's *person*?

Lossky rejects the view that a person or *hypostasis* can contain other persons or *hypostases*, as parts of "a kind of supra-person." He holds that the theological definition of a person or *hypostasis* implies "an absolute difference, an ontological irreducibility."[19] One person cannot be substituted for another without annihilating personal distinctiveness.

Zizioulas disputes this, pointing to biblical passages such as Matt 18:20, "Where two or three gather in my name, there am I with them."[20] But Lossky comments on this text as if anticipating this objection. "The Lord did not say 'I contain them in me' or 'They are in me,' . . . but precisely 'I am in the midst of them,' as a person who is *with other* persons who surround him."[21]

Zizioulas also appeals to the "in Christ" passages in the writings of John and Paul. The intercommunion and coinherence of persons is indeed a central theme in the Johannine and Pauline writings. Christians are described as being "in Christ" (*en Christō*) and Christ (or God) is said to be "in us" (John 6:56; 14:20; 15:4; Rom 8:1, 10; 2 Cor 5:17; 13:5; Gal 2:20; Col 1:27; 1 John 3:24; 4:13; 4:16).

But these passages can hardly mean the annihilation of our personal identity, still less the Eastern religious notion of the merging of the droplets of our individuality in an amorphous ocean of primordial being or a *nirvana* of nonexistence. As Lossky says, that would be "a blessedness in which there would be no blessed."[22] We must surely understand the "in Christ" passages as implying the fulfillment of our personal identity and uniqueness in the fullness of Christ's person. The risen and ascended Christ promises each of his faithful followers a unique personal identity: "I will give that

---

19. Lossky, "Catholic Consciousness," 188.
20. Zizioulas, *Communion and Otherness*, 74–75.
21. Lossky, "Catholic Consciousness," 189, italics original.
22. Lossky, *Mystical Theology*, 166.

person a white stone with a new name written on it, known only to the one who receives it" (Rev 2:17).

Zizioulas insists that our union with God and with one another is not brought about by Christ's assumption of our nature, but by Christ's communion and coinherence with us *in his own person*. It is the problem of the relationship between the *Logos* and the *logoi*, the one and the many. "The 'many' are not united in the *nature* of the 'one' but in his *person*—both in ecclesiology and in Christology the unity is *hypostatic* [personal]. . . . Christ unites not via *nature* but 'hypostatically,' i.e., via *personhood*."[23]

Zizioulas quotes the Byzantine theologian Maximus the Confessor, to the effect that "*natures can unite only because they possess a hypostasis [person]; the principle of unity is not nature but person.*"[24] The mystery of interpersonal communion is that it involves persons as *wholes*, not just as parts of a whole. Such union can only happen at the dimension of persons, not at the sub-personal level of nature.

Zizioulas does not seem to recognize that Lossky affirms this. Lossky explicitly says that Christ's recapitulation of our humanity is *in his person*, not merely by his assumption of our generic human nature. In the passage already quoted, Lossky says that "human nature" is "reunited in the *hypostasis* of Christ." It is "an '*enhypostasised*' nature": it exists in Christ's *hypostasis* or person. Our identity as human persons, he says, is "not suppressed" or "mingled" "with the divine person of Christ."[25] On the contrary, we "attain to perfection" as persons—"become fully *personal*"—in the unity of the nature that Christ assumed.[26] "The church, the new body of humanity, . . . is one nature in Christ, yet includes many human *hypostases*."[27]

## Universality and Freedom

"Life in Christ," Zizioulas continues, "means placing all our relations, in and through which we obtain our personal identity, in the *hypostasis* [person] of

---

23. Zizioulas, *Communion and Otherness*, 74, italics original.

24. Zizioulas, *Communion and Otherness*, 74–75, italics original. The quotation from Maximus is undocumented, but seems to be from his *Theological and Polemical Opuscula*, 14. Historian of doctrine Jaroslav Pelikan observes of this passage, "The single divine hypostasis of the Logos was constitutive of the union in the God-man, taking up into that union a perfect human nature, which was not a hypostasis on its own but achieved hypostatic and personal reality in the union" (Pelikan, *Christian Tradition*, 2:89).

25. Lossky, *Mystical Theology*, 165, my italics.

26. Lossky, *Mystical Theology*, 167, italics original.

27. Lossky, *Mystical Theology*, 166, my italics.

Christ. Christ is the only one that can guarantee . . . the eternal survival of every being we regard as unique and indispensable, for he is the only one in whom death, which threatens the particular with extinction, is overcome. It is for this reason that Christ can claim absolute uniqueness for himself to the point of demanding from us that we cease, for his sake, to regard any other being (father, mother, wife, children, etc. Matt 10:37; Luke 14:26) as unique and indispensable. It is not that he wants to exclude in this way anyone we love uniquely, but rather that he is the only one who can hypostasize them and give them eternal being."[28]

As the incarnate Son of the creator of all human beings, Christ's claim is universal. "I am the way and the truth and the life. No one comes to the Father except through me" (John 14:6). "Salvation is found in no one else, for there is no other name under heaven given to mankind by which we must be saved" (Acts 4:12). As the one who became incarnate for the salvation of all human beings, Christ's claim is universal and all-embracing. It is an invitation and challenge to people everywhere.

Is such a universal claim intrinsically coercive? In the aftermath of the totalitarian ideologies of the twentieth century, Zizioulas is sensitive to this point. He believes that "if unity is attached to nature and not hypostasis, a totalitarian ontology, so much and so rightly feared by post-modernity, becomes inevitable. If unity takes place at the hypostatic [personal] level, . . . the fear of such a totalitarian ontology is dispelled."[29]

Zizioulas claims that Lossky's schema of Christ-nature-unity versus Spirit-person-diversity is "problematic" and has totalitarian implications.[30] It is a strange and hostile charge, which the evidence does not support. Lossky's view accords with patristic tradition. Gregory of Nyssa similarly defined the distinctive contributions of the Son and the Spirit to the work of redemption. The economy of the Son, says Gregory, concerns humanity as a whole (*katholou*), which he recapitulates in his hypostasis; the economy of the Holy Spirit concerns each individual human being (*epi menous*), who he brings into the fullness of Christ's recapitulation.[31]

Moreover, not only does Lossky affirm that our human nature is *hypostasized* in the person of Christ, as we have just seen. Lossky also emphasizes the Holy Spirit's role in engaging our free response as we are united with Christ. He says that God's grace conveyed to us by the Spirit comes to us, not

---

28. Zizioulas, *Communion and Otherness*, 75, italics original.
29. Zizioulas, *Communion and Otherness*, 75.
30. Zizioulas, *Communion and Otherness*, 74–75.
31. J. P. Migne, *Patrologia Graeca*, 44, 1312c, cited by Philippou, "The Mystery of Pentecost," 88.

as an external force imposed from without, but as an "inward flowering."[32] "It is in this freedom that we acknowledge the deity of the Son, made manifest to our understanding through the Holy Spirit dwelling in us." If this were not so—if God's grace did not come to believers inwardly and freely by means of the Spirit—then "either they would be annihilated in being united to the person of Christ, or else the person of Christ would be imposed upon them from without."[33]

Indeed, it is Zizioulas's scheme that seems authoritarian, not Lossky's. Miroslav Volf argues that personal faith and individual response has no place in Zizioulas's theology.[34] But the Holy Spirit, whose distinctive ministry Lossky extols, is the agent of freedom (2 Cor 3:17), the very basis of free association and agreement (*sobornost*).[35] For Lossky, as for the New Testament writers, the Holy Spirit is the source of freedom. The Spirit respects the integrity and liberty of creatures. Unlike pagan cults, the Spirit moves us freely to acknowledge the Lordship of Christ (1 Cor 12:3). The Spirit removes the veil of unbelief from our minds, leads us to confess Christ, and freely transforms us into his likeness (2 Cor 3:16-18). The Spirit inspires the free response of persons—the very antithesis of coercion—as we bear witness to the universal claims of Jesus Christ.[36]

## The Two Hands of God

Zizioulas warns against setting the ministry of the Spirit in opposition to that of the Son. He sees this polarization in the common assertion that "the

---

32. Lossky, *Mystical Theology*, 170.
33. Lossky, *Mystical Theology*, 170.

34. Volf, *After Our Likeness*, 95-96. Even where Zizioulas does discuss faith, he insists that it is "not the action of an individual on their own" (Zizioulas, *Lectures in Christian Dogmatics*, 34).

35. *Sobornost*, a Russian word with no exact English equivalent, means "conciliarity" or "collegiality," unity based on freedom, love, and truth. It was used by the modern Russian Orthodox theologians, Alexei Khomiakoff ("The Church Is One," 192-222) and Sergei Bulgakov (*The Orthodox Church*, 59-86), to affirm the unity of many persons in the fellowship of the church. It echoes the conciliar agreement of the Jerusalem Council: "It seemed good to the Holy Spirit and to us" (Acts 15:28).

36. The role of human freedom has been especially emphasized by the émigré Russian writer Nicolas Berdyaev, in response to Communist totalitarianism: "Christ . . . must be freely accepted and it is by a free spiritual act that we must come to him. . . . He wants us to accept him freely, he desires the unforced love of man, and he can never compel anyone for he always has regard for our freedom. . . . It is not enough to accept truth, that is to say, God; it must be freely accepted. Freedom cannot be the result of constraint." (Berdyaev, *Freedom and the Spirit*, 126-27).

Holy Spirit has nothing to do with the traditional institution of the church, or that the gospel cannot be confined within institutional frameworks." He sees it too in the contrast between "the supposed freedom of charismatic ecclesial communities, and the churches with 'institutional' apostolic and episcopal ministry."[37]

Zizioulas seems to be reacting against the dynamism and unmanageability of Spirit-inspired movements. A more irenic view would hold that the institutional and charismatic dimensions of the church are not opposed to one another but are complementary.[38] Theologically, though, Zizioulas is surely correct: our understanding of the church "is not a matter of either Christ or the Spirit, but of all the persons of the Trinity in indivisible unity. . . . The role of the Holy Spirit should never lead us into an ecclesiology not founded in Christ: ecclesiology cannot be *Spirit*-centered because the church is the recapitulation of everything *in Christ*."[39]

We may acknowledge this theological truism, yet grant the cogency of Lossky's argument that the Holy Spirit has a distinctive personalizing role in the divine economy within the recapitulation of everything in Christ. Christ is the *head* of the body. But he is not its totality, supplanting or suppressing its individual parts. Christ's body is comprised of many members. The Spirit's distinctive ministry is to these many and varied members. The Spirit both integrates them into the one body of Christ and allots to each one individually their various personal charisms (1 Cor 12:11-13). As Lossky says, "there is the need in the church for another dispensation than that of the Son, who recapitulates the unity of nature—for a dispensation which is directed to each human person in particular, consecrating personal multiplicity in the unity of the body of Christ. This is the dispensation of the Holy Spirit, the Pentecostal aspect of the church."[40]

Lossky wishes to resist any understanding of the unity and catholicity of the church in which "persons are . . . absorbed in a supra-Person, that of Christ or that of the Spirit."[41] He sees the first tendency, to absorb persons in Christ, in the ecclesiology of the nineteenth-century Catholic theologian Johann Möhler,[42] and it is also evident in Zizioulas's thinking. He sees the latter tendency, to absorb persons in the Spirit, in the reaction of

---

37. Zizioulas, *Lectures in Christian Dogmatics*, 149.

38. So Congar (*I Believe in the Holy Spirit*, 2:11) and Hocken (*Pentecost and Parousia*, 111–12).

39. Zizioulas, *Lectures in Christian Dogmatics*, 150, italics original.

40. Lossky, "Catholic Consciousness," 189.

41. Lossky, "Catholic Consciousness," 191.

42. Möhler, *Unity in the Church*.

the nineteenth-century Russian Slavophile theologian Alexei Khomiakoff.[43] "The mystery of the catholicity of the church is realized in the plurality of personal consciousnesses as an accord of unity and multiplicity, in the image of the Holy Trinity which the church realizes in her life."[44]

It is not an either-or, but a both-and. "Both dispensations—of the Son and of the Spirit—are inseparable; they mutually condition one another since one without the other is unthinkable. One cannot receive the Holy Spirit without being a member of the body of Christ. . . . Personal multiplicity is crowned by the Holy Spirit *only* in the unity of the body of Christ."[45]

So Lossky develops his creative insight into the dual nature of the divine economy of salvation. "The work of Christ concerns human nature, which he recapitulates *in his hypostasis*. The work of the Holy Spirit, on the other hand, concerns persons, being applied to each one singly. . . . The one lends his *hypostasis* to the nature, the other gives his divinity to the persons. Thus, the work of Christ unifies; the work of the Holy Spirit diversifies. . . . The work of Christ and the work of the Holy Spirit are therefore inseparable."[46]

Lossky's thought provides a profound theological integration of the New Testament's testimony to the ministry of the Holy Spirit, which Pentecostal and charismatic theology should embrace. The church has a dual character. It reflects what we might describe as the stereoscopic nature of God's activity. It is a work of the Father's "two hands." It is both the body of Christ and the fellowship of the Holy Spirit.

---

43. Khomiakoff, "The Church is One."
44. Lossky, "Catholic Consciousness," 192.
45. Lossky, "Catholic Consciousness," 190, my italics.
46. Lossky, *Mystical Theology*, 166-67, my italics.

## 12

# The Spirit Will Guide You into All Truth

*The mysterious nature of the Holy Spirit eludes our comprehension and theological formulations. But the worldwide Pentecostal-charismatic movement of recent times has drawn attention to many aspects of the Spirit's person, presence, power, and activity that the church's traditional pneumatology have overlooked. This concluding chapter gathers together these insights in the order that they have appeared in this book. It is time for systematic theology to respond to the challenge of the renewal movement and incorporate what has been learned in charismatic experience into its formulation of the person and activity of the Holy Spirit.*

THE HOLY SPIRIT IS numinous and mysterious, the hidden member of the Godhead. This may have contributed to the lack of development of the doctrine of the Spirit in classical theology. The very nature of the Spirit eludes our understanding and resists our formulation. Both the Hebrew word *rûach* and the Greek word *pneuma*, which we translate as "spirit," mean, among other things, a movement of air, breath, or wind. To write about the Holy Spirit is as difficult as capturing breath or chasing the wind.

The essence of the Spirit is elusive. If the Spirit is divine and holy, the Lord and giver of life, then by definition, this is a reality surpassingly transcendent, yet as intangible and intimate to us as life itself. "The wind blows wherever it pleases," says Jesus. "You hear its sound, but you cannot tell where it comes from or where it is going" (John 3:8). Even as the Spirit influences us, the Spirit is indefinable, mysterious, in its sublime origin and inward moving. This study has revealed biblical evidence of this elusiveness in the use of verbal forms instead of nouns to describe the Spirit's operations, in the transcendent nature of the Spirit's activities, or in the miraculous charisms and varieties of personal experience which the Spirit bestows upon God's people.

On the other hand, this inquiry has also documented surprising emphases, consistencies, progressions, and patterns in the biblical record of the Holy Spirit. These are not the insights of enthusiasts claiming a new revelation. They are present in the revealed text itself. But they have lain dormant, unrecognized until brought to our attention in the remarkable global outpouring of the Holy Spirit that comprises the contemporary Pentecostal-charismatic movement. What was shrouded in darkness and obscurity has emerged into the light of day, full of color, shape, movement, and beauty. This vibrant landscape is a challenge to the academy. Can theology catch up with these discoveries and integrate them into a fuller understanding and description of the Holy Spirit? This chapter summarizes and presents them in the order I have discussed them in this book.

The first challenge to theology posed by the contemporary outpouring of the Holy Spirit is to recognize the eschatological significance of this event. The initial outpouring of the Holy Spirit on the apostolic community assembled at the feast of Pentecost in Jerusalem marked the "firstfruits" of the ingathering of the nations foretold in the prophecy of Joel (Joel 2:28-29, Acts 2:17-18). So, too, the renewal of the Spirit's signs and wonders in our time draws attention to the ripening harvest of evangelism that will mark the end of the age before the coming day of the Lord (Joel 2:31; Acts 2:20). As the "early rains" in the land of Israel germinate the seed, so the "latter rains" swell the grain for harvest (Joel 2:23). The outpouring of the Holy Spirit on "all flesh," indiscriminately of distinctions of sex, age, or social status (Joel 2:28-29), together with the parallel phenomenon of the return of the Jewish people to their land (Joel 3:1), point to the fulfillment of Joel's prophecy in our time. History is moving to its culmination in the *acharit ha-yamim* or "end of days" before the return of the Lord.

Many factors combine to suggest that this contemporary global outpouring of the Spirit, as Peter Hocken has affirmed, is a sovereign grace of God for the renewal of the whole church for its witness and mission as we enter the last days. It is a movement spanning all geographic regions, all ethnic groups, and all sectors of the church. It is a spontaneous movement without the usual influences of human organization, though these have assisted its dissemination. This suggests that a divine grace is at work in the Pentecostal-charismatic movement for the renewal of the church in all aspects of its life, thought, and mission. Even the insights gathered in this book provide evidence of a divine inspiration at work, for they have arisen in the spontaneity of charismatic experience, not just from the scholarly theological study of the Scriptures.

The earliest references in the Bible to the activity of the Spirit point to the role of the Spirit as the perfecter of creation and of human beings. The Spirit "hovers" over the creation, moving the creature teleologically from an imperfect and unfinished condition to a finished and perfected state (Gen 1:2). Even before the role of the Spirit in human creativity is first recorded (Exod 31:1–11), the Spirit is the creative artist who moves history and humanity from their incomplete and provisional form to their ultimate destiny. This is the real theological foundation for the later role of the Spirit in healing and restoration, as well as the Spirit's creative role in praise, singing, music, drama, and renewing the folk arts.

The Scriptures bear witness to a progressive development in the relationship between the Creator and the creature. This progression is denoted by the prepositions "on," "with," and "in." In contrast to all forms of pantheistic religion, the Bible describes the Spirit of God as transcendent, acting "on" or "upon" people, but not actually indwelling them until the dramatic change in relationship that takes place with the birth of Jesus the Messiah, the Word made flesh and the Son of God incarnate. There is no permanent indwelling of a human being by the Holy Spirit until the Spirit comes upon Jesus at the decisive event of his baptism in the Jordan by John the Baptist and "remains" on and in him, the source and secret of his wisdom and mighty works (John 1:32–34). So during Jesus' ministry the Spirit is "with" the disciples, his followers, and companions (John 14:17). Only after Jesus' ascension, when the Spirit is outpoured at Pentecost, does the Spirit come to live "in" them and indwell them as the Father had earlier indwelt Jesus (John 14:17, 20).

A strong case can be made for a charismatic understanding of the humanity of Christ. Far from performing miracles out of his divine nature as the Son of God, the evidence of the Scriptures supports the view that Jesus accomplished his mighty works in dependence on the power of the Holy Spirit (Acts 10:38). Having relinquished omnipotence and the power to work miracles when he became incarnate, Jesus received back these abilities in the limitations of our humanity, by means that are available to believers: through prayer, growing in knowledge of the Scriptures, relying on the Spirit, overcoming temptation, resisting society's expectations, and faithfully persevering in his discernment of God's call. Jesus is thus our exemplar for life and ministry, as well as our Savior from sin.

There is an illuminating analogy between the dual activity of the Spirit in Christ and in Christians. The Spirit's role in Jesus' virginal conception and birth parallels the Spirit's role in the new birth of the believer (John 1:13; 3:5–8). Similarly, the descent of the Spirit at Jesus' baptism which marks his installation as Messiah and inaugurates his public ministry parallels our initiation by the Spirit into a life of fresh effectiveness in service and ministry as his followers. Being born anew and being baptized in Holy Spirit are distinctive modes of the Spirit's presence and operation in our lives as believers, just as they were in Jesus, our prototype and example.

From this distinction between the Spirit's indwelling and empowerment comes a proper understanding of what the New Testament distinguishes as the "fruit" and "gifts" of the Holy Spirit. The fruit of the Spirit is the organic development of Christian character, which results from the influence of the indwelling life of the Spirit in believers. Character, like fruit, is an outgrowth of life and takes time to develop. But the gifts are the gratuitous and dynamic activities of the Spirit in and through believers as they worship, witness to, or serve the Lord. They are exercised on an as-required basis and are given freely without reference to a person's maturity or holiness. This is why immature Christians can exercise the gifts of the Spirit. It is also why Jesus indicates that he will not acknowledge those who have worked miracles if they do not have a relationship with him (Matt 7:21–23).

The distinction between the Spirit's indwelling and empowerment is supported by the use or omission of the definite article in references to (the) Holy Spirit in the text of the Greek New Testament. This feature is suppressed in Bible translations. References with the definite article generally refer to the Spirit as a person. They emphasize the Spirit's character and feelings. References without the definite article, on the other hand—the so-called anarthrous references—treat Spirit as an impersonal influence or power. This significant but overlooked feature of the Greek text supports the distinction between the Spirit's indwelling and empowerment; the former deriving from the Spirit's role in the new birth and the latter from being baptized in Holy Spirit. Recognition of this contrast would help remove misunderstandings between evangelical and Pentecostal Christians.

The text of the New Testament includes several other distinctive features in describing the activity of the Holy Spirit. When referring to the foundational initiatory experience, it does not use the noun form, "baptism of the Holy Spirit," but rather the verbal form, "baptize in (or with) Holy Spirit." This suggests that we are not dealing here with a theological construct but with a dynamic experience, a wind "blowing where it wills." Being baptized in Holy Spirit is an initiatory impartation, an inauguration into an entirely new realm of experience, rather than a static datum of Christian theology.

The New Testament descriptions of this dynamic activity of the Spirit always represent the Spirit as "filling," "falling on," or "coming upon" people, entering a person from without. It is never depicted as the release of something inherent in one's baptism, as Catholic and Anglo-Catholic charismatic writers persist in representing it, still less the realization of some innate spiritual potential as envisaged by New Age spirituality. Being baptized in Holy Spirit is not the outworking of some spiritual potential inherent in our human nature. It is the inworking of the divine grace of a transcendent Creator through the agency of his empowering Spirit.

In the light of these realities, as David Pawson has argued, we need to revise our understanding of the Holy Spirit's role in conversion and how we counsel new converts for salvation. The regenerating role of the Holy Spirit in conversion needs to be supplemented by recognition of the Holy Spirit's reinvigorating role in Christian living and the importance of the new believer being "baptized in" or "filled with" Holy Spirit from the start of their Christian life. The "full package" of Christian initiation involves turning from sin, believing in Jesus Christ, being baptized in water, and being baptized or filled with Holy Spirit. The redeeming work of Christ on the cross is necessary for salvation. The empowering work of the Holy Spirit is normative for effective service. In place of the commonly accepted notion in evangelistic counseling that conversion is "receiving Jesus into your heart," it should be stressed that conversion involves acknowledging Jesus as Lord and inviting the Holy Spirit into one's heart. Ideally, the new convert should be counseled to be baptized in Holy Spirit, in order to live a fully effective Christian life.

I have proposed a new and more insightful classification of spiritual gifts, based on Paul's threefold arrangement in 1 Corinthians 12:4–6: "There are different kinds of gifts (*charismata*), but the same Spirit distributes them. There are different kinds of service (*diakoniai*), but the same Lord. There are different kinds of working (*energēmata*), but in all of them and in everyone it is the same God at work." The *charismata* proper, the *manifestation gifts*, are the dynamic graces of the Holy Spirit revealed in charismatic gatherings or in pastoral ministry. The *ministry gifts* are the different types of complementary leaders the risen and ascended Lord gives to his church for its edification and upbuilding. The *motivational gifts* are the impulses or leadings implanted in us by a loving Father, to accomplish with joy the good works that God prepared beforehand for us to do (Eph 2:10). This classification is not only more biblical and more accurate than other proposed arrangements of the gifts. It is fully trinitarian, demonstrating the distinctive roles the three persons of the Godhead play in the lived experience of believers.

Transcending our historical existence, the Spirit is a foretaste of the age to come. The Spirit is the agent of Jesus' resurrection (Rom 1:4). The Spirit makes present in our experience the reality of the kingdom of God (Rom 14:17) and the powers of the coming age (Heb 6:4-5). The Spirit reveals "what is yet to come" (John 16:13). The Spirit is not the inner working of the historical process, as in the philosophy of Hegel and its child Marxism, but the coming of the *eschaton*, the in-breaking of the kingdom of God, into human history. The apostle Paul, particularly, identifies the Holy Spirit with the coming age when the travail and imperfection of the present order of creation are overcome in the glorious liberty of the children of God (Rom 8:18-23).

Theology must take more account of the reality that the person of the Holy Spirit does not become incarnate in human nature and is not an extension of the incarnation. Instead, as Vladimir Lossky argues, the Spirit conveys the divine nature to a multiplicity of human persons. On the day of Pentecost, the church is therefore constituted as a wonderful divine-human society: as both the body of Christ and the community of the Holy Spirit. The Son is the basis of the church's unity. The Spirit is the source of its rich variety, the diversity of human persons and spiritual gifts. We who are redeemed by Christ are transformed into his likeness by the Holy Spirit, "from one degree of glory to another" (2 Cor 3:17-18, RSV). So we become like our Lord and share in the glory that is to come.

Finally, the Pentecostal-charismatic movement offers a fresh perspective on the *Filioque* dispute that has divided Christendom for a millennium. Everywhere, the outpouring of the Spirit gives rise to the spontaneous testimony that Jesus is Lord. This results in new initiatives in Christian mission and service, which show the reality and implications of Christ's Lordship. The move of the Spirit has a christocentric focus. At the same time, the renewal testifies to the independent agency of the Spirit as a unique divine person who blows wherever he wishes (John 3:8). This suggests that my proposal that the Spirit "proceeds *eternally* from the Father and *is sent in time by* the Son," may be a fitting way to affirm both the origin and mission of the Spirit in the Creed. With the Eastern Orthodox, we affirm that the Father is the unique source and origin of the Spirit (John 15:26). At the same time, with the Western Church, we affirm the distinctive christological orientation of the Spirit, bringing glory to Jesus by taking what is his and making it known to us (John 16:14-15).

Jesus promised that when the Spirit comes, "he will guide you into all the truth" (John 16:13). Some of the foregoing insights have been lost in the history of theology and recovered by the contemporary outpouring of the Holy Spirit. Other insights, particularly the nuances of language and grammar in the descriptions of the Spirit in the Greek New Testament, do not appear to have been recognized or reckoned with at any time in the earlier history of theology. In either case—the recovery of lost insights or the drawing attention to fresh insights—it is the sovereign activity of the Spirit that has brought about this fuller understanding.

The time has come for the church's theology and pneumatology to come to terms with the dynamic insights awakened by the surprising and ever-gracious Spirit in the global Pentecostal-charismatic renewal movement.

# Appendix 1

## *New Testament References to (the) Holy Spirit*

*The references to (the) Holy Spirit in the Greek New Testament divide almost equally between those that use the definite article and those that omit the article. Those that use the article (forty instances) generally refer to the personality or personhood of the Spirit, while those that do not (the anarthrous references, forty-nine instances) tend to treat Spirit as an impersonal influence or power. A notable feature is the number of matching pairs in close proximity in the biblical text. This list omits a few references with no theological significance.*[1]

| Person of the Spirit (with the definite article) | Power of Spirit (without definite article) |
|---|---|
| | "... she [Mary] was found to be pregnant through Holy Spirit." "... what is conceived in her [Mary] is from Holy Spirit." (Matt 1:18, 20) |
| | "... he [John the Baptist] will be filled with Holy Spirit even before he is born." (Luke 1:15) |

1. References are from the NIV (2011), omitting the definite article where it is absent in the Greek. Those with an asterisk are my own rendering, to highlight peculiarities in the Greek text.

| Person of the Spirit (with the definite article) | Power of Spirit (without definite article) |
|---|---|
| | "The angel answered her [Mary], 'Holy Spirit will come upon you, and power of Most High will overshadow you.'" (Luke 1:35) |
| | "Elizabeth was filled with Holy Spirit." (Luke 1:41) |
| | "His father Zechariah was filled with Holy Spirit and prophesied." (Luke 1:67) |
| "It had been revealed to him [Simeon] by the Holy Spirit.... Moved by the Spirit, he went into the temple courts." (Luke 2:26–27) | "... and Holy Spirit was upon him [Simeon]." (Luke 2:25) |
| | "I baptize you with water.... He will baptize you with Holy Spirit and fire." (Matt 3:11; Mark 1:8; Luke 3:16) |
| "... the Holy Spirit descended on him [Jesus] in bodily form like a dove." (Luke 3:22; Matt 3:16; Mark 1:10; cf. John 1:32) | |
| "'The man on whom you see the Spirit come down and remain...'" (John 1:33a) | "'... is the one who will baptize with Holy Spirit.'" (John 1:33b) |
| "... and was led by the Spirit into the wilderness." (Luke 4:1; Matt 4:1; Mark 1:12) | "Jesus, full of Holy Spirit, left the Jordan...." (Luke 4:1) |
| "... 'Flesh gives birth to flesh, but the Spirit gives birth to spirit.... So it is with everyone born of the Spirit.'" (John 3:6, 8) | "... 'no one can enter the kingdom of God unless they are born of water and Spirit.'" (John 3:5) |
| "God gives the Spirit without limit." (John 3:34) | |
| "Jesus returned to Galilee in the power of the Spirit." (Luke 4:14) | |
| "By this he meant the Spirit, whom those who believed in him were later to receive." (John 7:39) | "For there was no Spirit yet, because Jesus was not yet glorified." (John 7:39)* |
| "Jesus, full of joy through the Holy Spirit..." (Luke 10:21) | |
| | "... how much more will your Father in heaven give Holy Spirit to those who ask him!" (Luke 11:13) |

# APPENDIX 1—NEW TESTAMENT REFERENCES TO (THE) HOLY SPIRIT

| Person of the Spirit (with the definite article) | Power of Spirit (without definite article) |
|---|---|
| "Anyone who speaks against the Holy Spirit will not be forgiven." (Matt 12:32; Mark 3:29; cf. Luke 12:10) | "If it is by Spirit of God that I [Jesus] drive out demons, then the kingdom of God has come upon you." (Matt 12:28) |
| "Just say whatever is given you at the time, for it is not you speaking, but the Holy Spirit." (Mark 13:11, cf. Matt 10:20; Luke 12:12) | |
| "The Advocate, the Holy Spirit, whom the Father will send in my name, will teach you all things . . . ." (John 14:26) | |
| "When the Advocate comes . . . —the Spirit of truth who proceeds from the Father—he will testify about me." (John 15:26)* | |
| "When he, the Spirit of truth, comes, he will guide you into all the truth." (John 16:13) | |
| | "[Jesus] breathed on them and said, 'Receive Holy Spirit.'"(John 20:22) |
| "You will receive power when the Holy Spirit comes on you." (Acts 1:8) | "John baptized with water, but in a few days you will be baptized with Holy Spirit." (Acts 1:5) |
| ". . . the Scripture had to be fulfilled in which the Holy Spirit spoke long ago through David . . . ." (Acts 1:16) | |
| ". . . and began to speak in other tongues as the Spirit enabled them." (Acts 2:4b) | "All of them were filled with Holy Spirit . . . " (Acts 2:4a) |
| "Exalted to the right hand of God, he [Jesus] has received from the Father the promised Holy Spirit and has poured out what you now see and hear." (Acts 2:33) | |
| "Repent and be baptized, . . . and you will receive the gift of the Holy Spirit." (Acts 2:38) | |
| "And they were all filled with the Holy Spirit . . . ." (Acts 4:31) | "Then Peter, filled with Holy Spirit, . . . " (Acts 4:8) |
| "'Ananias, how is it . . . that you have lied to the Holy Spirit?'" (Acts 5:3) "'How could you conspire to test the Spirit of the Lord?'" (Acts 5:9) | |

| Person of the Spirit (with the definite article) | Power of Spirit (without definite article) |
|---|---|
| "We are witnesses of these things, and so is the Holy Spirit, whom God has given to those who obey him." (Acts 5:32) | |
| "'You always resist the Holy Spirit!'" (Acts 7:51) | "Stephen, full of Holy Spirit, . . ." (Acts 7:55) |
| "When Simon saw that the Spirit was given at the laying on of the apostles' hands, . . ." (Acts 8:18) | ". . . they prayed for the new believers there that they might receive Holy Spirit, . . . Then Peter and John placed their hands on them, and they received Holy Spirit." (Acts 8:15, 17) |
| "The Spirit told Philip, 'Go to that chariot and stay near it.'" (Acts 8:29) | |
| | "Brother Saul, the Lord—Jesus . . . —has sent me so that you may see again and be filled with Holy Spirit." (Acts 9:17) |
| ". . . encouraged by the Holy Spirit, it [the church in Judea, Galilee, and Samaria] increased in numbers." (Acts 9:31) | |
| "While Peter was still thinking about the vision, the Spirit said to him, . . ." (Acts 10:19) | |
| "While Peter was still speaking these words, the Holy Spirit came on all who heard the message. The circumcised believers . . . were astonished that the gift of the Holy Spirit had been poured out even on the Gentiles." (Acts 10:44–45) | "God anointed Jesus of Nazareth with Holy Spirit and power, . . ." (Acts 10:38) |
| "Surely no one can stand in the way of their being baptized . . . . They have received the Holy Spirit just as we have." (Acts 10:47) | |
| "The Spirit told me to have no hesitation about going with them." (Acts 11:12) | |
| "As I began to speak, the Holy Spirit came on them as he had come on us at the beginning." (Acts 11:15) | "Then I remembered what the Lord had said: 'John baptized with water, but you will be baptized with Holy Spirit.'" (Acts 11:16) |
| "Agabus stood up and through the Spirit predicted that a severe famine would spread over the entire Roman world." (Acts 11:28) | |

# APPENDIX 1—NEW TESTAMENT REFERENCES TO (THE) HOLY SPIRIT

| Person of the Spirit (with the definite article) | Power of Spirit (without definite article) |
|---|---|
| "... the Holy Spirit said, 'Set apart for me Barnabas and Saul.'" (Acts 13:2) | "He [Barnabas] was a good man, full of Holy Spirit and faith, ... " (Acts 11:24) |
| "The two of them, sent on their way by the Holy Spirit, ..." (Acts 13:4) | "Paul, filled with Holy Spirit, ..." (Acts 13:9) |
| "God ... showed that he accepted them by giving the Holy Spirit to them, just as he did to us." (Acts 15:8) | |
| "It seemed good to the Holy Spirit and to us ...." (Acts 15:28) | |
| "... having been kept by the Holy Spirit from preaching the word in the province of Asia. ... they tried to enter Bithynia, but the Spirit of Jesus would not allow them to." (Acts 16:6, 7) | |
| "When Paul placed his hands on them, the Holy Spirit came on them, and they spoke in tongues and prophesied." (Acts 19:6) | "'Did you receive Holy Spirit when you believed?' They answered, 'No, we have not even heard that there is Holy Spirit.'" (Acts 19:2) |
| "And now, compelled by the Spirit, I am going to Jerusalem .... I only know that in every city the Holy Spirit warns me that prison and hardships are facing me." (Acts 20:22–23) | |
| "Keep watch over yourselves and all the flock of which the Holy Spirit has made you overseers." (Acts 20:28) | |
| "Through the Spirit they urged Paul not to go to Jerusalem. ... The Holy Spirit says, 'In this way the Jewish leaders in Jerusalem will bind the owner of this belt ....'" (Acts 21:4, 11) | |
| "The Holy Spirit spoke the truth to your ancestors ...." (Acts 28:25) | |
| | "God's love has been poured out into our hearts through Holy Spirit, who has been given to us." (Rom 5:5) |
| "... through Christ Jesus the law of the Spirit who gives life has set you free from the law of sin and death." (Rom 8:2) | |

| Person of the Spirit (with the definite article) | Power of Spirit (without definite article) |
|---|---|
| "... have their minds set on what the Spirit desires." (Rom 8:5b) "... the mind governed by the Spirit is life and peace." (Rom 8:6) | "Those who live according to flesh have their minds set on what the flesh desires, but those who live in accordance with Spirit ..." (Rom 8:5a) |
| | "You, however, are not in flesh but in Spirit, since Spirit of God dwells in you." (Rom 8:9a)* |
| | "Anyone who does not have Spirit of Christ does not belong to him." (Rom 8:9b)* |
| "And if the Spirit of him who raised Jesus from the dead is living in you, he who raised Christ from the dead will also give life to your mortal bodies because of his Spirit who lives in you." (Rom 8:11) | "... if you live according to flesh, you will die; but if by Spirit you put to death the misdeeds of the body, you will live." (Rom 8:13) |
| "The Spirit himself testifies with our spirit that we are God's children." (Rom 8:16) | "... those who are led by Spirit of God are children of God." (Rom 8:14) "You received Spirit of adoption, by which we cry, *Abba*, Father." (Rom 8:15)* |
| "... we ourselves, who have the firstfruits of the Spirit, groan inwardly as we wait eagerly ... for the redemption of our bodies." (Rom 8:23) | |
| "... the Spirit helps us in our weakness.... the Spirit himself intercedes for us through wordless groans. And he who searches our hearts knows the mind of the Spirit, because the Spirit intercedes for God's people in accordance with the will of God." (Rom 8:26–27) | |
| | "... be aglow with Spirit." (Rom 12:11, RSV) |
| | "The kingdom of God is ... righteousness, peace and joy in Holy Spirit." (Rom 14:17) |
| | "... so that you may overflow with hope by power of Holy Spirit." (Rom 15:13) |
| "I urge you, ... by our Lord Jesus Christ and by the love of the Spirit." (Rom 15:30) | "... by power of signs and wonders, by power of Spirit." (Rom 15:19)* |

# APPENDIX 1—NEW TESTAMENT REFERENCES TO (THE) HOLY SPIRIT

| Person of the Spirit (with the definite article) | Power of Spirit (without definite article) |
|---|---|
| "... no one knows the thoughts of God except the Spirit of God." (1 Cor 2:11) | "This is what we speak, not in words taught by human wisdom but in words taught by Spirit." (1 Cor 2:13) |
| "Do you not know that your bodies are temples of the Holy Spirit, who is in you ...?" (1 Cor 6:19) | "... no-one who is speaking by Spirit of God says 'Jesus be cursed,' and no-one can say 'Jesus is Lord,' except by Holy Spirit." (1 Cor 12:3) |
| "[God] set his seal of ownership on us, and put his Spirit in our hearts as a deposit [*arrabōn*], guaranteeing what is to come." (2 Cor 1:22) | |
| "... the letter kills, but the Spirit gives life." (2 Cor 3:6) | |
| "Now the Lord is the Spirit, and where the Spirit of the Lord is, there is freedom. (2 Cor 3:17) | "And we all ... are being transformed into his image with ever-increasing glory, which comes from Lord, who is Spirit." (2 Cor 3:18) |
| "God ... has given us the Spirit as a deposit [*arrabōn*], guaranteeing what is to come." (2 Cor 5:5) | |
| "May the ... fellowship of the Holy Spirit be with you all." (2 Cor 13:14) | "... in Holy Spirit and in sincere love." (2 Cor 6:6) |
| "Did you receive the Spirit by the works of the law ...? Does God give you his Spirit and work miracles among you by the works of the law ...?" (Gal 3:2, 5) | "After beginning by means of Spirit, are you now trying to finish by means of the flesh?" (Gal 3:3) |
| "He [Christ] redeemed us ... so that by faith we might receive the promise of the Spirit." (Gal 3:14) | |
| "Because you are his sons, God sent the Spirit of his Son into our hearts, the Spirit who calls out, '*Abba*, Father.'" (Gal 4:6) | "For through Spirit we eagerly await by faith the righteousness for which we hope." (Gal 5:5) |
| "For the flesh desires what is contrary to the Spirit, and the Spirit what is contrary to the flesh." (Gal 5:17) | "Walk by Spirit, and you will not gratify the desires of the flesh." (Gal 5:16) |
| "The fruit of the Spirit is love, joy, peace ...." (Gal 5:22) | "Since we live by Spirit, let us keep in step with Spirit." (Gal 5:25) |
| "When you believed, you were marked in him with a seal, the promised Holy Spirit, who is a deposit [*arrabōn*] guaranteeing our inheritance ...." (Eph 1:13–14) | |

| Person of the Spirit (with the definite article) | Power of Spirit (without definite article) |
|---|---|
| "Make every effort to keep the unity of the Spirit through the bond of peace." (Eph 4:3) | "And in him you too are being built together to become a dwelling in which God lives by Spirit." (Eph 2:22) |
| | "[The mystery of Christ] has now been revealed by Spirit to God's holy apostles and prophets." (Eph 3:5) |
| "Do not grieve the Holy Spirit of God." (Eph 4:30) | "Do not get drunk on wine . . . . Instead, be filled with Spirit." (Eph 5:18) |
| "Take . . . the sword of the Spirit, which is the word of God." (Eph 6:17) | "And pray in Spirit on all occasions with all kinds of prayers and requests." (Eph 6:18) |
| | ". . . our gospel came to you not simply with words but also with power, with Holy Spirit and deep conviction . . . . You welcomed the message . . . with the joy given by Holy Spirit." (1 Thess 1:5–6) |
| "The Spirit clearly says that in later times some will abandon the faith . . . ." (1 Tim 4:1) | "Guard the good deposit that was entrusted to you—guard it with the help of Holy Spirit who lives in us." (2 Tim 1:14) |
| | "He saved us through the washing of rebirth and renewal by Holy Spirit." (Titus 3:5) |
| | "God also testified to it [salvation] by signs, wonders and various miracles, and by gifts of Holy Spirit distributed according to his will." (Heb 2:4) |
| "So, as the Holy Spirit says: 'Today, if you hear his voice, do not harden your hearts . . . .'" (Heb 3:7-8) | "It is impossible for those . . . who have shared in Holy Spirit . . . , and who have fallen away, to be brought back to repentance . . . ." (Heb 6:4–6) |
| ". . . the prophets, . . . trying to find out the time and circumstances to which the Spirit of Christ in them was pointing . . . ." (1 Pet 1:10–11) | ". . . those who have preached the gospel to you by Holy Spirit sent from heaven." (1 Pet 1:12) |
| | ". . . prophets, though human, spoke from God as they were carried along by Holy Spirit." (2 Pet 1:21) |

| Person of the Spirit (with the definite article) | Power of Spirit (without definite article) |
|---|---|
| "This is how you can recognize the Spirit of God.... This is how we recognize the Spirit of truth.... And it is the Spirit who testifies, because the Spirit is the truth." (1 John 4:2, 6; 5:6) | |
| | "... by building yourselves up in your most holy faith and praying in Holy Spirit." (Jude 20) |
| | "On the Lord's Day I was in Spirit" (Rev 1:10) |

# Appendix 2

## Charismatic Renewal in New Zealand

*In my country, New Zealand, charismatic renewal may have begun earlier and had a greater penetration of the historic churches than anywhere else in the world. It also had a remarkable global reach. To acknowledge this will mean that historians need to make adjustments to their established narrative of the global charismatic renewal movement. It is as if the Gospel had first to reach "the ends of the earth," before it could echo back to Jerusalem (Acts 1:8). I am currently writing a history of the charismatic renewal movement in New Zealand, provisionally titled "Where Morning Dawns." This is a summary of my research and preliminary findings.*

IN NEW ZEALAND, THE earliest leaders in the mainstream churches to be baptized in the Holy Spirit were Frank Garratt, a Brethren elder, on the fourteenth day of an extended fast in 1951,[1] and Noel Billinghurst, a trainee for the Methodist ministry, in 1952.[2] Baptist lay pastor Trevor Chandler was baptized in the Spirit in 1956 and Murray Robertson, then a Presbyterian Bible Class leader but destined to become an influential Baptist pastor, in 1960. Douglas Watt, minister of Greyfriars Presbyterian Church, Mt. Eden, Auckland, was baptized in the Spirit in 1963 at the hands of David du Plessis

1. Ian Garratt, "Shut Out, Yet Empowered," 90.
2. Billinghurst, "Testimony," 4.

while visiting the Netherlands and began a healing ministry. Early in 1966, Owen Woodfield, minister of St. John's Methodist Church, Bryndwr, received the gift of tongues while hosting du Plessis in Christchurch.

Describing the New Zealand Christian scene in 1978, *Operation World* said that the impact of charismatic renewal "has been greater than any other English speaking nation."[3] The first Catholic Life in the Spirit Seminar, at Liston House, Auckland in February 1973, attended by several hundred excited people, may have been the largest held anywhere in the world. By 1974, following the introduction of Life in the Spirit Seminars, between 40 and 50 percent of the clergy in the Auckland Anglican diocese were said to be sympathetic to charismatic renewal.[4] By 1989, after the first John Wimber conferences, some 70 percent of Baptist churches identified with the charismatic movement.[5] A decade later, at the height of the impact of Presbyerian Renewal Ministries, it was stated that the renewal had impacted half of New Zealand's Presbyterian congregations.[6]

Charismatic renewal produced the largest churches of their affiliation in New Zealand: the largest Anglican (St. Christopher's, Christchurch), Baptist (Spreydon, Christchurch), Methodist (Opawa, Christchurch), and Presbyterian churches (Hornby, now Hope, Christchurch), and the largest rural church (Oxford Baptist).[7]

Sensing an incipient move of God during his visit to New Zealand, English Bible teacher Arthur Wallis convened a groundbreaking conference at Massey University, Palmerston North in August 1964. The speakers were all laymen who had been baptized in the Holy Spirit. Campbell McAlpine, Milton Smith, and Wallis himself were Brethren; Tom Marshall was Baptist. Trevor Chandler, Joy Dawson, Clive Lovatt, Rob Wheeler, Neville Winger, and Frank Houston shared in the testimony meetings. In his opening address, Wallis stressed that the conference was not convened "to cause any individual to leave his denomination, church, assembly or fellowship." Rather, he believed that God desired to reveal "a manifestation of [his] power and glory . . . through his church to a waiting world."[8]

In the event, the Brethren movement in New Zealand rejected the contemporary move of the Holy Spirit, leading many charismatic Brethren

---

3. Johnstone, *Operation World*, 318.
4. Auckland diocesan report, cited in Ward, *Losing Our Religion?* 72.
5. Bolitho, *Meet the Baptists*, 37.
6. Hocken, "Charismatic Movement," *NIDPCM* 514.
7. Murray Robertson's influence may be seen in the fact that the pastors of every one of these churches attended his fortnightly Thursday afternoon support group during his ministry at Spreydon Baptist.
8. Wallis et al., *I Will Build My Church*, 2; Steel, *Milton Smith*, 137–39.

to form independent Christian fellowships or join Baptist churches.⁹ The ensuing movement of the Spirit occurred in less likely contexts.

While Ray Muller was Anglican chaplain at Massey University, Palmerston North (1965–67), a student revival took place, and some 5 percent of the entire student body were baptized in the Holy Spirit.[10] After being baptized in the Spirit during the visit of Dennis Bennett, High Church vicar Kenneth Prebble made St. Paul's Anglican into a leading center of renewal in Auckland (1966–74).[11] Forbidden by Bishop Gowing from having charismatic meetings in people's homes, Herbert Boniface introduced renewal into his evening service, turning St. Margaret's, Hillsborough into another leading Anglican charismatic church in Auckland. John Balchin's statesmanlike twenty-eight-year ministry (1966–94) oversaw the development of three satellite congregations and led First Presbyterian Church, Papakura to become the second-largest Presbyterian church in New Zealand.[12] During Graeme Coad's ten-year ministry, Mount Maunganui Baptist (1971–81) became something of a Jesus People church, with many conversions among surfers and skydivers.[13]

Some churches grew to be outstanding examples of renewal. As a result of Murray Robertson's forty-year ministry (1968–2009), Spreydon Baptist Church, Christchurch became a model of holistic renewal, evangelism, and community ministries for many churches throughout New Zealand and Australia.[14] In contrast to the Brethren rejection of the gifts of the Holy Spirit, Brian Hathaway, a gifted secondary school teacher and teachers' college lecturer, led Te Atatu Bible Chapel, a Brethren assembly in West Auckland, in a renewal notable for its integration of evangelical, charismatic, and social justice concerns (1982–2004).[15] My baptism in the Holy Spirit in 1981, amid the trauma of two church schisms, introduced renewal at Hornby (now Hope) Presbyterian Church, Christchurch. Under my successors Murray Talbot (1988–2013) and Hamish Galloway (2011–2020), it has grown to be the leading multi-site Presbyterian community church in New Zealand.[16]

---

9. Lineham, "Tongues Must Cease," 1–48.
10. Bennett, *Nine O'Clock in the Morning*, 196.
11. Merritt, *To God be the Glory*, 25.
12. Millward, *John Balchin*, 60, 89–92, 108.
13. Coad and Knudsen, *Fire at the Mount*.
14. Ward, *Against the Odds*.
15. Hathaway, *Beyond Renewal*; Hocken, "Charismatic Renewal," *NIDPCM* 514.
16. Reid, *Thus Far*.

Renewal organizations brought international speakers to New Zealand and were effective in disseminating charismatic renewal among the churches. After eighteen months in England working with Michael Harper and the Fountain Trust, Ray Muller returned to New Zealand and founded Christian Advance Ministries (CAM). Under his leadership (1972–75), followed by Cecil Marshall (1975–80) and David Harper (1981–85), CAM ran summer schools which impacted all the churches, especially Anglican, Catholic, and Presbyterian. In 1980 Fr. Cecil Dennehy convened a meeting of Catholic diocesan renewal leaders to form the National Service Committee for Catholic charismatic renewal. For ten years (1982–92), Ray Taylor, deputy director (later director) of the Employers Federation, was chairman of the Paraclete Trust (later Presbyterian Renewal Ministries), which hosted five visits by Delores Winder and saw the emergence of a chain of Presbyterian regional renewal churches throughout the country. Anglican Renewal Ministries, founded in 1982 by Don Battley and Ray Muller, played a similar role in the Anglican Church. Its successor, New Wine, has organized well-attended Summer Festivals but has been less effective in local church renewal.[17]

Inspired by the 1989 Lausanne Congress on World Evangelization in Manila, Baptist church growth leader Bruce Patrick instigated and oversaw the historic Vision New Zealand Congresses of 1993, 1997, 1999, 2002, 2005, 2008, and 2011. For these, he edited the notable series of books of background papers and research, *New Vision New Zealand* (vols. 1–4). He did this while leading Auckland's Baptist Tabernacle from a demoralized remnant of eighty to a thriving fellowship of over seven hundred people in five congregations (1993–2009).

Many New Zealanders were at the forefront of creative songwriting in the early days of charismatic renewal. David and Dale Garratt's pioneering three-volume compilation, *Scripture in Song* (1976, 1981, and 1988), was globally disseminated. Notable musicians were Stephen Bell-Booth, Brent Chambers, Wayne Drain, Kirsten Fordyce, Richard Gillard, Mike and Viv Hibbert, Jeff Rea, Jules Riding, John Smith, Vicki Trustrum, and Natalie Yule-Yeoman. Bruce McGrail, Rob Packer, and David Lyle Morris have been influential worship leaders. Riding is the only one to have made a career out of Christian music, recently touring Europe on several occasions.

A feature of the New Zealand charismatic renewal movement has been its global influence. Barry Kissell left New Zealand in 1959 and trained for the Anglican ministry in England. While on the staff of St. Andrew's, Chorleywood, he founded and directed its faith sharing ministry. He took teams

---

17. Battley, *No Way Back*.

to hundreds of churches in twenty-five countries, evangelizing and teaching on the renewing power of the Holy Spirit. Trevor Chandler left New Zealand in 1973 and founded an independent Pentecostal fellowship in Brisbane that grew into the network of Christian Life Churches in Australia. Frank Houston moved from Lower Hutt to Sydney in 1977 and founded the Christian Life Centre. In 1983 it established a daughter church, Hills Christian Life Centre. Under the leadership of his son, Brian Houston, this grew into Hillsong Church. Hillsong has had a global impact, developing an influential contemporary worship music ministry and planting churches in London, New York, Ottawa, Seattle, Buenos Aires, Moscow, Kiev, Tel Aviv, Budapest, Stockholm, and Copenhagen.[18]

After living in a Manila slum, Viv Grigg founded Servants to Asia's Urban Poor in 1983 to plant churches among the poor of Asia's megacities. A prophetic voice, he has coordinated the global AD2000 Movement cities network, written *Companion to the Poor* (1984), *Cry of the Urban Poor* (1992), and *The Spirit of Christ and the Postmodern City* (2009), and featured in the film *Poor Wise Man* (2018). An authority on transformational revivals, he is now Professor of Urban Leadership at William Carey International University in Pasadena, California.

Many New Zealand charismatic churches are involved in global mission. Spreydon Baptist sent mission teams to Papua New Guinea, the Philippines, Hong Kong, India, and Zambia. Seventy-two people went from Spreydon Baptist as missionaries overseas—a staggering output for a single church.[19] In 1993–94 in St. Alban's, Palmerston North, a much smaller church, a missions support group led by missions intern Joseph Bateson (a convert from a Latin-rite Catholic family) grew to twenty-five young adults, seventeen of whom went on to serve overseas, alongside my three mission trips to Eastern Europe after the fall of Communism.[20]

Several New Zealanders have maintained international healing ministries, particularly Bill Subritzky, Cecilie Graham, and Fr. John Rea, SM. Ray Comfort and Winkie Pratney became influential youth evangelists in the United States. Many New Zealanders served overseas with Youth with a Mission (YWAM), notably Jeff Fountain in the Netherlands, who became director of YWAM Europe in 1990, and John Dawson in the United States, who became international president of YWAM in 2003. Peter Dean and Keith Warrington have given long service to YWAM in Germany, as have Stevie and Tracey Wilson in France, and Barry and Kay Austin in the United

---

18. Riches and Wagner, *The Hillsong Movement*; Bryan, "Hillsong's Global Appeal."
19. Ward, *Against the Odds*, 76.
20. Yule, *Serendipity*, 35.

Kingdom. Other New Zealanders with long records of service in YWAM include Larry and Barbara Baldock, Judy Hayden, Alan and Joanne McLean, Jenny Moores, and Don Stephens.

Jeff Fountain is now director of the Schuman Centre for European Studies, seeking to return the European Community to its Christian basis. In 1990, John Dawson founded the International Reconciliation Coalition (IRC). In 1995, on the nine hundredth anniversary of the First Crusade, he led a pilgrimage which retraced the steps of the Crusaders and apologized to communities along the route for wrongs done in the name of Jesus. Other initiatives have included prayer journeys to the slave ports of West Africa, to places where Native Americans were massacred, and to sites where aborigines were mistreated in Australia. Dawson, together with Evan Thomas, a New Zealand Messianic pastor at Beit Asaph, Netanya, Israel, worked with Towards Jerusalem II to help return the global church to its Jewish roots.

Prayer for Israel NZ (1986–2019), founded by Murray Dixon, was one of the earliest Christian groups in the world to support the Messianic community in Israel. In 2019 it merged with Celebrate Messiah, the recently established New Zealand branch of Chosen Ministries. Its leader, Scott Brown, laughed at by his friends when he left the United States to do Jewish evangelism in New Zealand, has been astonished to find that more Jews are becoming believers in *Yeshua* through New Zealand's network of Christian hospitality to Israeli backpackers than anywhere else on earth. He says, "It is unlike anything I have experienced in thirty years of Jewish evangelism."[21]

For a small country, this influence is quite remarkable. Like the South Island's braided rivers, streams of renewal have influenced all branches of the New Zealand church. New Zealanders are a nation of pioneers, adaptable, resilient, ready to improvise and make do. We are not perceived as a threat to others, politically or culturally. The charismatic renewal tapped into a generation ready and willing to serve their Lord with resourcefulness and innovation. It illustrates that people open to the Holy Spirit accomplish far more than human organization alone could achieve.

---

21. Speaking at "Simcha 2018," Celebrate Messiah conference, Palmerston North, 24 November 2018.

# Appendix 3

## *Five Prayers to the Holy Spirit*

### 1. Hymn to the Hidden Mystery

Come, true light.
Come, eternal life.
Come, hidden mystery.
Come, nameless treasure.
Come, ineffable reality.
Come, incomprehensible face.
Come, everlasting exultation.

Come, unfading light.
Come, trusty expectation of all
who are going to be saved.
Come, awakening of those who sleep.
Come, resurrection of the dead.
Come, mighty one who always creates,
who recreates and who transforms
all things by his will alone.

Come, invisible and untouchable,
and in every way intangible.
Come, you who always remain immutable,
and who at every hour are wholly altered,
and are coming to us who lie in hell,

## APPENDIX 3 — FIVE PRAYERS TO THE HOLY SPIRIT

you who are above all the heavens.
Come, most beloved name
repeated again and again,
a name entirely forbidden for us to speak
or to know the very person you are,
the kind or quality.

Come, eternal joy.
Come, imperishable crown.
Come, purple of our great God and King.
Come, crystalline cincture set with gems.
Come, unapproachable sandal.
Come, royal, purple robe
and truly autocratic right hand!

Come, you whom my miserable soul
has desired and desires.
Come, the alone to the alone,
because I am alone, as you see!
Come, you who separated me from everyone
and made me alone on the earth.

Come, you who have become desire itself in me
and who made me desire you,
the utterly unapproachable one.
Come, my breath and my life.
Come, consolation of my dejected soul.
Come, my joy and glory,
and endless luxury.

Introductory prayer to the *Hymns of Divine Love*,
Symeon the New Theologian (949–1072)[1]

---

1. Symeon, *Divine Eros*, 33, to which I have added the title and stanza divisions. Reproduced by permission of St. Vladimir's Seminary Press, Crestwood, NY.

## 2. Veni, sancte Spiritus

Come, thou holy Paraclete,
And from thy celestial seat
Send thy light and brilliancy:
Father of the poor, draw near;
Giver of all gifts, be here;
Come, the soul's true radiancy.

Come, of comforters the best,
Of the soul the sweetest guest,
Come in toil refreshingly:
Thou in labour rest most sweet,
Thou art shadow from the heat,
Comfort in adversity.

O Thou light, most pure and blest,
Shine within the inmost breast
Of thy faithful company.
Where thou art not, man hath nought;
Every holy deed and thought
Comes from thy divinity.

What is soilèd, make thou pure;
What is wounded, work its cure;
What is parchèd, fructify;
What is rigid, gently bend;
What is frozen, warmly tend;
Straighten what goes erringly.

Fill thy faithful, who confide
In thy power to guard and guide,
With thy sevenfold mystery.
Here thy grace and virtue send:
Grant salvation in the end,
And in heaven felicity.

Pentecost sequence from the Roman Missal
Thirteenth century
Translated from the Latin by John Mason Neale (1818–66)[2]

## 3. Prayer of the Council Fathers

We are here before you, O Holy Spirit, conscious of our innumerable sins, but united in a special way in your holy name. Come and abide with us. Deign to penetrate our hearts.

Be the guide of our actions, indicate the path we should take, and show us what we must do so that, with your help, our work may in all things be pleasing to you.

May you be our only inspiration and the overseer of our intentions, for you alone possess a glorious name together with the Father and the Son.

May you, who are infinite justice, never permit that we be disturbers of justice. Let not our ignorance induce us to evil, nor flattery sway us, nor moral and material interest corrupt us. But unite our hearts to you alone, and do it strongly, so that, with the gift of your grace, we may be one in you and may in nothing depart from the truth.

Thus, united in your name, may we in our every action follow the dictates of your mercy and justice, so that today and always our judgments may not be alien to you and in eternity we may obtain the unending reward of our actions.

Amen.

This prayer, believed to have been composed by Isidore of Seville (c560–636), was used before every meeting of the preparatory commissions and council sessions of the Second Vatican Council (1962–65).[3]

## 4. Song to the Holy Spirit

Lord, Holy Spirit,
You blow like the wind in a thousand paddocks,
Inside and outside the fences,
You blow where you wish to blow.

---

2. *English Hymnal*, No. 155. Public domain.

3. Abbott, *Documents of Vatican II*, xxii. Reproduced by permission of Crossroad Publishing.

## APPENDIX 3 — FIVE PRAYERS TO THE HOLY SPIRIT

Lord, Holy Spirit,
You are the sun who shines on the little plant,
You warm him gently, you give him life,
You raise him up to become a tree with many leaves.

Lord, Holy Spirit,
You are the mother eagle with her young,
Holding them in peace under your feathers.
On the highest mountain you have built your nest,
Above the valley, above the storms of the world,
Where no hunter ever comes.

Lord, Holy Spirit,
You are the bright cloud in whom we hide,
In whom we know already that the battle has been won.
You bring us to our Brother Jesus
To rest our heads upon his shoulder.

Lord, Holy Spirit,
You are the kind fire who does not cease to burn,
Consuming us with flames of love and peace,
Driving us out like sparks to set the world on fire.

Lord, Holy Spirit,
In the love of friends you are building a new house,
Heaven is with us when you are with us.
You are singing your song in the hearts of the poor.
Guide us, wound us, heal us. Bring us to the Father.

James K. Baxter, "Song to the Holy Spirit" (1972)[4]

---

4. Baxter, *Thoughts about the Holy Spirit*, 23; *Collected Poems*, 572. Reproduced by permission of the James K. Baxter Trust.

## 5. Prayer for the World

### 1. King of the Universe

Almighty God—Father, Son, and Holy Spirit—as a united worldwide body of believers, we are gathered today to honor and glorify your name. We bow before your throne of grace and acknowledge that you are the Creator of heaven and earth. You existed through all eternity and in you all things hold together. There is no one like you, holy and righteous in all your ways. We submit to your authority and sovereignty as the King of the universe and pray with one voice to enthrone you in our hearts and to honor you before the world.

> *Lord God, you alone are worthy of our praise and adoration. We worship you.*

### 2. Our Father in Heaven

Our Father in Heaven, thank you for loving the world so greatly that you gave your only Son, Jesus Christ, to die on the cross for our sins, so that we could be reconciled to you. Thank you for giving us the right to call you Father, because of our faith in Jesus Christ as our Savior. Nothing, not even principalities and powers, is able to separate us from your love which you demonstrated in your Son, Jesus Christ.

> *Thank you Father for adopting us into your family. We now cry, Abba Father!*

### 3. Lord of All the Earth

Lord Jesus Christ, you alone are worthy to open the scroll of history, for you were slain and have redeemed us to the Father by your blood. Thank you for interceding for us as our High Priest. As we stand before you from many tribes and nations, we confess that you are head of the church and Lord of every created thing in heaven and on earth. Come, and draw followers to serve you from every tribe and language. May these become your inheritance in all the earth. Let your kingdom be established in every nation of the world, so that governments will rule with righteousness and justice. May your gospel be made known to every person on earth. May your blessing bring transformation amidst every people. And may your name be great, from the rising of the sun to its setting.

> *Jesus Christ, you are the Savior of the world and the Lord of all.*

## 4. Have Mercy on Us

Father of mercy and grace, we acknowledge that we have sinned and that our world is gripped by the power of sin. Our hearts are grieved by injustice, hatred, anger and violence. We are shamed by the oppression, racism and bloodshed in our land. We weep because of the loss of innocent life in war and terrorism, abortion, persecution and senseless murders. Our hearts are broken by every rejection of Christ as Lord and Savior. As we stand before you, we know that your gaze beholds all things. Our homes are broken by selfishness and immorality. Our lives are polluted by greed, idolatry and sexual sin. Our churches are divided by rebellious pride. All the sins that we may find in our world, you have found among your people. We have grieved your heart and brought shame to your name. We approach your throne of grace in this hour of need. We ask for your mercy and your help to truly repent.

*God of mercy, pour out your grace. Forgive our sins. Heal our land.*

## 5. Pour out Your Spirit

Spirit of the living God, we confess that we can do nothing apart from you. Living God, pour out your Spirit upon all flesh. Empower the church to be transformed into the image of Jesus Christ. Release your power to bring healing to the sick, freedom to the possessed, comfort to those who mourn and release for those who are oppressed. Come and melt the hearts of people to love again. Answer the call of the homeless, the hungry, the helpless, and the dying. Enfold orphans, widows, and the elderly in your arms. Display your mercy and provide for our needs. Give us wisdom and insight in every sphere of life so that we will find solutions to the complex problems of the world. Help us to use the resources of the earth for the well-being of all. Pour your love into our hearts, fill us with compassion, and let the power of the Holy Spirit characterise our lives.

*Holy Spirit, we need your comfort and guidance. Come and transform our hearts.*

## 6. Deliver us From Evil

Lord Jesus Christ, because you were dead, but are now risen, and because the Father has given you a name above all names, you will defeat all powers of evil. You have declared that the gates of hell will not prevail against your church. We pray for deliverance from demonic oppression. We pray for the tearing down of the strongholds and ideologies that hinder and resist the spreading of the knowledge of God. We resist the plan of the enemy to keep nations in darkness and pray that you will remove the veil that covers the peoples. We ask for open doors so that the gospel can enter every nation. Restrain the evil that promotes violence and death. Break the hold of slavery, tyranny, and disease. Fill us with courage to fearlessly and faithfully preach your word. Give us a spirit of intercession to cry out on behalf of the lost.

*Almighty God, deliver us from evil and the Evil One.*

## 7. Come Lord Jesus

King of Glory, come to the nations of the world. You have promised long ago that you would come to restore all things. We welcome you to finish your work in our cities, our peoples, and our nations. We now lift our voices in unison with believers from across the face of the earth—from Africa, from the Middle East, from North and South America, from Asia, from Europe, from Australia, New Zealand, and the Pacific Islands—together we cry:

> *Lift up your heads, O you gates! Be lifted up ancient doors so that the King of glory may come in!*

As your deeds increase throughout the earth, and as your blessings abound to all the nations, they will seek you, asking, "Who is this King of glory?" Together we will answer:

> *He is the Lord Almighty! Blessed is He who comes in the name of the Lord!*

Come fill the earth with your glory as the waters cover the sea. The Spirit and the Bride say:

> *Amen! Come Lord Jesus!*

Prayer prepared for the Global Day of Prayer on Pentecost Sunday, 4 June 2006. The previous year, on Pentecost Sunday, 15 May 2005, Christians from 156 of the 220 nations of the world united across denominational and cultural boundaries for the first Global Day of Prayer.[5]

---

5. From *Intercessors for New Zealand* newsletter, edited by Brian Caughley (June 2006), 6–8, to which I have added subheadings. Reproduced by permission of Global Day of Prayer, Johannesburg, South Africa.

# Glossary

***ad extra***
Latin for "external, outward," referring to the actions of God outside his own being, in relation to the universe and in salvation history. See also **economic Trinity**.

***ad intra***
Latin for "internal, inward," referring to the inner life and relations of the Godhead. See also **immanent Trinity**.

**Adoptionism**
The view that Jesus was a virtuous man chosen by God, whose piety was approved by God when the Holy Spirit descended on him at his baptism, giving him power for his ministry, and who was declared to be Son of God by his resurrection. It was condemned as a heresy by the Synod of Antioch (268), though its advocates claimed it was the view handed down by the apostles.

**anarthrous**
Text in which the noun is used without the article.

**anthropic principle**
The cosmological principle that theories of the universe must take account of the extraordinarily narrow constraints within which life in general and human life in particular can exist.

**apophatic**
The view, held particularly by the Eastern Orthodox Church, that the inner depths of God or of a person are mysterious and cannot be exhaustively known or described in terms of human categories (from the Greek *apophasis*, "negation of being").

## apostle
Apostles, not limited to the Twelve, have a distinct calling by Christ, are missionary pioneers and church founders, distinguished by signs, wonders, and miracles, and recognized as authoritative by the churches they have established.

## *arrabōn*
A term used by Paul (2 Cor 1:22; 5:5; Eph 1:14) to describe the role of the Holy Spirit awakening in us the hope of our ultimate salvation. A legal and commercial term meaning "deposit," "down payment," "first installment," or "pledge," it refers to the first part of the purchase price paid in advance, which secures legal entitlement to the item purchased. See also **firstfruits**.

## baptism in the Holy Spirit
The common term for the initial experience of being impacted by the Holy Spirit, as opposed to subsequent infillings of the Spirit. The New Testament uses the verb "baptize in (or with) Holy Spirit" rather than the noun, and omits the definite article, indicating that this is a dynamic experience of empowerment, not a doctrinal concept.

## begetting
The bringing into existence of a being with the same nature as oneself, also known as "**generation**," in contrast to "making" or "creating," which is the bringing into existence of a being with a different nature than oneself.

## cataphatic
The view, held particularly by Reformed theology in distinction from **apophatic**, that God or a person can be truly known and described by their self-disclosure, by their revelation of themselves (from *kataphasis*, "affirmation of being").

## cessationism
The view that miracles and the charismatic gifts of the Holy Spirit ceased in the Christian church after the age of the apostles and the formation of the biblical canon.

## charismatic
Pertaining to the experience or gifts (*charismata*) of the Holy Spirit; an adherent of the charismatic movement.

**charismatic renewal movement**
Originally called neo-Pentecostalism, the movement of Christians in the historic churches who embrace the use of the *charismata*, the gifts of the Holy Spirit, as distinct from the adherents of the classical Pentecostal denominations.

**charisms or *charismata***
Direct actions of the Holy Spirit through people for their edification or the benefit of others, distinct from human talents and natural abilities. The word "charisms" comes from *charismata* (singular *charisma*), Greek for "gifts," "favors," or "gracelets" (from *charis*, "grace," "favor"); spiritual actions of power and ability performed by believers through the direct enabling of the Holy Spirit (Rom 12:6; 1 Cor 12:4, 9, 28, 30, 31).

**creation**
The act of bringing into existence something entirely new, that did not previously exist.

**dispensationalism**
The speculative eschatological system devised by John Nelson Darby in the 1830s which divides history into dispensations and separates the destiny of Jews and Christians. Popularized by the Scofield Reference Bible (1909), it reached the height of its influence in the 1970s with the publication of Hal Lindsey's book *The Late, Great Planet Earth* (1970), the best-selling prophecy book of all time.

**distinguishing between spirits (*diakriseis pneumaton*)**
The spiritual ability to distinguish between divine, human, and demonic powers (1 Cor 12:10).

**economic Trinity**
The three persons of the Godhead as they are involved in the divine **economy**, God's action in creation, revelation, and redemption.

**economy**
God's plan of salvation (Greek, *oikonomia*), hidden from eternity in God (Eph 3:9), but now, in the fullness of time, realized and revealed in Christ (Eph 1:10).

## *empneumatosis*

A term, meaning "inspiriting," suggested by John McIntyre[6] to denote the Holy Spirit's activity in the world and in human persons, on analogy with the term "**incarnation**" as used of the entry of God the Son into the world and humanity.

## *enhypostatos*

A patristic Greek word meaning "being or existing in a person." It signifies that human nature is not united with God *independently of the person (anhypostatos)* of the *Logos*, the incarnate Son of God, but only *in the person (enhypostatos)* of the *Logos*.

## eschatological

Having to do with the "last things," God's purpose for our future destiny.

## *eschaton*

The final event of the divine plan, the consummation of all things.

## essentialism

The philosophical view that things have a given set of attributes and characteristics that make them what they are, closely associated with the view that things have a real existence independently of our perceptions or constructs of them.

## evangelical

Christians who emphasize personal conversion, growth in holiness, the importance of evangelism, and the authority of the Bible (from *euanggelion*, "gospel" or "good news").

## faith (*pistis*), gift of

The spiritual gift of confidence that God will intervene powerfully in a particular situation (1 Cor 12:9), as distinct from the "saving faith" by which one becomes and lives as a Christian.

## *Filioque*

Latin for "and the Son," the clause which was added to the Nicene Creed by the Western or Catholic Church without the consent of the Eastern Church, that the Spirit "proceeds from the Father *and the Son*."

---

6. McIntyre, *Shape of Pneumatology*, 208.

### firstfruits
An agricultural term used by Paul to describe how the Spirit awakens in us the hope of our coming redemption (Rom 8:23). Just as firstfruits anticipate the full and completed harvest, so the Holy Spirit dwelling in us is both the present enjoyment of salvation and the pledge of its ultimate consummation. See also ***arrabōn***.

### folk arts
Sometimes restricted to the visual arts of traditional cultures, the term is used here of other participatory expressions of popular creativity such as drama, dance, music, songwriting, and worship leading, in contrast to performance based music and art.

### generation (see **begetting**)

### glorification
The biblical term for our future destiny and felicity (Rom 8:30), used by the Western Church where the Eastern Orthodox use the term ***theōsis***. It refers to our ultimate transformation, when we are raised imperishable, put on immortality, are clothed in splendor, and participate in God's resplendent glory (1 Cor 15:42–43, 52–53). As Jesus, risen and ascended, is already glorified (John 12:16, 23; 13:31–32; 17:1, 5), so Christians, when he returns, will be like him, seeing him as he really is (1 John 3:2).

### *glossolalia* (see **tongues, speaking in**)

### grace
The (or a) free, unearned, and undeserved favor of God.

### guidance (*kubernēseis*), gifts of
The spiritual gift of oversight, the plural implying the ability to give repeated instances of wise counsel and guidance for the community (1 Cor 12:28).

### healings (*charismata iamatōn*), gifts of
Paul describes this spiritual gift in the plural (1 Cor 12:9), implying that no one has a permanent gift of healing or a habitual power to heal people, but that each divine healing is a distinct charism or gift of grace.

### *hypostasis* (plural *hypostases*)
The patristic Greek term for "person," applied to the persons of the Godhead, Father, Son, and Holy Spirit, who are distinguished from each other

by the incommunicable personal attributes of being unbegotten, begotten, or proceeding (paternity, generation, or spiration).

**hypostatic union**
The union of the two natures, divine and human, in the person (*hypostasis*) of the incarnate Son of God.

**immanent Trinity**
The inner life and relations of the three persons of the Godhead.

**incarnation**
The embodiment of the Son of God in human flesh (Greek *ensarkosis*), assuming human nature and becoming a human being (John 1:14).

**interpretation of tongues (*hermēneia glossōn*)**
The spiritual gift of interpretation, not normally a word for word translation, conveying the essential sense of a message in **tongues**. Paul discourages speaking in **tongues** in a public meeting unless accompanied by interpretation (1 Cor 14:27–28), and treats **tongues** plus interpretation as the equivalent of prophecy (1 Cor 14:5).

**latter days**
The end of the age, referred to in the Bible as the "end of days" (*acharit hayamim*, Isa 2:2; Mic 4:1), "last day" (*eschatē hemera*, John 6:39–40, 44, 54), or "later times" (*huterois kairois*, 1 Tim 4:1) and characterized as a time of growing apostasy, turmoil, and social distress.

***logos***
Word, reason, or the rational faculty in human beings. The *Logos* refers to the second person of the Trinity, who enlightens every human being (John 1:9) and who became incarnate as the one who "became flesh and made his dwelling among us" (John 1:14).

**Messiah**
The hoped-for Spirit-anointed Jewish deliverer and world leader (Hebrew *Māshiach*, Greek *Christos*, "anointed one"), foretold in many biblical prophecies (2 Sam 7:12, 16; Pss 2, 72; Isa 11:1–4; 42:1–4; 61:1–3) and fulfilled by Jesus (Luke 4:18–19; 24:46).

**millennium**
The thousand-year earthly reign of the Messiah, spoken of in many biblical prophecies (e.g. Ps 72; Isa 2:1–5; Zech 14:16; Acts 3:21; Rev 20:1–6) and by

the second-century theologian Irenaeus (*Against Heresies*, 5.31.1–36.3), but eclipsed in historic Christian teaching by Augustine's identification of the triumphant church with the kingdom of God. The reemergence of Israel has led to a revival of millennial expectation by charismatic teachers such as Derek Prince, David Pawson, and Peter Hocken.

**miracles (*energēmata dunameōn*)**
The Pauline term "deeds of power" is the divinely given ability to perform signs, wonders, miracles, and exorcisms, often a sign of the ministry of an apostle (2 Cor 12:12).

**nature**
The basic inherent character, properties, or qualities of something (Greek *phusis*, Latin *natura*). Human nature is the humanity of each and every human being, assumed by the person of Christ (the *Logos*) in the **incarnation** (John 1:14).

**ontological**
Having to do with the nature of being, with how things are.

**paraclete**
The Greek word used in John's Gospel of the Holy Spirit (*paraclētos*, John 14:16, 26; 15:26; 16:7), meaning one who is called to stand beside us, a person summoned to our aid, someone who appears on our behalf (Latin *advocatus*, "advocate"). The word alludes to a defence counsel in a legal trial, and means "advisor," "advocate," or "helper," rather than the term "comforter" used in the King James Version.

**patristic**
Having to do with the early Christian theologians or church fathers.

**Pentecostal**
Christians who are members of the original Pentecostal denominations, who pioneered the rediscovery of baptism in the Holy Spirit, evidenced by speaking in tongues, prophecy, healing, and deliverance.

***perichoresis***
The Greek term (*perichōrēsis*, meaning "rotation," "proceeding around") for the mutual indwelling, interpenetration, or coinherence of the three persons of the Trinity in one another (Latin *circumincessio*, circumincession).

## person, personhood

In contemporary culture, the word "person" means little more than "an individual human being." But in Christian theology, used both of the persons of the Godhead and of human persons created in God's image, the concept of personhood has a relational quality, denoting both the incommunicable depth and uniqueness of a person and a person's capacity for self-transcendence, creativity, and relationship with other persons.

## pneumatology

The branch of theology that deals with the Holy Spirit.

## procession

The theological term (Greek *ekporeusis*, Latin *processio*), sometimes called "**spiration**," which denotes the manner of the Spirit's origin from the God the Father, in contrast to "**generation**," the origin of the Son from the Father.

## prophecy, prophesying (*prophēteia*)

The gift, inspired by the Holy Spirit, of speaking spontaneously on behalf of God with precise relevance to a person or situation, which discloses the hidden secrets of people's lives, clarifies a situation, or reveals future events. Wayne Grudem defines it as "speaking human words to report something God brings to mind."[7]

## prophet

Prophets, as described in the New Testament, are those who exercise a proven record of speaking spontaneously on behalf of God, usually independent of formal church leadership.

## protological

Having to do with origins and "first things."

## recapitulation

The reprise, summing up or gathering up of all things in the eschatological consummation in Christ, referred to in the New Testament as the "regeneration" (*palingenesia*, Matt 19:28) or "restoration" (*apokatastasis*, Acts 3:21) of all things.

## regeneration

The inner renewal or "new birth" by the Holy Spirit (John 3:3–8; Titus 3:5; 1 Pet 1:3) which makes a person a Christian, imparting eternal life (John

---

1. Grudem, *The Gift of Prophecy*, 67, 89, 167.

3:15–16) or a share in the divine nature (2 Pet 1:4), and so making a human person a child of God (John 1:12; 1 John 3:1–2) and a member of God's family (Rom 8:15–17).

**replacement theology**
The doctrine, deriving from the second-century apologists and prevalent in the historic churches of Christendom, that the Christian church has replaced or superseded the Jewish people in God's purposes because of their rejection of their Messiah.

**restorationism**
Christian belief in the return of the Jewish people to their land and to their Lord in the **latter days**, based on biblical prophecy, which predated the rise of Christian **dispensationalism** and secular Zionism by two and a half centuries.

**sanctification**
The inner and ongoing transformation of a Christian's mind, actions, character, and relationships by the Holy Spirit which follows regeneration (Rom 8:1–14; 12:1–2; Eph 5:18—6:9), resulting in progress in overcoming the sinful nature and its desires (Gal 5:16–26), greater love for others, a desire to serve God, growth in holiness, and an ever-increasing likeness to Christ (2 Cor 3:18).

**singing in the Spirit ("*jubilate*")**
Singing without words or in tongues with a full heart, strangely beautiful when in harmony with others.

***sobornost***
A Russian word with no exact English equivalent, meaning "conciliarity" or "collegiality": unity and agreement based on freedom, love, and truth. It was used by the modern Russian Orthodox theologians Alexei Khomiakoff and Sergei Bulgakov to denote the unity of many persons in the fellowship of the church.

**spiration**
An alternative Latin term for the "**procession**" of the Holy Spirit, the distinctive manner of the Spirit's origin from the Father, evoking the metaphor of breathing, the etymology of "spirit," and the concept of inspiration.

**spiritual gifts**
The generic term for the divine graces freely and variously given by God to build up the individual believer and the Christian community. These have

a threefold structure and include the dynamic charisms involving the direct inspiration of the Holy Spirit (the "manifestation gifts" or *charismata* proper), the "ministry gifts" bestowed by the risen Lord for the upbuilding of his church, and the "motivational gifts" or callings which reveal the special providence of God the Father.

*starets* (plural *startsy*)
A spiritual counselor in the Russian Orthodox tradition, specially gifted with the ability to read the secrets of the human heart.

**teleological**
Showing evidence of design, purpose, and intentionality in the world.

*theōsis*
The term used by the theologians of the Eastern Orthodox Church to refer to the Christian's **sanctification** and **glorification**. It means "deification," "divinization," or "participation in the divine nature" (2 Pet 1:3–4), but not in a pantheistic sense. It does not imply any impairment of our humanity or of God's divinity. Just as the Son of God became incarnate as a human being without ceasing to be divine, so we are called to become children of God, without ceasing to be fully and truly human.

**tongues (*glossōn*), speaking in**
Speech inspired by the Holy Spirit: speaking sounds in, or that resemble, a language not learned by or known to the speaker, in prayer, praise, or prophecy. Chiefly beneficial for personal edification, tongues has the same value as **prophecy** when accompanied by the **interpretation of tongues**. George Montague suggests its relationship to prayer is like abstract art to painting,[8] just as Harvey Cox likens the Pentecostal phenomenon to jazz compared with compositional music.[9]

**word of knowledge (*logos gnōseōs*)**
A spiritual gift of insight into a person's life or what God is doing in a meeting, not known by natural means.

**word of wisdom (*logos sophias*)**
A spiritual gift of discernment that provides an instantly recognizable solution to a difficult pastoral problem or situation.

---

8. Montague, *The Spirit and His Gifts*, chapter 2.
9. Cox, *Fire from Heaven*, 143–57.

# Bibliography

Abbott, Walter M., ed. *The Documents of Vatican II*. New York: Herder & Herder, 1966.
Allen, Roland. "Pentecost and the World." In *The Ministry of the Spirit: Selected Writings*, edited by David M. Paton, 1–61. Cambridge: Lutterworth, 2006.
Anderson, Allan Heaton. *To the Ends of the Earth: Pentecostalism and the Transformation of World Christianity*. New York: Oxford University Press, 2013.
Athanasius. *The Letters of Saint Athanasius Concerning the Holy Spirit to Bishop Serapion (359-60)*. Translated with introduction and notes by C. R. B. Shapland. London: Epworth, 1951.
Baly, Denis. *The Geography of the Bible: A Study in Historical Geography*. London: Lutterworth, 1957.
Barrett, David B. "Statistics, Global." In *DPCM* 810-30.
———. "The Worldwide Holy Spirit Renewal." In *The Century of the Holy Spirit: 100 Years of Pentecostal and Charismatic Renewal, 1901-2001*, edited by Vinson Synan, 381–414. Nashville: Thomas Nelson, 2001.
Barrow, John. *The Origin of the Universe*. London: Weidenfeld & Nicolson, 1994.
Barth, Karl. *Church Dogmatics*. Edited by Geoffrey W. Bromiley and Thomas F. Torrance, translated by Geoffrey W. Bromiley et al. Vol. I, Part 1—Vol. IV, Part 4. Edinburgh: T. & T. Clark, 1956-75.
———. *The Resurrection of the Dead*. Translated by H. J. Stenning. London: Hodder & Stoughton, 1933.
Bartleman, Frank. *Azusa Street: An Eyewitness Account*. Centennial ed. 1906-2006. Introduction by Vinson Synan. Gainesville, FL: Bridge-Logos, 2006.
Basil the Great. *On the Holy Spirit*. Translated by David Anderson. Crestwood, NY: St. Vladimir's Seminary, 1980.
Battley, Don. *No Way Back: A Personal History of Charismatic Renewal in the New Zealand Anglican Church*. Auckland: Castle, 2019.
Baxter, James K. *Autumn Testament*. Wellington: Price Milburn, 1972. Republished in *Complete Prose*, edited by John Weir, 3:471-80. Wellington, NZ: Victoria University Press, 2015.
———. *Collected Poems of James K. Baxter*. Edited by J. E. Weir. Wellington, NZ: Oxford University Press, 1981.
———. *Thoughts about the Holy Spirit*. Wellington, NZ: Futuna, 1973. Republished in *Complete Prose*, edited by John Weir, 3:512-36. Wellington, NZ: Victoria University Press, 2015.
Beall, Patricia, and Martha Keys Barker. *The Folk Arts in Renewal*. London: Hodder & Stoughton, 1980.

Bennett, Dennis J. *Nine O'Clock in the Morning.* Eastbourne, UK: Kingsway, 1971.

Berdyaev, Nicolas. *Freedom and the Spirit.* Translated by Oliver Fielding Clarke. London: Geoffrey Bles, 1935.

Bessenecker, Scott. *The New Friars: The Emerging Movement Serving the World's Poor.* Downers Grove: InterVarsity, 2006.

Bettelheim, Bruno. *The Children of the Dream.* London: Macmillan, 1969.

Billinghurst, Noel. "Testimony." In *Logos Magazine*, an early charismatic magazine published in Christchurch, NZ, 1.3 (February 1967) 4–7.

Bittlinger, Arnold, ed. *The Church is Charismatic: The World Council of Churches and the Charismatic Renewal.* Geneva: World Council of Churches, 1981.

———. *Gifts and Graces: A Commentary on 1 Corinthians 12–14.* Translated by Herbert Klassen. London: Hodder & Stoughton, 1967.

———. *Gifts and Ministries.* London: Hodder & Stoughton, 1974.

Bolitho, Elaine E. *Meet the Baptists: Postwar Personalities and Perspectives.* Auckland: Christian Research Association of NZ, 1993.

Bratsiotis, N. P. "*bāśār.*" In *TDOT* 2:317–32.

Brook, John. "The Charismatic Contribution." *The Paraclete*, a newsletter for the charismatic renewal within the Presbyterian Church of New Zealand, 4 (1976) 8–14.

Brown, Raymond. "The Paraclete in the Fourth Gospel." *New Testament Studies* 13 (1967) 113–32.

Bruner, Frederick Dale. *A Theology of the Holy Spirit: The Pentecostal Experience and the New Testament Witness.* London: Hodder & Stoughton, 1970.

Bryan, Clint. "Hillsong's Global Appeal, Explained by Sociologists." *Christianity Today* 23 Jan 2019.

Bühler, Jürgen. "In the Footsteps of Messiah—Why We Celebrate the Feast." ICEJ Friday Feature, 4 Oct 2019. https://int.icej.org/news/headlines/friday-feature-footsteps-messiah---why-we-celebrate-feast.

Bulgakov, Sergei. *The Orthodox Church.* Crestwood, NY: St. Vladimir's Seminary, 1988.

Burgess, Stanley M. *The Holy Spirit: Eastern Christian Traditions.* Peabody, MA: Hendrikson, 1989.

Busch, Eberhard. *Karl Barth: His Life from Letters and Autobiographical Texts.* Translated by John Bowden. London: SCM, 1976.

Calvin, John. *Institutes of the Christian Religion.* Edited by John T. McNeill, translated by Ford Lewis Battles. 2 vols. London: SCM, 1961.

Campbell, Theodore C. "The Doctrine of the Holy Spirit in the Theology of Athanasius." In *SJT* 27 (1974) 408–40.

Campenhausen, Hans von. "Der urchristliche Apostelbegriff" [The Early Christian Understanding of the Apostolate]. *Studia theologica* 1 (1948–49) 96–130.

Casdorph, H. Richard. *The Miracles.* Plainfield, NJ: Logos, 1976.

Chambers, J. B. *Is Any Sick Among You?* Carterton, NZ: Roydhouse & Son, 1975.

Christenson, Larry. *Speaking in Tongues and Its Significance for the Church.* Minneapolis: Bethany, 1968.

Clark, Steve. *Baptized in the Spirit and Spiritual Gifts.* Pecos, NM: Dove, 1969.

Coad, Beverley, and Jeanette Knudsen. *Fire at the Mount.* Palmerston North, NZ: Mountain Peak, 2010.

Cohen, Akiva. "Messianic Jews and the Land of Israel." In *Introduction to Messianic Judaism: Its Ecclesial Context and Biblical Foundations*, edited by David J. Rudolph and Joel Willitts, 107–15. Grand Rapids: Zondervan, 2013.

Congar, Yves. *I Believe in the Holy Spirit.* Vol. 1, *The Experience of the Spirit.* Vol. 2, *Lord and Giver of Life.* Vol. 3, *The River of Life Flows in the East and in the West.* Translated by David Smith. New York: Seabury, 1983.

Cox, Harvey. *Fire from Heaven: The Rise of Pentecostal Spirituality and the Reshaping of Religion in the Twenty-First Century.* Cambridge, MA: Da Capo, 1995.

Cranfield, C. E. B. *A Critical and Exegetical Commentary on the Epistle to the Romans.* Vol. 1. Edinburgh: T. & T. Clark, 1985.

Dallimore, Arnold. *The Life of Edward Irving: Forerunner of the Charismatic Movement.* Edinburgh: Banner of Truth, 1983.

David, George. *The Eclipse and Rediscovery of Person.* New Delhi: TRACI, 1976.

Davies, Paul. *The Goldilocks Enigma: Why is the Universe Just Right for Life?* London: Allen Lane, 2006.

Dayton, Donald W. *Theological Roots of Pentecostalism.* Grand Rapids: Zondervan, 1987.

Deere, Jack. *Surprised by the Power of the Spirit.* Grand Rapids: Zondervan, 1993.

Di Sabatino, David. *Frisbee: The Life and Death of a Hippie Preacher.* DVD. Lake Forest, CA: Jester, 2006.

———. *The Jesus People Movement: An Annotated Bibliography and Resource.* 2nd ed. Lake Forest, CA: Jester, 2004.

Dorries, David. "West of Scotland Revival." In *NIDPCM* 1189–92.

Dragas, George. "Holy Spirit and Tradition: The Writings of St. Athanasius." In *Sobornost* 1 (1979) 51–72.

Duin, Julia. *Days of Fire and Glory: The Rise and Fall of a Charismatic Community.* Baltimore: Crossland, 2009.

Dunn, James D. G. *The Acts of the Apostles.* Grand Rapids: Eerdmans, 2016.

———. *Baptism in the Holy Spirit: A Re-examination of the New Testament Teaching on the Gift of the Spirit in relation to Pentecostalism Today.* London: SCM, 1970.

———. *Jesus and the Spirit: A Study of the Religious and Charismatic Experience of Jesus and the First Christians as Reflected in the New Testament.* London: SCM, 1975.

Durran, Maggie. *The Wind at the Door: The Story of the Community of Celebration, Home of the Fisherfolk.* Eastbourne, UK: Kingsway, 1986.

Ellis, E. Earle. "The Role of the Christian Prophet in Acts." In *Apostolic History and the Gospel: Biblical and Historical Essays Presented to F. F. Bruce on His 60th Birthday,* edited by W. W. Gasque and R. P. Martin, 55–67. London: Paternoster, 1970.

*English Hymnal.* Edited by Percy Dearmer. Musical editor, Ralph Vaughan Williams. 2nd ed. London: Oxford University Press, 1933.

Enroth, Ronald M., et al. *The Jesus People: Old-Time Religion in the Age of Aquarius.* Grand Rapids: Eerdmans, 1972.

Farrer, Austin. *A Celebration of Faith.* London: Hodder & Stoughton, 1970.

Ferguson, Ron, and Mark Chater. *Mole under the Fence: Conversations with Roland Walls.* Edinburgh: St. Andrew, 2006.

*First Love: A Historic Gathering of Jesus Music Pioneers.* Two DVD and two CD set. Monument, CO: Exploration Films, 1998.

Florovsky, Georges. "The Idea of Creation in Christian Philosophy." In *Eastern Churches Quarterly* 8 (1949) Supplementary Issue 2, "Nature and Grace," 53–77.

———. "St. Gregory Palamas and the Tradition of the Fathers." In *Collected Works* 1:105–20. Belmont, MA: Nordland, 1972.

Flusser, David, and R. Stephen Notley. *The Sage from Galilee: Rediscovering Jesus' Genius.* Grand Rapids: Eerdmans, 2007.

Foster, Richard. *Freedom of Simplicity*. London: SPCK, 1981.
Francis, D. Pitt. "The Holy Spirit—a Statistical Enquiry." *Expository Times* 96 (1985) 136–37.
Francis, Pope. "Address to the Renewal in the Holy Spirit Movement." St. Peter's Square, Rome, 3 Jul 2015. http://w2.vatican.va/content/francesco/en/speeches/2015/july/documents/papa-francesco_20150703_movimento-rinnovamento-spirito.html.
Fruchtenbaum, Arnold G. *Yeshua: The Life of the Messiah from a Messianic Jewish Perspective*. Abridged. San Antonio: Ariel Ministries, 2017.
Garratt, Ian. "Shut Out, Yet Empowered." In Bev Montgomery and George Bryant, *Transformed Lives: The Move of God that Shook the New Zealand Church*, 87–96. Auckland: Castle, 2010.
Garrison, David. *A Wind in the House of Islam: How God is Drawing Muslims around the World to Faith in Jesus Christ*. Monument, CO: Wigtake, 2014.
Gee, Donald. *Spiritual Gifts in the Work of Ministry Today*. Springfield, MO: Gospel Publishing, 1963.
Goll, James. *Releasing Spiritual Gifts Today*. New Kensington, PA: Whitaker, 2016.
Goode, Reema. *Which None Can Shut: Remarkable True Stories of God's Miraculous Work in the Muslim World*. Carol Stream, IL: Tyndale, 2010.
Graham, Billy. *The Holy Spirit: Activating God's Power in Your Life*. Glasgow: Collins, 1980.
———. *The Jesus Generation*. Grand Rapids: Zondervan, 1971.
"The Greek and Latin Traditions Regarding the Procession of the Holy Spirit." *Catholic International* 7 (1996) 36–43.
Green, Gene L., et al., eds. *The Spirit over the Earth: Pneumatology in the Majority World*. Majority World Theology Series. Grand Rapids: Eerdmans, 2016.
———, eds. *The Trinity Among the Nations: The Doctrine of God in the Majority World*. Majority World Theology Series. Grand Rapids: Eerdmans, 2015.
Green, Michael. *I Believe in the Holy Spirit*. London: Hodder & Stoughton, 1975.
Griffin, Winn. *Gracelets: Being Conduits of the Extravagant Acts of God's Grace*. Woodinville, WA: Harmon, 2015.
Grigg, Viv. *Companion to the Poor*. Sutherland, NSW: Albatross, 1984.
———. *Cry of the Urban Poor*. Monrovia, CA: MARC, 1992.
———. *The Spirit of Christ and the Postmodern City: Transforming Revival among Auckland's Evangelicals and Pentecostals*. Wellington, NZ: Urban Leadership Foundation, 2009.
Grudem, Wayne A. *The Gift of Prophecy in the New Testament and Today*. Westchester, IL: Crossway, 1988.
Guth, Alan H. "Inflationary Universe: A Possible Solution to the Horizon and Flatness Problems." *Physical Review D* 23 (1981) 347.
Habets, Myk. *The Anointed Son: A Trinitarian Spirit Christology*. Princeton Theological Monograph Series 129. Eugene, OR: Pickwick, 2010.
———, ed. *Ecumenical Perspectives on the Filioque for the Twenty-First Century*. London: T. & T. Clark, 2014.
Hadamard, Jacques. *The Psychology of Invention in the Mathematical Field*. Princeton, NJ: Princeton University Press, 1945.
Harper, Michael. *As at the Beginning: The Twentieth-Century Pentecostal Revival*. London: Hodder & Stoughton, 1965.
———. *A New Way of Living: How the Church of the Redeemer, Houston, Found a New Life-Style*. London: Hodder & Stoughton, 1973.

Harrell, David Edwin. *All Things Are Possible: The Healing and Charismatic Revivals in Modern America*. Bloomington, IN: Indiana University Press, 1975.
Hathaway, Brian. *Beyond Renewal: The Kingdom of God*. Milton Keynes, UK: Word, 1990.
Hawthorne, Gerald F. *The Presence and the Power: The Significance of the Holy Spirit in the Life and Ministry of Jesus*. Dallas, TX: Word, 1991.
Hebblethwaite, Brian. *The Incarnation: Collected Essays in Christology*. Cambridge: Cambridge University Press, 1987.
Hendry, George S. *The Holy Spirit in Christian Theology*. Rev. ed. London: SCM, 1965.
Heppe, Heinrich. *Reformed Dogmatics, Set Out and Illustrated from the Sources*. Translated by G. T. Thomson. London: Allen & Unwin, 1950.
Heron, Alasdair I. C. *The Holy Spirit in the Bible, in the History of Christian Thought and in Recent Theology*. London: Marshall, Morgan & Scott, 1983.
Heschel, Abraham. *The Prophets*. 2 vols. New York: Harper & Row, 1962.
Hill, Clifford. *Prophecy Past and Present: An Exploration of the Prophetic Ministry in the Bible and the Church Today*. Rev. ed. Guildford, UK: Eagle, 1995.
Hocken, Peter. *Azusa, Rome, and Zion: Pentecostal Faith, Catholic Reform, and Jewish Roots*. Eugene, OR: Pickwick, 2016.
———. *The Challenges of the Pentecostal, Charismatic and Messianic Jewish Movements: The Tensions of the Spirit*. Abingdon, UK: Routledge, 2016.
———. "Charismatic Movement." In *DPCM* 130–60.
———. "Charismatic Movement." In *EC* 1:404–8.
———. "Charismatic Movement." In *NIDPCM* 477–519.
———. *The Glory and the Shame: Reflections on the Twentieth-Century Outpouring of the Holy Spirit*. Guildford, UK: Eagle, 1994.
———. *Pentecost and Parousia: Charismatic Renewal, Christian Unity, and the Coming Glory*. Eugene, OR: Wipf & Stock, 2013.
Hoffmeyer, John F. "Trinity." In *EC* 5:540–51.
Hollenweger, Walter J. *Der erste Korintherbrief, eine Arbeitshilfe zur Bibelwoche* [The First Letter to the Corinthians: An Aid for Bible Week]. Klingenmünster: Volksmissionarisches Amt der Pfälzischen Landeskirche, 1965.
———. "Pentecostalism." In *EC* 4:144–51.
———. *The Pentecostals*. London: SCM, 1972.
Irving, Edward. *Christ's Holiness in Flesh: The Form, Fountain Head, and Assurance to us of Holiness in the Flesh*. Edinburgh: John Lindsay, 1831.
———. "Facts Connected with Recent Manifestations of Spiritual Gifts." *Fraser's Magazine* (Jan 1832) 759–60.
———. *The Orthodox and Catholic Doctrine of our Lord's Human Nature*. London: Baldwin & Craddock, 1830.
Israel College of the Bible. "Findings of New Research on the Messianic Movement in Israel." A 2017 research project on Messianic Jews in Israel. https://www.oneforisrael.org/bible-based-teaching-from-israel/findings-of-new-research-on-the-messianic-movement-in-israel/.
James, M. R. *The Apocryphal New Testament*. Oxford: Oxford University Press, 1980.
Jeremias, Joachim. *Jesus' Promise to the Nations*. London: SCM, 1958.
Johns, Jackie David. "Pentecostal Churches." In *EC* 4:137–44.
Johnson, Todd M., and Peter F. Crossing. "Christianity 2013: Renewalists and Faith and Migration." *IBMR* 37 (2013) 32–33.

Johnson, Todd M., et al. "Christianity 2019: What's Missing?" *IBMR* 43 (2019) 92–102.

Johnstone, Patrick. *Operation World: A Day-to-Day Guide to Praying for the World.* Bromley, UK: STL, 1978.

Jones, Charles Edwin. "The Jesus People." In *DPCM* 491–93.

Kelsey, Morton T. *Tongue Speaking: An Experiment in Spiritual Experience.* New York: Doubleday, 1965.

Khomiakoff, Alexis S.. "The Church Is One" (c1850). In *Russia and the English Church during the Last Fifty Years,* edited by W. J. Birkbeck, 192–222. London: Society for Promoting Christian Knowledge, 1895.

Kilian, Sabbas J. "The Holy Spirit in Christ and in Christians." In *American Benedictine Review* 20 (1969) 99–121.

King, Tim. "The Feast: Walking in Faith with God for 39 Years." *Word from Jerusalem* (Nov/Dec 2017) 8.

Konrad, Ulrich. *Mozarts Schaffensweise: Studien zu den Werkautographen, Skizzen und Entwürfen* [Mozart's Method of Composition: Studies of the Autograph Scores, Sketches and Drafts]. Göttingen: Vandenhoeck & Ruprecht, 1992.

Kraft, Charles H. *Christianity with Power: Your Worldview and Your Experience of the Supernatural.* Ann Arbor, MI: Servant, 1989.

Kuyper, Abraham. *The Work of the Holy Spirit.* Translated by Henri de Vries. New York: Funk & Wagnalls, 1900.

Lawson, James G. *Deeper Experiences of Famous Christians.* New Kensington, PA: Whitaker, 1998.

Lewis, C. S. *Mere Christianity.* London: Collins Fontana, 1955.

———. *Reflections on the Psalms.* London: Collins Fontana, 1961.

Lineham, Peter J. "Tongues Must Cease: The Brethren and the Charismatic Movement in New Zealand." *Christian Brethren Research Fellowship Journal* 96 (1982) 1–48.

Lloyd-Jones, Martyn. *The Christian Warfare: An Exposition of Ephesians 6:10–13.* Edinburgh: Banner of Truth, 1976.

———. *Life in the Spirit in Marriage, Home and Work: An Exposition of Ephesians 5:18–6:9.* Edinburgh: Banner of Truth, 1974.

Long, Zeb Bradford, and Douglas McMurry. *The Collapse of the Brass Heaven: Rebuilding Our Worldview to Embrace the Power of God.* Grand Rapids: Chosen, 1994.

Lossky, Vladimir. "Catholic Consciousness: Anthropological Implications of the Dogma of the Church." In *In the Image and Likeness of God,* 183–94. London: Mowbrays, 1975.

———. *The Mystical Theology of the Eastern Church.* Translated by members of the Fellowship of St. Alban and St. Sergius. Cambridge: James Clarke, 1957.

———. "The Procession of the Holy Spirit in Orthodox Trinitarian Doctrine." In *In the Image and Likeness of God,* 71–96. London: Mowbrays, 1975.

———. "Redemption and Deification." In *In the Image and Likeness of God,* 97–110. London: Mowbrays, 1975.

———. "Tradition and Traditions." In *In the Image and Likeness of God,* 141–68. London: Mowbrays, 1975.

———. *The Vision of God.* Translated by Asheleigh Moorhouse. London: Faith Press, 1963.

Macchia, Frank D. *Baptized in the Spirit: A Global Pentecostal Theology.* Grand Rapids: Zondervan, 2006.

———. *Jesus the Spirit Baptizer: Christology in Light of Pentecost*. Grand Rapids: Eerdmans, 2018.

MacEwan, Neven. *When the Crowd Stops Roaring: The Inspirational Memoir of an Extraordinary All Black*. Ruawai, NZ: Wild Side, 2019.

MackIntosh, H. R. *The Doctrine of the Person of Christ*. 2nd ed. Edinburgh: T. & T. Clark, 1913.

MacNutt, Francis. *Healing*. Notre Dame, IN: Ave Maria, 1974.

Mahrenholz, Christhard, et al, eds. *Handbuch zum evangelischen Kirchengesangbuch* [Companion to the Protestant church hymnbook]. Göttingen: Vandenhoeck & Ruprecht, 1958.

Maloney, George. *The Mystic of Fire and Light: St. Symeon the New Theologian*. Denville, NJ: Dimension, 1975.

Marty, Martin E. "The Pentecostal Phenomenon." In *Encyclopaedia Britannica Yearbook 1973*, 592–93. Chicago: Encyclopaedia Britannica, 1973.

McDonnell, Kilian. *Charismatic Renewal and the Churches*. New York: Seabury, 1976.

———. *The Other Hand of God: The Holy Spirit as the Universal Touch and Goal*. Collegeville, MN: Liturgical, 2003.

McIntyre, John. "The Holy Spirit in Greek Patristic Thought." *SJT* 7 (1954) 353–75.

———. *The Shape of Pneumatology: Studies in the Doctrine of the Holy Spirit*. Edinburgh: T. & T. Clark, 1997.

McNair Scott, Benjamin G. *Apostles Today: Making Sense of Contemporary Charismatic Apostolates; A Historical and Theological Appraisal*. Eugene, OR: Pickwick, 2014.

Menzies, William W., and Robert P. Menzies. *Spirit and Power: Foundations of Pentecostal Experience*. Grand Rapids: Zondervan, 2000.

Merritt, N. F. H. *To God be the Glory: The First 10½ years of the Charismatic Renewal in St. Paul's*. Auckland: St. Paul's Outreach Trust, 1981.

Meyendorff, John. *Byzantine Theology: Historical Trends and Doctrinal Themes*. London: Mowbrays, 1975.

———. *Christ in Eastern Christian Thought*. Crestwood, NY: St. Vladimir's Seminary, 1975.

———. *St. Gregory Palamas and Orthodox Spirituality*. Translated by Adele Fisk. Crestwood, NY: St. Vladimir's Seminary, 1974.

———. *A Study of Gregory Palamas*. Translated by George Lawrence. 2nd ed. Leighton Buzzard, UK: Faith Press, 1974.

Meyer, Werner. *Der erste Brief an die Korinther* [The First Letter to the Corinthians]. 2 vols. Zurich: Zwingli, 1945.

Miller, Elmer C. *Pentecost Examined by a Baptist Lawyer*. Springfield, MO: Gospel, 1936.

Miller, John. *A Simple Life: Roland Walls and the Community of the Transfiguration*. Edinburgh: St. Andrew, 2014.

Millward, Steve. *John Balchin: A Biography*. Papakura, NZ: Steve Millward, 1994.

Möhler, Johann. *Unity in the Church, or, The Principles of Catholicism: Presented in the Spirit of the Church Fathers of the First Three Centuries*. Translated by Peter C. Erb. Washington, DC: Catholic University of America Press, 2016.

Montague, George T. *The Spirit and His Gifts: The Biblical Background of Spirit-Baptism, Tongue-Speaking, and Prophecy*. New York: Paulist, 1974.

Mühlen, Heribert. *A Charismatic Theology: Initiation in the Spirit*. London: Burns & Oates, 1978.

———. *Der Heilige Geist als Person in der Trinität, bei der Inkarnation und im Gnadenbund* [The Holy Spirit as Person in the Trinity, in the Incarnation and in the Covenant of Grace]. Münster: Aschendorff, 1966.

———. *Una Mystica Persona: Die Kirche als das Mysterium der Identität des Heiligen Geistes in Christus und den Christen* [One Mystical Person: The Church as the Mystery of the Identity of the Holy Spirit in Christ and in Christians]. Munich: Ferdinand Schöning, 1964.

Myer, Ron. *Fivefold Ministry Made Practical.* Lititz, PA: House to House, 2006.

Nissiotis, Nikos A. "The Importance of the Doctrine of the Trinity for Church Life and Theology." In *The Orthodox Ethos*, edited by A. J. Philippou, 32–69. Oxford: Holywell, 1964.

Norton, Robert. *Memoirs of James and George Macdonald of Port Glasgow.* London: John F. Shaw, 1840.

O'Connor, Edward D. *The Pentecostal Movement in the Catholic Church.* Notre Dame, IN: Ave Maria, 1971.

O'Donnell, John J. "In Him and over Him: The Holy Spirit in the Life of Jesus." *Gregorianum* 70 (1989) 25–45.

Pain, Timothy. *Prophecy: A Re-reading of Scripture.* Eastbourne, UK: Kingsway, 1986.

Paris, Nyalle. "Wind of Change: A Theological Reflection on Charismatic Renewal at Hornby Presbyterian Church, 1974–1986." Research essay, Otago University, Dunedin, NZ, 2006.

Parrinder, Geoffrey. *Jesus in the Qur'ān.* London: Faber & Faber, 1965.

Pawson, David. *The Normal Christian Birth.* London: Hodder & Stoughton, 1989.

———. *Truth to Tell.* London: Hodder & Stoughton, 1977.

———. *Unlocking the Bible.* London: Harper Collins, 2003.

———. *When Jesus Returns.* London: Hodder & Stoughton, 1995.

Pelikan, Jaroslav. *The Christian Tradition.* Vol. 2, *The Spirit of Eastern Christendom.* Chicago: University of Chicago Press, 1974.

Penrose, Roger. *The Emperor's New Mind: Concerning Computers, Minds and the Laws of Physics.* Oxford: Oxford University Press, 1989.

———. *The Road to Reality: A Complete Guide to the Laws of the Universe.* London: Jonathan Cape, 2004.

Pickerill, Don. *Motivational Gifts.* 4th ed. Greenacre, NSW, Australia: Calvary Chapel, n.d. [late 1970s].

Philippou, Angelos J. "The Mystery of Pentecost." In *The Orthodox Ethos*, edited by A. J. Philippou, 70-97. Oxford: Holywell, 1964.

Pinnock, Clark H. *Flame of Love: A Theology of the Holy Spirit.* Downers Grove: InterVarsity, 1996.

Plowman, Edward E. *The Jesus Movement: Accounts of Christian Revolutionaries in Action.* London: Hodder & Stoughton, 1972.

Prince, Derek. *Israel and the Church: Parallel Restoration.* Charlotte, NC: Derek Prince Ministries, n.d.

Pulkingham, Graham. *Gathered for Power.* London: Hodder & Stoughton, 1973.

Rad, Gerhard von. "The Beginnings of Historical Writing in Ancient Israel" (1944). In *The Problem of the Hexateuch and Other Essays*, translated by E. W. Trueman Dicken, 166–204. Edinburgh: Oliver & Boyd, 1966.

Rahner, Karl. *Theological Investigations.* Vol. 18, *God and Revelation.* London: Darton, Longman & Todd, 1983.

———. *The Trinity*. New York: Crossroad, 1997.
Ranaghan, Kevin, and Dorothy Ranaghan. *Catholic Pentecostals*. Paramus, NJ: Paulist, 1969.
Rausch, David A. *Messianic Judaism: Its History, Theology and Polity*. New York: Edwin Mellen, 1982.
Rea, John. *Proclaim with Wonders: The Role of Miracles in the Work of Evangelisation*. Otane, Hawkes Bay, NZ: Pleroma, 2013.
———. *Witness to Wonders: Healings and Miracles Today*. East Keilor, VIC, Australia: Comsodar, 2005.
———. *Wonders Still Abounding: An Account of Signs and Wonders Witnessed over the Past Few Years*. Otane, Hawkes Bay, NZ: Pleroma, 2018.
Reid, Michael. "But By My Spirit: A History of the Charismatic Renewal in Christchurch, 1960-1985." PhD diss., University of Canterbury, Christchurch, NZ, 2003.
———. *Thus Far . . . A Centennial History of Hornby Presbyterian Church, 1908-2008*. Christchurch, NZ: Verve, 2008.
Rengstorf, Karl H. "Apostolos." In *TDNT* 1:407-47.
Riches, Tanya, and Tom Wagner, eds. *The Hillsong Movement Examined: You Call Me Out Upon the Waters*. London: Palgrave Macmillan, 2017.
Riss, Richard M. *A Survey of 20th-Century Revival Movements in North America*. Peabody, MA: Hendrickson, 1988.
Ritschl, Dietrich. "Holy Spirit." In *EC* 2:577-83.
Rookmaaker, Hans R. *Modern Art and the Death of a Culture*. London: InterVarsity, 1970.
Roxborogh, John. "As at the Beginning in Britain: Michael Harper, Edward Irving and the Catholic Apostolic Church." *Theological Renewal* 11 (1979) 17-23.
Ruthven, Jon. *On the Cessation of the Charismata: The Protestant Polemic on Postbiblical Miracles*. Journal of Pentecostal Theology Supplement Series 3. Sheffield: Sheffield Academic, 1993.
Sandford, John, and Paula Sandford. *The Elijah Task: A Call to Today's Prophets and Intercessors*. Tulsa, OK: Victory, 1986.
Satyavrata, Ivan. *The Holy Spirit: Lord and Life-Giver*. Nottingham: InterVarsity, 2009.
———. "The Spirit Blows Where It Wills: The Holy Spirit's Personhood in Indian Christian Thought." In *The Spirit over the Earth: Pneumatology in the Majority World*, edited by Gene L. Green et al., 34-57. Majority World Theology Series. Grand Rapids: Eerdmans, 2016.
Scheeben, Matthias. *The Mysteries of Christianity*. St. Louis, MO: Herder, 1946.
Scotland, Nigel. *Charismatics and the New Millennium: The Impact of Charismatic Christianity from 1960 into the New Millennium*. Guildford, UK: Eagle.
Sherrill, John L. *They Speak with Other Tongues*. London: Hodder & Stoughton, 1965.
Siecienski, A. Edward. *The Filioque: History of a Doctrinal Controversy*. Oxford Studies in Historical Theology. Oxford: Oxford University Press, 2010.
Smail, Thomas A. *The Forgotten Father*. London: Hodder & Stoughton, 1980.
———. *Like Father, Like Son: The Trinity Imaged in Our Humanity*. Grand Rapids: Eerdmans, 2005.
———. *Reflected Glory: The Spirit in Christ and Christians*. London: Hodder & Stoughton, 1975.
Smith, Chuck, and Tal Brooke. *Harvest*. Old Tappan, NJ: Chosen, 1987.

Smith, George Adam. *The Historical Geography of the Holy Land*. 27th ed. London: Hodder & Stoughton, 1931.

Smith, Kevin John. *The Origins, Nature, and Significance of the Jesus Movement*. Lexington, KY: Emeth, 2011.

Soloviev, Vladimir. *Russia and the Universal Church*. Translated by Herbert Rees. London: Geoffrey Bless, 1948.

"Spirit and Power: A 10-Country Survey of Pentecostals." Pew Research Center, 5 October 2006. https://www.pewforum.org/2006/10/05/spirit-and-power/.

Staniloae, Dumitru. "The Holy Spirit in the Theology and Life of the Orthodox Church." In *Sobornost* 7 (1975) 4–21.

Steel, Natalie. *Milton Smith: A Man after God's Heart*. Auckland: Castle, 2003.

Stott, John R. W. *Baptism and Fullness: The Work of the Holy Spirit Today*. 2nd ed. Leicester: InterVarsity, 1975.

———. *The Spirit, the Church, and the World: The Message of Acts*. Downers Grove: InterVarsity, 1990.

Strachan, Gordon. *The Pentecostal Theology of Edward Irving*. London: Darton, Longman & Todd, 1973.

———. "Theological and Cultural Origins of the Nineteenth-Century Pentecostal Movement." In *Theological Renewal* 1 (1975) 17–28.

Suenens, Léon Joseph. *A New Pentecost?* Translated by Francis Martin. New York: Seabury, 1974.

Sullivan, Francis A. *Charisms and Charismatic Renewal: A Biblical and Theological Study*. Dublin: Gill & Macmillan, 1982.

Swete, H. B. *The Holy Spirit in the Ancient Church*. London: Macmillan, 1912.

———. *The Holy Spirit in the New Testament*. London: Macmillan, 1909.

———. *On the History of the Doctrine of the Procession of the Holy Spirit*. Cambridge: Deighton, Bell, 1876.

Symeon the New Theologian. *Divine Eros: Hymns of St. Symeon the New Theologian*. Translated by Daniel K. Griggs. Crestwood, NY: St. Vladimir's Seminary, 2010.

Synan, Vinson. *The Century of the Holy Spirit: 100 Years of Pentecostal and Charismatic Renewal, 1901–2001*. Nashville: Thomas Nelson, 2001.

———. *In the Latter Days: The Outpouring of the Holy Spirit in the Twentieth Century*. Ann Arbor, MI: Servant, 1984.

———. "Presbyterian and Reformed Charismatics." *DPCM* 724–26.

———. "Presbyterian and Reformed Charismatics." *NIDPCM* 995–97.

Taylor, John V. *The Go-Between God: The Holy Spirit and the Christian Mission*. London: SCM, 1972.

Taylor, Ray. "Chairman's Letter." *Renewal News* (formerly *The Paraclete*) 2 (1987) 9.

Taylor, Vincent. *The Person of Christ in New Testament Teaching*. London: Macmillan, 1958.

Temple, William. *Readings in St. John's Gospel*. London: Macmillan, 1945.

Thiselton, Anthony C. *The Holy Spirit—in Biblical Teaching, through the Centuries, and Today*. Grand Rapids: Eerdmans, 2013.

Thunberg, Lars. *Microcosm and Mediator: The Theological Anthropology of Maximus the Confessor*. Lund: Gleerup, 1965.

Torrey, Rueben A. *What the Bible Teaches: A Thorough and Comprehensive Study of What the Bible Has to Say Concerning the Great Doctrines of Which It Treats*. New York: Fleming H. Revell, 1898.

Trousdale, Jerry. *Miraculous Movements: How Hundreds of Thousands of Muslims Are Falling in Love with Jesus*. Nashville: Thomas Nelson, 2012.
Turner, Max. "Holy Spirit." In *Dictionary of Jesus and the Gospels*, edited by Joel B. Green and Scot McKnight, 341–51. Downers Grove: InterVarsity, 1992.
UPCUSA. *The Work of the Holy Spirit*. Report of the Special Committee on the Work of the Holy Spirit. Philadelphia: UPCUSA, 1970.
Verney, Stephen. *Fire in Coventry: How Love, Prayer, and the Holy Spirit Completely Transformed a Congregation*. London: Hodder & Stoughton, 1974.
Villafañe, Eldin. *The Liberating Spirit: Toward an Hispanic American Pentecostal Social Ethic*. Grand Rapids: Eerdmans, 1993.
Visser 't Hooft, W. A. *Rembrandt and the Gospel*. London: SCM, 1958.
*Viva Cristo Rey*. Video presented by Fr. John Bertolucci. Prepared for Pope John Paul II. Dallas, TX: Catholic Charismatic Services, 1981.
Volf, Miroslav. *After Our Likeness: The Church as the Image of the Trinity*. Grand Rapids: Eerdmans, 1998.
Vos, Howard F. "Adoptionism." In *EDT* 13–14.
Wagner, C. Peter. *Signs and Wonders Today: The Story of Fuller Theological Seminary's Remarkable Course on Spiritual Power*. Altamonte Springs, FL: Creation House, 1987.
———. *The Third Wave of the Holy Spirit: Encountering the Power of Signs and Wonders Today*. Ann Arbor, MI: Servant, 1988.
———. *Your Spiritual Gifts Can Help Your Church Grow*. Ventura, CA: Regal, 1974.
"Wagner-Modified Houts Questionnaire." Pasadena, CA: Charles E. Fuller Institute of Evangelism and Church Growth, 1979.
Wainwright, Arthur W. *The Trinity in the New Testament*. London: SPCK, 1962.
Wallis, Arthur, et al. "I Will Build My Church." Massey Conference Report, Palmerston North, NZ, August 1964.
Walls, Roland. "St. Gregory Palamas." In *SJT* 21 (1968) 435–48.
Ward, Kevin R. *Against the Odds: Murray Robertson and Spreydon Baptist Church*. Auckland: Archer, 2016.
———. *Losing Our Religion? Changing Patterns of Believing and Belonging in Secular Western Societies*. Eugene, OR: Wipf & Stock, 2013.
Ware, Kallistos T. "Orthodoxy and the Charismatic Movement." In *Eastern Churches Review* 5 (1973) 182–86.
Warfield, B. B. *Miracles: Yesterday and Today, True and False*. Grand Rapids: Eerdmans, 1953.
Watson, David. *One in the Spirit*. London: Hodder & Stoughton, 1973.
Watson, Merv, and Merla Watson. *Songs from Jerusalem*. Vols. 1 and 2. Toronto: Gordon V. Thompson Music, 1984, 1985.
Wenders, Wim, and Juliano Ribeiro Salgado. *The Salt of the Earth: A Journey with Sebastião Salgado*. DVD. Paris: Decia Films, 2014.
Westcott, B. F. *The Gospel According to St. John*. London: John Murray, 1882.
Whitley, H. C. *Blinded Eagle: An Introduction to the Life and Teaching of Edward Irving*. London: SCM, 1955.
Wilkerson, David, et al. *The Cross and the Switchblade*. Old Tappan, NJ: Fleming H. Revell, 1963.
Williams, Don. *Bob Dylan: The Man, the Music, the Message*. Old Tappan, NJ: Fleming H. Revell, 1985.

———. *Signs, Wonders, and the Kingdom of God: A Biblical Guide for the Reluctant Skeptic*. Ann Arbor, MI: Servant, 1989.
Williams, J. Rodman. "Baptism in the Holy Spirit." In *DPCM* 40–48.
———. "Baptism in the Holy Spirit." In *NIDPCM* 354–63.
———. *Renewal Theology: Systematic Theology from a Charismatic Perspective*. Vol. 2, *Salvation, the Holy Spirit, and Christian Living*. Grand Rapids: Zondervan, 1990.
Wimber, Carol. *John Wimber: The Way It Was*. London: Hodder & Stoughton, 1999.
Wimber, John. "Some Notable Personalities: Their Practices and Pitfalls." *Signs and Wonders and Church Growth*, section 8. Placentia, CA: Vineyard Ministries International, 1984.
Wimber, John, and Kevin Springer. *Power Evangelism: Signs and Wonders Today*. London: Hodder & Stoughton, 1985.
———. *Power Healing*. London: Hodder & Stoughton, 1986.
Winder, Delores, and Bill Keith. *Jesus Set Me Free*. Safety Harbor, FL: Fellowship Foundation, 1982.
———. *Surprised by Healing: One of the Greatest Healing Miracles of the 21st Century*. Shippensburg, PA: Destiny Image, 2013.
Winer, Robert I. *The Calling: The History of the Messianic Jewish Alliance of America, 1915–1990*. Wynnewood, PA: Messianic Jewish Alliance of America, 1990.
Yocum, Bruce. *Prophecy*. Ann Arbor, MI: Word of Life, 1976.
Yule, Rob. *The Discovery of the Beginning: How the Greatest Scientific Discovery of Our Time Points to the Creator*. Affirm Booklet 19. Tauranga, NZ: Affirm, 2006.
———. "Icons as Christian Art." In *ERT* 6 (1982) 202–14.
———. "Letter to the Editor: The Regathering of Israel." *DayStar* 6 (2006) 6.
———. "More Pages from a Bohemian Diary." Unpublished journal of a trip to the Czech Republic, 1996.
———. "Orthodox Spirituality: An Outline of its Characteristic Features." In *Latimer* 73 (1981) 12–21.
———. "Recent Writing on Christian Spirituality: An Article Review." In *SJT* 28 (1975) 588–98.
———. *Restoring the Fortunes of Zion: Essays on Israel, Jerusalem, and Jewish-Christian Relations on the Fiftieth Anniversary of the Six-Day War*. Bloomington, IN: WestBow, 2017.
———. *The Return of Jesus: Earthing the Christian Hope*. Affirm Booklet 6. Auckland: Affirm, 1998.
———. *Serendipity: A Brief Memoir in Pictures*. Palmerston North, NZ: Kirya Publications, 2014.
Zizioulas, John D. *Being as Communion: Studies in Personhood and the Church*. London: Darton, Longman & Todd, 1985.
———. *Communion and Otherness: Further Studies in Personhood and the Church*. Edited by Paul McPartlan. London: T. & T. Clark, 2006.
———. "Human Capacity and Human Incapacity: A Theological Exploration of Personhood." In *SJT* 28 (1975) 401–47.
———. *Lectures in Christian Dogmatics*. Edited by Douglas H. Knight. London: T. & T. Clark, 2008.

# Index of Names

Agabus (prophet), 116, 174
Allen, Roland, 91
Ananias (early Christian), 173
Anderson, Allan Heaton, 205,
Anderson, John, 154
Anselm, Archbishop of Canterbury, 89, 135
Aquinas, Thomas. *See* Thomas Aquinas
Aristotle, 30
Athanasius, Bishop of Alexandria, 122, 123, 135, 145, 153
Augustine, Saint, 25, 111, 142, 143, 144, 145, 155, 200
Austin, Barry and Kay, 184

Bach, Johann Sebastian, 34
Bacon, Francis, 37
Baker, Heidi and Rolland, 27
Balchin, John, 182
Baldock, Larry and Barbara, 185
Baly, Denis, 6
Barker, Martha Keys, 39
Barnabas (prophet), 116
Barrett, David B., 4–5
Barrow, John, 30
Barth, Karl, xx, 57, 67–68, 82, 143–46
Bartleman, Frank, 7, 8, 9
Basil the Great, 79, 122, 123, 132
Bateson, Joseph, 184
Battley, Don, 183
Baxter, James K., 35, 190
Beall, Patricia, 39
Bell-Booth, Stephen, 183
Bennett, Dennis J., xviii, 14, 16, 182
Berdyaev, Nicolas, 161

Bertolucci, John, 17
Bessenecker, Scott, 26
Bettelheim, Bruno, 26
Bezalel (artisan), 34
Billinghurst, Noel, 180
Bittlinger, Arnold, 16, 83, 99–101, 104–12, 113, 114, 116, 117, 119
Blessit, Arthur, 18
Blumhardt, Johann Christoph, 70
Boethius (philosopher), 154
Bolitho, Elaine E., 181
Boniface, Herbert, 182
Booth William, 70
Bradford, George C. (Brick), 15
Bredesen, Harald, 15
Breward, Ian, xix
Brook, John B., ix, xvi, xxi, 110
Brooke, Tal, 18
Brown, James, 15
Brown, Raymond E., 73
Brown, Scott, 185
Bruner, Frederick Dale, 14, 64, 66, 91
Bryan, Clint, 184
Bühler, Jürgen, 39
Bulgakov, Sergei, 161, 202
Bunyan, John, 70
Busch, Eberhard, 145
Bush, Luis, 21, 117

Caesar Augustus, 124
Calvin, John, 116
Campbell, Mary, 54
Campenhausen, Hans von, 115
Casdorph, H. Richard, 13
Cash, Johnny, 19

# INDEX OF NAMES

Caughley, Brian, 193
Chambers, Brent, 183
Cambers, J. B. (Jim), 106
Chandler, Trevor, 180, 181, 184
Charlemagne, Emperor, 139
Chater, Mark, 150
Chernoff, Joel, 20
Chernoff, Martin, 20
Chernoff, Yohanna, 20
Christensen, Larry, 15
Clapton, Eric, 19
Clark, Paul, 19
Clark, Stephen (Steve), 17, 88, 91, 97–98
Clark, Terry, 12, 23
Clement of Alexandria, 135
Coad, Beverley, 182
Coad, Graeme, 182
Coghill, Rick, 20
Cohen, Akiva, 20
Collins, Jamie Owens, 23
Collins, John, 16
Comfort, Ray, 184
Congar, Yves, 22, 73, 124, 126, 127, 130–31, 135, 139, 140, 162
Cornelius (centurion), 44, 61, 89
Cox, Harvey, 3–4, 203
Cranfield, C. E. B., 133
Crossing, Peter F., 5
Crouch, Andraé, 19, 23
Cyril of Alexandria, 130–31

Dali, Salvador, 36
Dallimore, Arnold, 23
Daniel, 42
Dante Alighieri, 9
Darby, John Nelson, 6, 196
David, King, 37–38, 42, 43, 45, 80, 115
Davies, Paul, 32
Dawson, John, 184–85
Dawson, Joy, 181
Dean, Peter, 184
Deere, Jack, 87
Dennehy, Cecil, 183
Di Sabatino, David, 19, 84
Dixon, Murray, 185
Dorries, David W., 54
Drain, Wayne, 183
Dunn, James D. G., iv, 68, 101, 108

Dylan, Bob, 18, 19

Ehrlich, Rudolf, 146
Ekblad, Bob and Gracie, 27
Eldad (elder), 40
Ellis, E. Earle, 117
Enroth, Ronald M., 19
Euripides, 92

Farrer, Austin, 53
Fénelon, Francois, 70
Ferguson, Ron, 150
Finklestein, Joe and Debbie, 20
Finney, Charles, 70
Florovsky, Georges, 134, 138, 147
Flusser, David, 53
Fordyce, Kirsten, 111, 183
Foster, Richard, 26
Fox, Matthew, 31
Fountain, Jeff, 184–85
Francis, D. Pitt, 81
Frisbee, Lonnie, 18, 83–84
Fruchtenbaum, Arnold G., 60–61

Galloway, Hamish, 182
Garratt, David and Dale, 23, 183
Garratt, Frank, 74, 180
Garratt, Ian, 74, 180
Garrison, David, 21
Gee, Donald, 16, 108
Geering, Lloyd, xv
Giacumakis, George, 38
Gideon (leader), 41, 42, 45
Gillard, Richard, 183
Girard, Chuck, 19, 23
Goll, James W. (Jim), 103
Gordon, A. J., 70
Gothard, William W. (Bill), 118
Graham, Billy, 19, 117, 125
Graham, Cecilie, 184
Green, Keith, 19, 23
Green, Melody, 23
Green, Michael, 58
Gregory of Nazianzus, 51
Gregory of Nyssa, 135, 160
Grigg, Viv, 27, 184
Grudem, Wayne A., 108, 110, 201
Gummer, Paul, xxi

# INDEX OF NAMES

Guth, Alan, 32
Guthrie, Arlo, 19
Guyon, Madame, 70

Habets, Myk, 49, 58, 60, 142–43
Hadamard, Jacques, 36
Harper, David, 183
Harper, Michael, xvi, 16, 183
Hathaway, Brian, 26–27, 182
Havergal, Francis Ridley, 70
Hawthorne, Gerald F., 49, 51, 52–53, 58, 59–60
Hayden, Judy, 185
Hebblethwaite, Brian, 52
Hegel, G. W. F., 169
Hendry, George S., 73, 144
Heppe, Heinrich, 133
Heron, Alasdair I. C., 22, 31, 50
Herring, Annie, 19, 23
Heschel, Abraham, 110
Hewett, James A., 116
Hibbert, Mike and Viv, 183
Hilary of Poitiers, 140
Hill, Clifford, 118
Hocken, Peter, x, 6, 8, 12, 13–14, 15, 17, 20–21, 22–25, 26, 27–28, 86–87, 89, 94, 114–15, 116, 150, 162, 165, 181, 182, 200
Hoeven, Jan Willem van der, 38
Hollenweger, Walter J., 112
Honeytree, Nancy, 19, 23
Houston, Brian, 184
Houston, Frank, 181, 184
Houts, Richard F., 101
Hussein, Saddam, 9

Irenaeus, Bishop of Lyons, 123, 135, 200
Irving, Edward, 50–51, 52, 54
Isaiah (prophet), 46–47, 92
Isidore of Seville, 189

James, M. R., 53
James, Russell, xviii
Jeremias, Joachim, 48
Jesus. *See* Index of Subjects
Joel (prophet), 1–3, 5–9
John (gospel writer), ix, 64, 73, 76, 77, 158

John the Baptist, 44, 45, 48–49, 56–57, 59, 61, 63, 86, 87, 148–49, 166
John of Damascus, 123, 138, 157
Johnson, Todd M., 4–5,
Johnstone, Patrick, 181
Jones, Charles Edwin, 83
Joseph (patriarch), 9, 42
Joshua (leader), 42, 45
Judas (prophet), 116

Kaiser, Glenn, 19
Keaggy, Phil, 19
Keith, Bill, 13
Kelsey, Morton J. 112
Khomiakoff, Aleksei S., 161, 163, 202
King, Tim, 39
Kissell, Barry, 183
Knight, George A. F., 41
Knudsen, Jeanette, 182
Konrad, Ulrich, 36
Kraft, Charles H., 87
Krchňak, Michal, 105
Kuhlman, Kathryn, 13
Kuyper, Abraham, 33

Lawson, James G., 70
Lee, Edward, 3
Leontius of Byzantium, 157
Lewis, C. S., 73, 138
Lindsey, Hal, 24, 196
Lineham, Peter J., 182
Lloyd-Jones, D. Martyn, 69, 132
Long, Zeb Bradford (Brad), 87
Lossky, Valdimir, xi, 74, 123, 127–32, 135, 139, 142–43, 147, 152–53, 156, 157–63, 169
Lovatt, Clive, 181
Lucius (prophet), 116
Luke (gospel writer), 53, 55–56, 60–61, 90
Lyle Morris, David, 183

McAlpine, Campbell
Macchia, Frank D., 50, 57, 68
McCracken, Sarah, 105
McDonald, James, 54
McDonnell, Kilian, 17, 148
MacEwan, Neven, 78

McGrail, Bruce, 183
McGuire, Barry, 23
McIntyre, John, 73, 122, 126–27, 146, 149–50, 151, 154–55, 197
MackIntosh, H. R., 50
Mackay, John A. 15
McLean, Alan and Joanne, 185
McNair Scott, Benjamin G., 116
Manaen (prophet), 116
Mansfield, Darrell, 23
Mao Tse-tung, 9
Marshall, Cecil, 183
Marshall, Tom, 181
Martin, Francis, 109
Martin, Ralph P., 17
Mary (mother of Jesus), 55–56, 64, 134, 149
Matthew (gospel writer), 56
Matison, Don, 18
Maximus the Confessor, 135, 140, 157, 159
Medad (elder), 40
Meissner, Linda, 18–19
Merritt, N. F. H., 182
Meyer, Werner, 109
Meyendorff, John, 122, 128
Miller, Elmer C., 87,
Millward, Steve, 182
Moegling, Bud, 18
Möhler, Johann, 162
Montague, George T., 203
Moody, D. L., 70
Moores, Jenny, 185
Morrow, Peter, 110
Moses (lawgiver), 2, 40, 41
Mozart, Wofgang Amadeus, 36, 153
Mühlen, Heribert, 51–52, 57, 59, 93, 127–28
Müller, George, 70
Muller, Ray, 182, 183
Myer, Ron, 116

Nathan (prophet), 45
Neale, John Mason, 189
Nebuchadnezzar, King, 42
Nissiotis, Nikos A., 81, 141
Norman, Larry, 19
Norton, Robert, 54

O'Connor, Edward D., 17
O'Donnell, John J., 60
Oholiab (artisan), 34
Osterberg, Arthur, 7
Othniel (leader), 42

Packer, Rob, 183,
Pain, Timothy, 108
Paris, Nyalle, xvii, xx
Parrinder, Geoffrey, 53
Patrick, Bruce, 183
Paul (Saul) (apostle), 2, 9, 49, 56, 57, 71, 74, 76, 77, 81, 82, 83, 90–91, 92, 96, 97–103, 105–118, 122, 130, 131–32, 133–34, 154, 156, 158, 168, 169, 195, 198, 199, 200
Pawson, J. David, x, 25, 56, 81, 91, 94, 102, 125, 168, 200
Pederson, Duane, 19
Pelikan, Jaroslav, 135, 159
Penrose, Roger, 32, 36
Peter (apostle), 2, 14, 44–45, 61, 74, 87–88, 89, 116, 134
Petersen, Paul, xviii–xix
Pharaoh, 42
Philip (evangelist), 116
Philippou, Angelos J., 160
Pickerill, Don, 120
Pinnock, Clark H., 33, 62, 66, 124, 128, 145, 148
Plessis, David J. du, 16, 180–81
Plowman, Edward E., 19
Pontius Pilate, 124, 148
Pope Francis, 27
Pope John XXIII, 16
Pope John Paul II, 17
Pope Leo III, 139
Pratney, Winkie, 184
Prebble, Kenneth, 182
Prince, Derek, 6, 105, 200
Pulkingham, Graham, xvi
Pullinger, Jackie, 27, 112
Putin, Vladimir, 147

Rad, Gerhard von, 37
Rahner, Karl, 126, 143, 145–46
Ranaghan, Kevin and Dorothy, 17, 93
Rausch, David A., 20

Rea, Jeff, 183
Rea, John, 101, 105, 106, 184
Reid, Michael, xvii, 182
Rembrandt Harmensz van Rijn, 34, 36, 37, 153
Rengstorf, Karl H., 115
Riches, Tanya, 184
Riding, Jules, 183
Riss, Richard M., 8
Robertson, Lindsay, 60,
Robertson, Murray, xx, 21, 26, 78, 180, 181, 182
Rookmaaker, Hans R., 37
Rosen, Moishe, 20
Ruthven, Jon, 87

Salgado, Juliano Ribeiro, 9
Salgado, Sebastião, 9
Samson (leader), 42-43, 45, 80, 84, 85
Samuel (prophet), 37
Sanford, John and Paula, 117-18
Satyavrata, Ivan, 76
Saul (convert), 115, 116,
Saul, King, 37-38, 42-43, 45, 80
Savonarola, Girolamo, 70
Scheeben, Matthias, 126
Seraphim of Sarov, 107
Seymour, William Joseph, 3, 7, 8
Shakarian, Demos, 14
Sherrill, John, 17
Sider, Ronald J., 27
Siecienski, A. Edward, 140, 143
Silas (prophet), 116
Simila, Adrian, 18
Smail, Thomas A. (Tom), xix, 16, 33, 35, 53-54, 63, 64-65
Smith, Charles (Chuck), 18,
Smith, George Adam, 6
Smith, John, 183
Smith, Kevin John, 19
Smith, Milton, 181
Solomon, King, 31, 38, 46, 104
Soloviev, Vladimir, 147
Spence, Sir Basil, 34
Spittler, Russell P., 83, 97
Stalin, Joseph, 9
Staniloae, Dumitru, 140, 149
Steel, Natalie, 181

Stephens, Don, 185
Stone, Jean, 14
Stonehill, Randy, 19, 23
Stookey, Paul, 19
Stott, John R. W., 16, 68-69, 82-83, 89, 90, 94
Strachan, Gordon, 50-51, 54
Subritzky, Wilfred Allen (Bill), 184
Suenens, Cardinal Léon-Joseph, 17, 27
Sullivan, Francis A., 69, 91, 98-100, 102-5, 109-13
Sutherland, Graham, 34-35
Swete, H. B., 73, 81
Symeon the New Theologian, 124, 128-29, 187
Synan, H. Vinson, 15

Talbot, Janice, xvii
Talbot, John Michael, 19
Talbot, Murray, xi, xvii, xx, 182
Tallon, Jeff, 32
Taylor, John V., 92
Taylor, Ray, xx, 183
Taylor, Vincent, 52
Temple, William, 64, 73
Theodotus (theologian), 50
Theophilus of Antioch, 123
Thiselton, Anthony C., 82, 101, 106, 107, 114
Thomas Aquinas, 69, 143
Thomas, Evan, 185
Thomas, Richard (Rich), 17
Thunberg, Lars, 135
Torrance, James, 146
Trustrum, Vicki, 111, 183

Vermeer, Jan, 36
Verney, Stephen, 34
Vianney, Jean-Baptist (Curé d'Ars), 107
Villafañe, Eldin, xx, 27, 146
Visser't Hooft, Willem A., 37
Vos, Howard F., 50
Vrubel, Stefan, 105

Wagner, C. Peter, 5, 101
Wagner, Tom, 184
Wallis, Arthur R., 181
Walls, Roland, 11, 146, 150

## INDEX OF NAMES

Ward, Elizabeth (Liz), xxi
Ward, Kevin, 181, 182, 184
Ward, Matthew, 19, 23
Ware, Kallistos T., 147
Warfield, B. B., 87
Warrington, Keith, 184
Watson, David C. K., 16, 39, 92
Watson, Merv and Merla, 38–39
Watt, Douglas, 180
Wenders, Wim, 9
Wesley, John, 70
Westcott, B. F., 80
Wheeler, Rob, 181
Whitaker, Robert C., 15
Whitefield, George, 70
Wilkerson, David, 17
Williams, Don, 18
Williams, J. Rodman, 93–94
Wilson, Stevie and Tracey, 184
Wimber, Carol, 84
Wimber, John, 4, 18, 78, 82, 84, 181

Winder, Delores, 12–13, 183
Winer, Robert I., 20
Winger, Neville, 181
Winkler, Richard, 15
Wise, Ted and Liz, 18
Woodfield, Owen, 182
Woollcombe, Kenneth, 146

Yule, Andrew (Andy), xxi
Yule, Christene, x, xvi, xviii-ix, 154.
Yule, Robert M. (Rob), ix-xi, xv-xxi, 6, 19, 24, 25, 30, 37, 51, 52, 58, 63, 66, 78, 91, 93–94, 104–5, 107, 112, 120, 125–26, 140–41, 148–49, 154, 169, 182, 184.
Yule-Yeoman, Natalie, 183

Zadok (priest), 38
Zizioulas, John D., 74, 125–26, 129, 140–41, 152, 153–56, 158–62

# Index of Subjects

312 Azusa Street, Los Angeles, 3

AD2000 Movement, 117, 184
adoptionism, 50, 194
"all flesh", 2, 6, 165, 192,
*anamnēsis* ("memorial," remembering the past), 78, 130
*anarthrous* ("without the article"). *See also* definite article, 81, 167, 171, 194
Anglican Renewal Ministries (NZ), 183
anointing, 42, 43, 45, 48–49, 58, 60, 61, 62, 101, 128
anthropic principle, 31, 194
apocalyptic scenes, 9
apophatic, 145, 194
apostle, 113, 114–16, 117, 118, 195, 200
appropriation of spiritual gifts, 79, 90
The Ark, Seattle, 18
*arrabōn* ("down payment," longing for the future), 130, 134, 177, 195
artistic creativity, 33–40
Auckland Anglican Diocese, 181
Auckland Assembly of God (now Victory Convention Centre), 78
authoritarian tendencies, 147

baptism
  in water, 18, 83, 92–93, 130, 149, 166,
  Jesus', 44–45, 48, 50, 51, 52, 56–58, 59, 73, 80, 84, 123, 194
  and regeneration, 68
  and repentance, 56–57, 91
  symbolism of, 92–93

baptism in the Holy Spirit, ix, 12, 17, 25, 27, 65, 67–69, 86–95, 195, 200
  administered through prayer with laying on of hands, 90
  Barth's understanding of, 67–68
  distinct experience, 90–91
  empowerment for service, 25, 62–63, 65, 68, 79, 83, 84
  foundational significance of, x, 12, 25, 27, 86–87
  initiatory experience, 68, 88, 94
  instances of, ix, xviii-xix, 14–17, 24, 27, 70, 74, 180–82
  New Testament terminology of, 92–93, 94, 167, 195
  metaphorical significance of, 89
  "peculiar definiteness" of New Testament references, 91
  profound experience, 91–93
  and regeneration, 67–69, 79, 167–68
  Stott's understanding of, 68–69
  verbal form of descriptions, 68, 86, 94, 165, 167, 195
Baptist Tabernacle, Auckland, 183
baptize (*baptizō*) ("to plunge," "sink," "overwhelm"), 92–94
*baptō* ("to splash"), 92
*bara* ("to create"), 30
beauty, 30, 34, 165
Beelzebul, 60
"*began* to speak in other tongues", 90
begetting, 138–39, 195
Beit Asaph, Netanya, Israel, 185
Bible study, 17, 23, 26
Bible translations, 21, 80–81, 167

Body of Christ (*sōma Christou*), 21, 89, 99–100, 121, 128, 129–30, 149, 162–63, 169
Boeing Company, xviii
*Brahman* (impersonal absolute), 76
Byzantine Church, 34, 122, 135, 148, 152–53

Calvary, 62, 63
Calvary Chapel, Costa Mesa, California, 18, 83–84
capacity for God, 56, 65
cataphatic, 195
Catholic charismatic renewal, 16–17, 26, 183
Catholic Church, El Paso, Texas, 17
Catholic National Service Committee (NZ), 183
catholicity, 162–63
Celebrate Messiah (NZ), 185
celibacy, 83, 101
Central Europe, 26
cessationism, 16, 24, 74, 87, 111, 116, 195
chaos to cosmos, x, 29–33
charisma and character, 43, 83–85, 167
*charisma, charismata*, charisms. See spiritual gifts
charismatic renewal movement, 11–28
  "current of grace", 27
  evaluation of, 27–28
  features of, 22–27
  focus on Jesus, 22
  grace for whole church, 27–28, 165–66
  in New Zealand, 180–85
  in Roman Catholic Church, 16–17
  surprises of, 13–22
Chosen Ministries, 185
Christ (*Christos*), 22–23, 34–35, 42, 48–53, 55–59, 191–93, 199
  ascension ministries of, 114
  "in Christ", 74, 158–59
  parallel between Christ and Christians, 64–67, 167
  testified to by the Spirit, 122–24, 140–41, 169

  uniqueness and universality of, 159–60
Christendom, decline of, 36, 150
Christian Advance Ministries (NZ), 183
Christian art, 34
Christian initiation, 66, 67, 69, 86, 91, 125, 168
Christian Life Churches (Australia), 184
Christian World Liberation Front (CWLF), Berkeley, California, 19
Christians
  "children of God", 64, 67, 125, 131, 133–35, 151, 169, 203
  "coworkers with God", 79
  heirs of God's glory, 131
  "participants in the divine nature", 127, 128, 129, 131, 132, 133, 134, 202, 203
  recipients of eternal life, 64, 65, 125, 131, 133, 201
Christlike character, 83
Christmas tree analogy, 83, 85, 97
church, 89, 100, 111, 129–31, 146–48, 161–63
  body of Christ, 121, 129–30, 149, 157, 159, 163, 169
  community of the Spirit, 121, 129–30, 149, 163, 169
  constituted by the Spirit, 121, 126–28, 129, 162
  divine-human society, 169
  historic church(es), xx, 20, 25, 27–28, 66, 68, 91, 146–49, 164, 180, 200, 202
  instituted by Christ, 129
  institutional and charismatic, 162
  "kind of incarnation of the Holy Spirit" (Scheeben), 126
  leadership of, 96, 99, 113, 114–18, 168, 195, 203,
  "one mystical person" (Mühlen) 128
  renewal of, 1, 6, 11–12, 14–17, 27–28, 38–39, 91, 148, 150, 165–66, 181–84, 196
  spiritual organism, not just earthly institution, 147
Church Missionary Society (CMS), 93

Church of the Nativity, Bethlehem, 110
Church of the Redeemer, Houston, Texas, xvi, 26
Church of Scotland, 16, 50
*circumincession*, 124, 200
Communism, fall of, 26, 184
Community of Celebration, Cumbrae, Scotland, 26, 39
community
  personal differentiation in, 99, 131
  rediscovery of, 25-26, 27
conversion(s), 3, 12, 18, 19, 21, 26, 84, 182
  acknowledging Jesus as Lord, 168
  baptism in water, 91, 168
  believing in Jesus Christ, 91, 168
  divine change, 67
  full initiation, 66-67, 91, 168
  receiving the Holy Spirit, 66-67, 90, 91, 125, 168
  repentance from sin, 91, 168
cooperation with God, 78-79, 82, 98, 136
Corinthian church, 98, 100, 107, 109, 111-12
Corona del Mar, California, 18, 83
counseling new converts, 66-67, 91, 168
counterculture, 17-18, 20
Coventry Cathedral, 34
*creatio ex nihilo* ("creation out of nothing"), 30, 35
creation, 29-30, 32-33, 73, 78, 122-23, 133-34, 135, 138-39, 145, 151, 156, 166, 169, 196
creative inspiration, 29, 33, 36-37
creativity, x, xvii, 19, 23, 30, 33-36, 37, 39-40, 131, 153-54, 155, 166, 198, 201
Czech Republic, 18, 19, 105

Davidic worship, 38-39
death threats, 21
Decade of Evangelism, 21
definite article, use or omission of, 71, 78, 80-81, 82, 84, 86, 87, 167, 171-79
dehumanization, 36-37

deliverance, 18, 24, 25, 45, 51, 58, 60, 74, 193, 200
devil, the, xviii, 35, 44, 59, 61, 74, 75, 193
*diakoniai* ("services," "ministries"), 99, 100, 114, 168
discernment, 12, 52, 102, 103, 109, 167, 203
dispensationalism, 6, 25, 93, 196
distinguishing between spirits (*diakrisis pneumaton*), gift of, 102, 108, 196
dreams, 3, 7, 21
Dunsandel, NZ, xix

early church, ix, xvi, xvii, 90-91, 116-17
"early rain" (*ha yôre*) 2, 5-6, 165
Eastern Orthodox Church, ix, xi, xx, 58, 121, 122, 132, 134, 137, 139-41, 145-47, 149, 152-53, 169, 194, 197, 198, 202, 203
Eastern religions, 18, 139
economic Trinity, 138, 144-45, 196
economy (*oikonomia*), 99, 126, 129, 140-41, 145-46, 149, 152, 160, 162, 163, 196
ecstasy, ecstatic experiences, 98, 110
effectiveness, effective service, 24, 25, 27, 41, 55, 58, 60-61, 62-63, 65, 66-67, 79, 82, 84-85, 86, 87, 95, 96-97, 102, 103, 105, 106, 119, 149, 150, 167, 168
Emmanuel Community, Brisbane, Australia, 26
Emmaus College, Palmerston North, xix
*empneumatosis* ("inspiriting"), 197
encouragement (*paraclēsis*), gift of, 119
*energēmata* ("activities," "motivations"), 99, 100, 118-19, 168
*enhypostatos* ("in a person"), 157, 159, 160, 197
*ensarkosis* ("enfleshment," "incarnation"), 199
eschatological, xx, 1-2, 33, 115, 125, 126, 130, 150, 196, 197
eschatological expectation, 24, 93, 107, 165

*eschaton* (consummation of all things), 32, 107, 126, 150, 169, 197, 201
eternal life, 64–65, 125, 131, 133, 186
eternal salvation, 62, 67
European Charismatic Leaders Conference, 16
European Community, 185
evangelical(s), xv, xvi, xx, 5, 16, 20, 23, 55, 62, 67, 79, 81, 83, 84–85, 87, 97, 100, 114, 132, 140, 167, 182, 197
evangelism, evangelization, 21, 24, 26, 27, 39, 65, 66, 82, 102, 107, 117, 125, 165, 182, 183, 185, 197
evangelist, 4, 18, 24, 83, 113–14, 117, 118, 122
evangelistic counseling, 66, 91, 125, 168
evil, x, 9, 24, 25, 28, 38, 75, 189, 192–93
evil spirits, 40, 52, 59, 65
exorcism, 18, 24, 25, 45, 51, 58, 60, 74, 99, 106, 193, 200
experience, ix, x, xi, xv, xvii, xix-xx, xxi, 1, 2, 3, 13, 14, 17, 21, 22, 23, 24, 25, 27, 38, 39, 43, 52–53, 58–59, 66, 67–69, 69–70, 74, 75, 79, 84, 86–88, 89, 90–91, 92–95, 97, 101, 104, 105–6, 107, 110, 119, 120, 121–22, 125, 128, 134, 146, 153–54, 156–57, 164–66, 167–68, 169, 185, 195

faith (*pistis*), gift of, 83, 98, 99, 102, 103, 104, 197
faith, saving, 41, 68, 91, 104, 161, 191, 197
"faith seeking understanding" (*fides quaerens intellectum*)
fallen humanity, 2, 6, 51, 56, 57, 65, 124, 132–33, 156
Father, God the, xi, 23, 122, 124–25, 151
  and Jesus, 22, 23, 49, 51, 52, 57–58, 63, 71, 72–74, 75, 123, 124–25, 133, 160, 166, 169, 191, 192
  begets the Son, 138–39
  monarchy of, 139, 141–42
  not "given", 124
  not incarnate, 124–25
  not "sent", 125

originator, 33, 122–23, 151
our Father by adoption, 126, 131–32, 191
over all, 125, 130
sender of the Spirit, 72–75, 77, 87, 125
source of other divine persons, 137–41, 143, 149, 169, 201, 202
providence of, 96–97, 100, 168, 203
"two hands" of, 122–23, 157–58, 163
Feast of Tabernacles (*Sukkot*), 38, 73
*Filioque* clause, xi, 139–47, 149, 169, 197
First Crusade, 185
"firstfruits", 134, 165, 198
*First Love* (Jesus musicians reunion DVD), 12, 23
First Presbyterian Church, Chandler, Arizona 15
First Presbyterian Church, Invercargill, xx
First Presbyterian Church, Papakura, 182
First World War, 8, 9
Fisherfolk (music group), 39
fivefold ministries, 114–18
flesh (*sarx*), 2, 6, 43, 50–51, 53, 65, 132–33, 156, 165, 166, 192, 199
folk arts, 38, 39, 166, 198
forgiveness, ix, 24, 56, 62, 63, 87, 149
Fountain Trust (UK) 16, 183
freedom, 24, 37, 40, 47, 67, 94, 110, 119, 125, 131, 134, 136, 146, 148, 161, 192, 202
"fruit" of the Spirit, x, 22, 28, 71, 84, 104, 131, 167
  growth in Christ-likeness and holiness, 82–83, 97, 125, 131, 133, 197, 202
  organic development of Christian character, 82–83, 167
fruit tree analogy, 82, 85
fruitfulness, 62, 63, 82
Full Gospel Business Men's Fellowship International, 14
Fuller Theological Seminary, 18, 83

Geering controversy, xv
generation. *See* begetting

# INDEX OF SUBJECTS

"Gentile Pentecost", 89
gifts of the Spirit, x-xi, 6, 12, 15, 24, 25,
    28, 40, 43, 46, 67–68, 69, 71, 81,
    82–85, 86, 89–90, 95, 96–99,
    102–14, 125, 127, 128, 129, 131,
    132, 146, 167, 169, 182, 188,
    195–96, 202–3
  and Body of Christ, 88–89, 99
  Christmas tree analogy, 83, 97
  classification of, 98–101, 103,
    168–69
  dynamism of, x, 103, 113–14, 167,
    168, 203
  expressions of God's grace, 82–83,
    97, 167, 196
  for service in community, 95, 100
  inventory, x, 96, 98, 100–101
  manifestation gifts (*charismata*
    proper), 67–68, 96, 99, 102–14,
    168
  ministry gifts (*diakoniai*), 96, 99,
    100, 114–18, 168
  motivational gifts, (*energēmata*),
    xi, 96, 99, 100, 101–2, 118–20,
    168, 203
  and natural abilities, 100–102, 196
  not result of holiness, 82–84, 97
  Paul's threefold classification, 99,
    168
  permanency or impermanency of,
    113–14
  and personal fulfillment, 96–97,
    100, 119
  power gifts, 99, 103
  rediscovery of, 6, 12, 24, 25, 28
  revelatory gifts, 103
  trinitarian structure of, 99–100,
    168–69, 203,
  vocal gifts, 89, 103
giving away possessions, 69, 98, 112
giving or contributing (*metadotes*), gift
  of, 113, 118, 119
Global Day of Prayer, 193
glorification, 133–34, 198, 203
glory (*kābôd*), 7, 31, 57, 121, 124, 131,
  133–36, 169, 181, 193, 198
*glossolalia*. *See* tongues, speaking in
God. *See also* Father, Trinity

*ad intra* (in God), 138, 151, 194
*ad extra* (external to God), 124, 138,
  140, 145, 151, 194
glory (*kābôd*), 31, 121, 131, 134–36
"Godness of God", 145
grace of, x, xviii, xx, 6, 8, 9, 11, 16,
  24, 27–28, 48, 69, 78, 79, 82, 83,
  87, 94, 97, 100, 101, 105, 109,
  125, 127, 128, 130, 131–32, 133,
  134, 160–61, 165–66, 168, 188,
  192, 198, 202
immanence, 31
intimacy with, 23, 41, 48, 59, 84,
  123, 165
nearness, 38
participation in divine life of, 64,
  121, 128, 132, 134–35, 144, 146,
  203
rationalising of, 141–42, 143, 145
"stereoscopic" nature of activity of,
  163
time of opportunity, 10
transcendence, 31, 145
"two hands" of, 123, 129, 161, 163
wisdom of, 2, 8, 34, 42, 46, 107, 131
"God Squad" (Australia), 19
"Goldilocks effect", 32
"gracelet", 83, 97, 196
Greyfriars Presbyterian Church,
  Auckland, 180
guidance (*kubernēseis*), gifts of, 113–14,
  198
Gulag, 9
Gulf War, 9

hand analogy, 75
Harvest International Ministries, 18, 19,
  26, 105
  Bible School, Czech Republic, 18,
    105
healing(s), 12–13, 21, 54, 58
  absence of, 106
healings (*charismata iamatōn*), gifts of,
  102, 103, 105, 113, 198
heart, secrets of, 107, 116, 201, 203
Hillsong Church, 184
Hinduism, 76
hippies, 18–19

His Place, Hollywood, 18
history, historical process, 169
holiness, 11, 50–51, 52, 82, 83, 85, 97, 125, 131, 133, 134, 167, 197, 202
Holiness movement, 3, 4, 14
Hollywood Presbyterian Church, 18
Holocaust, the, 9
Holy Spirit
- abiding presence, 72–74
- acting person, 76–77
- activity, Evangelical and Pentecostal aspects of, 41, 55, 61–63, 65–67, 79, 81, 84–85, 167
- agent of enculturation, 150
- analogies of, 34, 46, 63, 73, 82–83, 85, 89, 124, 127, 128, 130–32, 167, 190
- "another *Paraclete*", 71, 72–73, 76, 146
- anticipates social change, 150
- as artist, 35, 166
- attitude to, 9–10, 132
- "autonomous Spirit", 151
- baptized in, ix, x, xviii-xix, 14, 15–17, 22–24, 27, 52, 62–63, 66–67, 68–69, 70, 74, 79, 84, 86–95, 96, 97, 110, 120, 128, 167–68, 180–82, 195
- blasphemy against , 60
- "bond of love" between Father and Son, 142
- breath who conveys the living Word 124
- brings fullness of life in Christ, 49, 61, 121, 122, 129, 160
- brings future (*eschaton*) into history, 107, 126, 150, 169
- and Christian unity, 46, 88–90, 120, 130, 148, 161–63
- communicates divine nature to multiplicity of human persons, xi, 121, 127–28, 129, 131–34, 157, 169, 201–2, 203
- communion between God and humans, 22, 131, 136, 144, 158–59
- communion in Godhead, 74, 144, 154, 156, 200
- community of (*koinōnia Pneumatōn*), 129–30
- compared to breath, 31, 78, 124, 132, 151, 164, 187, 202
- compared to fire, 34, 80, 88, 89, 124, 127, 132, 190
- compared to sunlight, 46, 132, 186, 188, 190
- compared to water, 34, 128, 130–31
- compared to wind, 34, 89, 124, 164
- concentrated in Jesus, 49, 61, 88
- continuing teacher, 75–76
- and conversion, 12, 67, 68, 81, 125, 168
- and creativity, x, 32–33, 33–36, 37–38, 39–40, 131, 166
- "direct inworking", 133
- distinctive operations of, xi, 66–67, 99, 124–26, 151, 152, 157, 160–61, 162, 167, 169
- distributed upon Christians, 88, 99, 102, 130, 168
- and diversity, 46, 127, 129–31, 148, 157, 169
- divinity of, 77, 122, 124, 127, 129, 132, 163, 188
- does not become incarnate, xi, 124, 126–28, 157, 169
- dynamism of, 130, 137, 147, 148, 151, 162
- empowering leaders, 29, 40–42, 43, 45
- empowerment for Christian service, ix, x, 51, 53–54, 55, 62–63, 65–67, 68, 75, 77–78, 79–80, 80–81, 83, 84, 94, 125–26, 128, 131, 149, 167, 168, 192, 195
- enabling power, 41, 56, 65, 71, 77–79, 87, 88, 89–90
- enhances uniqueness of human persons, 69, 99, 127, 131, 157
- "evangelist of the Trinity", 122
- external endowment, 41, 94, 168
- features highlighted by Pentecostal-charismatic movement, 149–51
- "first contact" with Godhead, 122
- "firstfruits" of coming redemption, 134, 198

## INDEX OF SUBJECTS

and freedom, 24, 40, 47, 67, 94, 125, 131, 134, 136, 146, 148, 160–61, 192
fruit of, 82–83, 84, 104, 131, 167
fullness of, 33, 49, 61, 63, 65, 67, 88–89, 94, 122, 129, 147, 148, 157, 160
fully personal, 142, 145, 148–51
gifts of, *See* gifts of the Spirit
"go-between God", 92
God's change agent, 136
and healing, 12–13, 21, 24, 44–45, 48, 51, 58, 60–61, 63, 65, 101, 102, 103, 105, 107, 113, 166, 181, 184, 192, 198
"hidden mystery", 124, 186
hides his personality, 121, 123–24, 125, 127–28
indwelling, 41, 42, 49, 50, 69, 71, 79, 82–83, 125, 126–28, 131, 132–33, 166–67
in Christians, 64–67, 68
in God's activity, 32–33, 60, 64, 66, 100, 121, 122–26, 161–63, 168
in human persons, xi, 125, 126–29, 131–32, 133–34, 152, 157–58, 159, 169
in Old Testament, x, 29–43, 45–48, 79–80, 131, 166
inspires artistic creativity, 29, 33–35, 37–39, 166
in Trinity, 35, 58, 77, 99–100, 122, 124–26, 129, 138, 139–46
and Jesus, 48–51, 55–63, 122–24 140–41, 169
and Jesus' birth, 55–56, 64–65, 167
and Jesus' Messiahship, 48–49, 58–59, 167
and Jesus' ministry, 49–51, 58, 59–61, 65, 66, 77, 167
*kenōsis* of coming into world, 128
and kingdom of God, 60, 65, 107, 169
liberator, 22, 51, 118, 125, 134, 151, 156
life giver, 31, 64–65, 76, 78, 82, 94, 121–22, 125, 128, 131–32, 133–36, 146, 147, 149, 164

makes Jesus known, 67, 71–72, 75, 138, 169
and newbirth, regeneration, 55, 64–66, 67–69, 79, 82, 84, 122, 125, 128, 167, 201–2
ordering creation, 30–33, 122–23, 135, 151, 166
organic analogies, 82, 85, 167
overcomes "desires of the flesh", 132–33, 202
perfecter of creation, 32, 151, 166
permanent indwelling, 29, 42, 44, 46, 48–49, 61, 166
as person, x, 76–78, 80–81, 84, 123–25, 127, 128, 131–32, 139, 142, 145, 146, 148–51, 164, 167, 169, 171–79, 187, 200
as power, ix, x, 7, 12, 25, 41, 44–45, 48, 51, 53, 54, 55–56, 58–61, 62–63, 65–67, 71, 77–78, 79–82, 84, 87, 164, 167, 171–79
prayers to, 123–24, 186–93
"preferential option" for the poor, 128
preparing the church for future challenges, 9, 150
procession of, 137, 138, 139–46, 201
recognisable personality, 146, 150–51, 169
renewing local churches, xvii, 14–16, 39, 114, 118, 148, 150
respects human freedom, 94, 131, 136, 148, 161
respects personal individuality, 69, 127, 158
reveals the Son, 77, 122–24 140–41, 146, 169
and sanctification, 82–83, 132–33, 134, 202
sevenfold gifts of, 46
stimulating mission, 6, 27, 62, 78, 116, 131, 148, 150, 165–66, 169, 184
supernatural signs of (sound, sight, speech), 88–89
temporary empowerment, 29, 42, 48, 83

Holy Spirit (*continued*)
  and *theōsis* ("deification"), 134–35, 198, 203
  transforms into divine likeness, 125, 133–36
  universal presence, 31, 71, 72–74, 77
  visible signs of, 48, 57, 78, 88–89, 123
  with or without definite article, 71, 78, 80–82, 84–85, 86, 87, 167, 171–79
  worldwide outpouring of, 1–3, 6, 8, 28, 148, 164, 191
Hornby Elim Church, Christchurch, xv
Hornby (now Hope) Presbyterian Church, Christchurch, x, xv, xvii, xix, xx, 181, 182
House of Immanuel, Bellingham, 18
humanity, xi, 2, 6, 12, 34, 37, 48–49, 50–51, 52–54, 56, 57, 60, 61, 64, 77, 122, 126, 128, 133, 134, 151, 156, 157, 159, 160, 166, 197, 100, 203
human nature, 51, 56, 127, 129–30, 131, 132, 133, 152, 153, 157–58, 159–60, 163, 169, 197, 199, 200
  trichotomist view of , 81
*Hymns of Divine Love* (Symeon), 124, 128, 187
*hypostasis* ("objective reality," "real being," "person"). *See also* person, 127, 130, 153, 157, 158–60, 163, 198–99
hypostatic union, 126, 128, 159, 199

iconography, 58
immanent Trinity, 138, 140, 144–46, 199
incarnation, xi, 50, 52–53, 55–56, 62, 65, 71, 73, 79, 122, 123, 124, 126–28, 131, 133–35, 144, 146, 150, 151, 153, 157, 160, 166, 169, 197, 199, 200, 203
"in Christ" (*en Christō*), 74, 158, 159, 162, 201
indwelling, 41, 42, 45, 49, 50, 69, 71, 79, 82–83, 125, 126–28, 131, 132–33, 166, 167
*Infancy Gospel of Thomas* 53

insight, 83, 98, 100, 101, 103, 104, 107, 119, 148, 166, 170, 192
Institute in Basic Life Principles, 118
intelligibility, 107–8, 109
intercession, 24, 101, 193
International Christian Embassy, Jerusalem, 38
International Reconciliation Coalition, 185
Internet, 21
interpretation of tongues (*hermēneia glossōn*), gift of, 63, 102, 109–13, 199, 203
inviting the Spirit, 67, 78, 168
Islam, Islamic world, 21, 150
"Isn't He Great" (inspired song), 111
Israel College of the Bible, 20,
Israel, restoration of, 3, 6, 19, 93, 115, 165, 200

Jerusalem Council, 161
Jerusalem, reunification of, 6, 19, 24
Jerusalem School of Synoptic Research, 53
Jesus Christ
  anointed with the Spirit. *See also* Jesus Christ, Messiah, 44–45, 47, 48–50, 55, 57, 58–59, 60–61, 77, 149, 199
  ascension, ix, xi, 44, 71, 72–74, 77, 125, 133, 135, 166, 198
  baptism, 48, 50, 51, 52, 56–59, 73, 80, 84, 88, 123, 166–67, 194
  Baptizer in the Spirit, ix, 25, 44, 49–50, 55, 61–63, 66, 77–78
  call and training of disciples, 56, 59, 72, 115
  claim of absolute uniqueness, 160, 161
  conflict with evil (one), 24, 50–51, 58, 59–60
  empowerment by the Spirit, 58, 59–61, 63, 65, 77, 149, 166–67
  exaltation of, 34, 50, 74, 125, 133, 135
  expels evil spirits, 51, 52, 59–60, 65
  focus on, 22–23, 28, 71–72, 75, 77, 123, 140, 169

forgives sins, 61, 62
heals the sick, 12, 51, 52, 54, 58, 59, 60–61, 65, 107
humanity of, 50–51, 52–53, 54, 56, 57, 64, 77, 126, 133, 134, 157, 159, 160, 166, 199, 200
humiliation of, 133, 135
identification with sinners, 51, 57, 58
incarnation of, 12, 50, 52–53, 55–56, 64, 126–27, 134–35, 157, 166
Jewish believers in, 19–20
Jewishness of, 53
knowledge and self-consciousness, 146
Messiah, 10, 20–21, 29, 44–50, 57, 58–61, 66, 73, 77, 107, 148–49, 166–67, 199
miracles, 50–51, 52, 53, 63, 102, 166
Muslims turning to, 21
Nazareth declaration, 26
obedience, 50, 52
only one who has defeated death, 160
our ministry exemplar, 53, 66, 167
pattern and prototype of Christian life, 51–54, 66–67, 167
and permanent indwelling of Spirit, 29, 41–42, 44, 46, 48–49, 61, 166
priestly role, 45, 52, 191
promise of the Spirit, 23, 25, 54, 63, 72–78, 87, 138, 140, 146, 170
prophetic teaching, 9, 151
public ministry, 44, 55, 56, 57, 58–61, 65, 167
resurrection, xv, 50, 73, 133, 135, 169, 194
return of, 24–25, 28, 93, 165, 193, 198
Savior from sins, 55, 57, 61–63, 107, 167, 191
"self-emptying" (*kenōsis*), 50, 52–53, 57, 128
sin-bearer, 57
sinlessness, 50–52, 57
Son of God, 50–51, 57–58, 61
Spirit-filled human being, 48–51, 57–58, 61, 88

story-teller, 37
Suffering Servant, 57–58
teaching about kingdom of God, 59–60, 65, 107
temptation of, 50–52, 58, 166
transfiguration, 57, 123,
virgin birth, 64, 84, 167
*Jesus* film, 21
Jesus music, 19, 23
Jesus People Army, Seattle, 19
Jesus People movement, xv, 17–19, 24, 26, 39, 83–84, 182
Jewish piety, 56
Jewish worship, 38–39
Jews for Jesus, 20
John Birch Society, 8
Juarez, Mexico, 17

Kampuchea, 9
kingdom of God, 25, 27, 59, 60, 65, 107, 169, 200
Ku Klux Klan, 8
*kibbutz* movement, 26
*kubernēseis* ("gifts of guidance"), 113–14, 198

Lamb (Messianic rock group), 20
Lamb of God Community, Christchurch, 26
lampstand (*menorah*), 34, 46
"Last Adam", 126
*The Late Great Planet Earth* (Lindsey), 25, 196
latter days, 1–3, 5–6, 24, 39, 151, 199
"latter rain" (*ha malkôsh*), 2, 5–6, 9, 165
Lausanne Congress on World Evangelization (Manila), 183
leadership, gift of. *See* management, gift of
Life in the Spirit Seminar, 181
light spectrum, 46
Liston House, Auckland, 181
The Living Room, San Francisco, 18
*logos* ("word," "reason"), 42, 126, 146, 157, 159, 197, 199
The Lord's Food Bank, 17
Love Song (music group), 19
Luke-Acts, 56

# INDEX OF SUBJECTS

Lutheran Charismatic Renewal Services (USA), 15

management or facilitation, gift of (*ho proistamenos*), 119
manifestation gifts, 67–68, 96, 102–14, 168
Mao's famine, 9
martyrdom, 69, 98
Marxism, 169
Massey University, Palmerston North, 181, 182
mercy, 47, 48, 189, 192
mercy (*eleos*), gift of, 99, 118, 119
Messiah (*Māshiach*), 10, 20–21, 29, 39, 44, 45–50, 57, 58–61, 77, 107, 148–49, 166–67, 199
messianic hope, 39, 45–46, 58
Messianic Judaism, 19–21, 60, 150, 185
messianic prophecies, 44, 45, 46–48, 59, 61
Middleton Grange School, Christchurch, xvi
midlife experiences of mature Christians, 70
millennium, 25, 199–200
ministry
    fivefold, 114, 117–18
    gifts, 96, 114–18, 168
    one-person, 118
    team, 26, 118
miracles 13, 21, 42, 50–52, 53, 63, 69, 83, 87, 102, 106, 107, 115–16, 149, 166, 167, 195
miracles (*energēmata dynameōn*), gifts of, 99, 102, 103, 106, 113, 200
mode of being (*Seinsweise*), 143
motivational gifts, xi, 96, 100, 103, 101–2, 118–20, 168, 203
Mount Maunganui Baptist Church, Tauranga, 182
Mount Vernon Reformed Church, New York, 15
Mount Zion, 38, 43
multiplication of food, 17
music, 12, 18, 19, 23, 34, 36, 37–40, 111, 112, 166, 183–84, 198, 203

nature (*ousia, natura*), xi, 2, 33, 50–51, 56, 61, 64–65, 81, 121, 122, 124, 127–34, 138–39, 141–43, 152, 156, 157–63, 166, 168, 169, 195, 197, 199, 200, 203
natural world, 31, 149, 150, 156
Navigator movement, xvi, 71
New Age movement, 168
new birth, ix, 55, 64–65, 66, 68, 79, 84, 125, 128, 167, 201
*New Vision, New Zealand*, 183
New Wine (NZ), 183
New Zealand, xv, xvii, xix, xx, xxi, 13, 15, 18, 23, 26, 32, 35, 41, 63, 74, 78, 92, 105, 106, 110, 111, 112, 121, 142, 180–85, 193
Nicene Creed, 139–40, 141, 144, 197
    revision of, 141, 148–49
*Nine O'Clock in the Morning* (Bennett), xviii
*nirvana*, 158
nuclear weapons, 34–35

Octorara Presbyterian Church, Parkesburg, Pennsylvania, 15
one-person ministry, 114, 118
Opawa Methodist Church, Christchurch, xviii, 181
order, x, 29, 30–32, 33, 135

pantheism, 76, 134, 139, 158, 166, 203
papacy, 139, 147
parable, 37
*paraclete* ("advocate," "helper"), 71–73, 75–77, 138, 139, 140, 146, 188, 200
Paraclete Trust (NZ), xx, xxi, 15, 183
passivity, 78–79
pastor, 113, 114, 117, 118
"Penrose number", 32
Pentecost, ix, 2, 41, 62, 63, 68, 69, 74, 78, 80, 87, 88, 89, 125, 127, 148–49, 165, 166, 169
Pentecostal(s), xv, 50, 55, 62, 66, 79, 81, 84, 93, 97, 101, 102, 108, 110, 128, 146, 162, 167, 184, 200
Pentecostal movement, ix, xviii, 1, 2, 3–9, 200, 203

eschatological significance, xx, 5–6, 9
fulfilment of Joel's prophecy, 5–9
inter-racial character, 8
origins of, 3–4
spread of, 4–5
statistics, 4–5
Pentecostal-charismatic movement, x, xi, xx, 3–9, 13–22, 87, 137, 148, 149–51, 163, 196
parallel with restoration of Israel, 6
theological implications of, 27–28, 149–51, 164–70
Pentecost sequence, 188–89
People of Praise, South Bend, Indiana, 26
perilous times, 1, 2, 9, 151, 199
percutaneous cordotomy, 13
*perichoresis*, 74, 124, 156, 200
person, ix, 37, 49, 51, 53, 72–73, 74, 76–77, 80–81, 96, 99, 121, 122, 123, 124–26, 137, 139, 141–43, 145, 146, 150–51, 152–56, 157–59, 160–61, 167, 171–79, 187, 194, 195, 197, 198, 201
person and nature, xi, 124, 127–30, 131–32, 133, 157–59, 160–61, 163, 169, 199, 200
*persona* ("role," "character," "person"), 153
personal communion, 74, 131, 136, 144, 150, 154–56, 158–59, 200
personal differentiation, 99, 130–31, 160, 162, 169
personal freedom and creativity, 30, 131, 148, 153–55, 161
personal fulfillment, 97, 100, 119, 134, 136, 158–59
personal integrity, 94, 132, 149, 151, 161
personhood, x, 76–77, 139, 152–56, 157–59
Pew Research Center, 22
*pneumatikon* ("matters of the Spirit"), 98
poetry, 23, 36, 37–38
poor, ministry to the, xviii, 8, 14, 17, 26–27, 46, 47, 128, 150, 184, 188, 190
Port Glasgow, Scotland, 54

post-conversion experiences of the Spirit, ix, 14–17, 27, 69, 70
Post Green Community, Dorset, England, 39
power (*dynamis*), ix, x, 4, 7, 12, 22, 25, 26, 41–42, 44–45, 48, 50–53, 54, 55–56, 58–59, 60–61, 62–63, 65–66, 67, 68, 73, 74, 77–79, 79–80, 80–81, 84, 86, 87, 89, 93–94, 99, 100, 102, 103, 106, 113, 117, 125–26, 149, 164, 167, 171–79, 188, 192, 196, 200
misunderstanding of, 82
praise of God, x, 22–23, 25, 27–28, 38–39, 43, 47, 89, 111, 166, 191, 203
prayer, xvi–xvii, xix, 7, 17, 21, 25, 31, 49, 52, 90, 99, 106, 107, 110, 112, 118, 122, 123–24, 135, 166, 185, 186–93, 203
Prayer for Israel (New Zealand), 185
"Prayer for the World" (Pentecost 2006) 191–93
Presbyterian Charismatic Communion (USA), 15
Presbyterian Church of (Aotearoa) New Zealand, xx, 13, 182
Presbyterian Renewal Ministries (New Zealand), ix, xxi, 13, 183
Presbytery of Annan, Scotland, 50
Presbytery of Phoenix, Arizona, 15
pride, 7, 62, 107, 110, 192
procession. *See* Holy Spirit, procession of
prophecy, biblical, 2, 5–9, 45, 46–48, 56, 59, 61, 93, 110, 165, 196, 202
prophecy, prophesying (*prophēteia*), gift of, 24, 69, 83, 91, 98, 99, 103, 107–110, 112, 113, 119, 199, 200, 201, 203
authority of, 108
prophet, 113, 116–18
*prosōpon* ("face," "character", "person"), 153
protological, 33, 201
psalter, 38, 43
psychosis, 12

Queen Street Assembly of God, Auckland, xv

rabbinic argument, 61
recapitulation, 159–60, 162, 201
racial discrimination, 8
racial integration, 8, 14
redemption 57, 78, 125, 133–35, 138, 146, 156, 158, 160, 196, 198
    downward movement (incarnation, *kenōsis*), 133, 135
    upward movement (glorification, *theōsis*), 133, 135
*Reflected Glory* (Smail), xix
regeneration. *See* new birth
relationship, 27, 29, 41, 48, 49, 58, 59, 61, 77, 81, 83, 95, 100, 114, 121, 123, 125, 131, 132, 137, 139–40, 142, 144, 145, 150, 151, 154–56, 159, 166, 167, 201, 202
renewal of congregational life, xvi, xvii, 14–15, 16, 17, 26, 111, 181, 182–83
restoration, 2, 6, 56, 93, 114, 166, 201, 202
restoration of Israel, 6, 93, 202
resurrection, xv, 50, 73, 133, 135, 149, 169, 186, 194
Resurrection Band, 19
revelation, xx, 117, 122, 124, 137, 143–46, 165, 195, 196
revival, xvi, xviii, 3–9, 18, 28, 39, 42, 54, 56, 114, 182, 184, 200
Riding Lights Theatre Company, 39
Roman Catholic Church, xx, 4, 16–17, 137, 139–40, 143, 146–47
*rûach* ("breath," "spirit," "Spirit"), 20, 30, 31, 42, 58, 164
Rwanda, 9

sacrament,
    definition of, 78
    baptism, 68–69
    bread and cup, 77
    Holy Spirit, 77–78
The Salt Company, Hollywood, 18
salvation, counseling new Christians for, 66–67, 79, 90, 125, 168

sanctification, 82, 132–33, 134, 202
San Francisco earthquake, 9
Sanhedrin (Jewish council), 60
Satan, 18, 24, 51
Schuman Centre for European Studies, 185
Scofield Reference Bible, 196
*Scripture in Song*, 23, 183
Second Chapter of Acts (music group), 19, 39
Second Vatican Council, 16, 189
Second World War, 9, 34
self-sufficiency, 62
Semi-Pelagianism, 79
Servants to Asia's Urban Poor, 27, 184
service, xvii, xix, 24, 25, 41, 42, 45, 53, 55, 58, 61, 62, 63, 65–67, 78, 79, 84, 86, 95, 96, 97, 99–100, 114, 117, 118, 149, 167, 168, 169, 184–85
serving (*diakonia*), gift of, 99, 100, 114, 117, 119, 168
shameful conduct, 8, 11, 192
*Shepherd of Hermas*, 50
signs and wonders, 5, 21, 78, 102, 107, 165
sinful humanity. *See* fallen humanity
singing in the Spirit (*jubilate*), xix, 39, 99, 111, 202
*sobornost* ("catholicity," "conciliarity"), 161, 202
social barriers, crossing of, 1, 8, 14, 17, 26–27, 46, 47, 184
Son of God, 49, 50–53, 56, 61, 64, 65, 126–27, 133, 134, 146, 150, 153, 157, 166, 194, 197, 199, 203
    alone becomes incarnate, 124–25, 157
    empties himself of divine prerogatives, 50–51, 52–53
    enters our fallen humanity and death, 52–53, 124, 157
    unites a divine person with human nature, 127, 157, 162–63
"Song to the Holy Spirit" (Baxter), 189–90
songwriting, 23, 37–38, 39, 183, 198
space-time, 73

## INDEX OF SUBJECTS

speaking in tongues (*glossolalia*), xv, 14, 23, 24, 89, 90, 98, 107, 109–12, 113, 200, 203
   in corporate gatherings, 110, 112, 199
   and ecstatic states, 110
   linguistic assessment of, 110
   with interpretation equal to prophecy, 112, 199
spiration. *See* Holy Spirit, procession
spiritual counsel, 24, 27, 46, 103, 107, 113, 198, 203
spiritual gifts. *See* gifts of the Spirit
*spirituque* ("and the Spirit"), 144
Spreydon (now South-West) Baptist Church, Christchurch, xx, 26, 78, 111, 181, 182, 184
St. Alban's Presbyterian Church, Palmerston North, xix, 184
St. Andrew's Church, Chorleywood, Hertfordshire, 183
St. Cuthbert's Church, York, 16, 39
St. John's Methodist Church, Christchurch, 181
St. Luke's Episcopalian Church, Seattle, 14
St. Margaret's Anglican Church, Hillsborough, 182
St. Mark's Church, Gillingham, Kent, 16
St. Mark's Episcopalian Church, Van Nuys, California, 14
St. Michael-le-Belfry Church, York, 39
St. Paul's Anglican Church, Auckland, 182
*starets*, 107, 203
"streams of living water", 73
succession narrative (Samuel), 37
supernatural realm, 24, 56, 64–65, 83, 89, 100–102, 125, 132
surprises, 6, 13–22
Synod of Antioch (268), 50, 194

tabernacle, 33–34, 38, 40
teacher, 75–76, 101, 102, 113–14, 117, 118
teaching (*didaskalia*), gift of, 99, 102, 117, 118–19

Te Atatu Bible Chapel, Auckland, 26, 118, 182
team ministry, xv, 13, 26, 43, 118, 120, 183, 184
technical skill, 35–37
*Te Deum*, 111
teleological, 32–33, 166, 203
Ten-Forty Window, 21
Tertiary Christian Studies Programme, xv, xvi
theophany, xx, 31,
*theōsis* ("deification"), 134–35, 198, 203
   parallel with incarnation, 134–35, 203
Third Council of Toledo (589), 139
tongues (*glossōn*), speaking in. *See* speaking in tongues
totalitarianism, 40, 160–61
Towards Jerusalem II, 185
trinitarian formulae
   "*from* the Father, *through* the Son, *in* the Spirit", 122
   "*in* the Spirit, *through* the Son, *to* the Father", 122
   "over all," "through all," and "in all", 122
Trinity. *See also* God, 35, 58, 74, 77, 96, 99, 122–24, 124–26, 129, 137, 139–43, 144–46, 153–55, 162, 163, 194, 196, 199
   "artist of", 35
   distinctive roles of three persons, 124–26
   Eastern view of, 141–43, 146–47
   economic Trinity, 122–24, 138, 144–46, 194, 196
   "evangelist of", 122
   Father as sole source of other persons, 139–43
   immanent Trinity, 137–38, 144–46, 194, 199
   modes of being (*Seinsweisen*), 143
   mutual indwelling of persons (*perichoresis, circumincession*), 74, 124, 156, 200
   "New Testament Trinity", 58
   "outward works are indivisble", 124

*Trinity* (continued)
  recognizable "personalities" of three persons, 137, 151
  social understanding of, 146
  "three persons in one essence", 141
  Western view of, 141, 143–46, 146–47
Trinity Episcopal Church, Wheaton, Illinois, 15
Trinity Lutheran Church, San Pedro, California, 15

United Presbyterian Church, USA, 15
unity, 85, 88–89, 120, 130, 141–43, 145, 148, 160
unity in diversity, 46, 100, 130, 148, 153, 161–63, 169, 202
universe, 29–33, 34, 35, 74, 139, 149, 191
  creation of, 30
  expansion rate, 32
  fine-tuning, 31–32

*Veni, sancte Spiritus* ("Come, thou holy Paraclete"), 188
Victoria University of Wellington, xv, xvi, 26
Vietnam War, 12, 18
The Vine, La Habra, Los Angeles, 18
Vineyard movement, 18, 83–84
virgin birth, 55, 64

Vision New Zealand Congresses, 183
visions, 3, 7, 21
*Viva Cristo Rey* (video), 17
vocal gifts of the Spirit, 89, 103
*Voice* magazine, 14
volition, 67, 94, 131, 136, 148, 149, 160–61
voluntary poverty, 69, 101

Wagner Modified Houts Questionnaire, 101
war, warfare, 9, 12, 18, 34–35, 156, 192
William Carey International University (Pasadena, CA), 184
wisdom, 2, 8, 34, 42, 46, 99, 103, 104, 107, 131, 146, 166, 192, 203
World Council of Churches, 16
Word of God Community (Ann Arbor, Michigan), 26
word of knowledge, insight (*logos gnōseōs*), 101, 103, 104, 203
word of wisdom, discernment (*logos sophias*), 42, 103, 104, 107, 203
worship leading, 118, 183, 198

York Minster, 39
Youth With a Mission (YWAM), xix, 184

Zionist movement, 6, 202

# Index of Biblical References

## Old Testament

### Genesis

| | |
|---|---|
| 1:1–5 | 29 |
| 1:1 | 30 |
| 1:2–3 | 123 |
| 1:2 | 31–33, 122, 166 |
| 1:21 | 30 |
| 1:26–27 | 35 |
| 1:26 | 51 |
| 1:27 | 30 |
| 1:28 | 51 |
| 2:7 | 31, 78 |
| 41:38 | 42 |

### Exodus

| | |
|---|---|
| 25:31–40 | 46 |
| 31:1–11 | 34, 166 |
| 31:3 | 34 |
| 35:30—36:1 | 34 |
| 35:31 | 34 |

### Leviticus

| | |
|---|---|
| 8:12 | 45 |
| 10:7 | 45 |
| 21:10 | 45 |
| 21:12 | 45 |

### Numbers

| | |
|---|---|
| 11:16–17 | 40 |
| 11:17 | 41, 80 |
| 11:24–30 | 40 |
| 11:25 | 41, 80 |
| 11:26 | 80 |
| 11:29 | 40, 80 |
| 27:15–23 | 42 |

### Deuteronomy

| | |
|---|---|
| 11:14 | 5 |
| 32:11 | 31 |

### Judges

| | |
|---|---|
| 3:9–10 | 42 |
| 6—7 | 42 |
| 6:33–35 | 42 |
| 6:34 | 41 |
| 13—16 | 43 |
| 14:6 | 42, 80 |
| 14:19 | 42, 80 |
| 15:14 | 80 |
| 16—19 | 85 |
| 16:20 | 42 |

## 1 Samuel

| | |
|---|---|
| 9—2 Samuel 9 | 43 |
| 9:2 | 43 |
| 10:1 | 45 |
| 10:6 | 80 |
| 10:10–13 | 42 |
| 10:10–11 | 80 |
| 10:23 | 43 |
| 13:14 | 43 |
| 16:13 | 37, 42, 45, 80 |
| 16:14 | 42 |
| 16:23 | 38 |
| 25:40–41 | 115 |

## 2 Samuel

| | |
|---|---|
| 7:12 | 45, 199 |
| 7:16 | 45, 199 |
| 10:4, 6 | 115 |
| 23:2 | 38 |

## 1 Kings

| | |
|---|---|
| 1:39 | 45 |
| 3:25 | 104 |

## 1 Chronicles

| | |
|---|---|
| 15:1—16:43 | 38 |

## 2 Chronicles

| | |
|---|---|
| 5:2–14 | 38 |
| 6:18 | 31 |
| 7:2 | 31 |

## Psalms

| | |
|---|---|
| 2 | 199 |
| 2:7 | 58 |
| 8:6 | 51 |
| 16:11 | 134 |
| 20:8 | 54 |
| 37:4 | 134 |
| 66:1 | 111 |
| 68 | 38 |
| 72 | 46, 199 |
| 95:1–2 | 111 |
| 104:27–30 | 31 |

## Proverbs

| | |
|---|---|
| 1:5 | 113 |
| 8:22–23 | 42 |
| 11:14 | 113 |

## Isaiah

| | |
|---|---|
| 2:1–5 | 199 |
| 2:2 | 199 |
| 11:1–4 | 46, 199 |
| 11:1–2 | 6 |
| 11:11–12 | 6 |
| 42:1–4 | 46–47, 199 |
| 42:1 | 49, 58 |
| 53:6 | 58 |
| 59:19 | 9 |
| 61:1–3 | 47–48, 199 |
| 61:1–2 | 59 |
| 63:10 | 76 |
| 64:4 | 92 |

## Jeremiah

| | |
|---|---|
| 31:27–34 | 6 |

## Ezekiel

| | |
|---|---|
| 11:17–20 | 6 |
| 36:24–30 | 6 |
| 36:25 | 62 |
| 36:26–27 | 79 |
| 36:27 | 62 |
| 37:1–14 | 6 |

| | | | |
|---|---|---|---|
| 37:14 | 79 | 3:5 | 56 |
| 39:29 | 80 | 3:11 | 94, 172 |
| | | 3:15 | 57 |
| | | 3:16–17 | 123 |
| **Daniel** | | 3:16 | 49, 172 |
| | | 4:1 | 24, 172 |
| 4:8 | 42 | 5:6 | 70 |
| 7:21 | 9 | 7:7 | 70 |
| 7:25 | 9 | 7:16 | 22 |
| | | 7:20 | 22 |
| | | 7:21–23 | 83, 167 |
| **Joel** | | 8:2–4 | 60 |
| | | 9:6 | 59 |
| 2:17 | xvii | 10:1 | 115 |
| 2:23 | 2, 5–6, 165 | 10:17–20 | 75 |
| 2:25 | 2 | 10:20 | 76, 173 |
| 2:28–32 | 2 | 10:37 | 160 |
| 2:28–29 | 7, 94, 165 | 11:11 | 56 |
| 2:28 | 2, 6, 80, 88 | 12:28 | 60, 173 |
| 2:30 | 9 | 12:29 | 59 |
| 2:31 | 2, 9, 165 | 12:31 | 60, 76 |
| 2:32 | 9, 88 | 12:32 | 173 |
| 3:1 | 6, 165 | 13:58 | 106 |
| | | 16:18 | 129 |
| | | 17:5 | 123 |
| **Micah** | | 17:20 | 104 |
| | | 18:20 | 158 |
| 4:1 | 199 | 19:28 | 115, 201 |
| | | 24:4–29 | 9 |
| | | 26:26–28 | 77 |
| **Zechariah** | | 28:19 | 141 |
| 14:16 | 39, 199 | | |
| | | **Mark** | |
| **Ecclesiasticus (Sirach)** | | 1:5 | 56 |
| | | 1:8 | 172 |
| 1:9–10 | 2 | 1:10 | 49, 172 |
| | | 1:12 | 172 |
| | | 1:15 | 60 |
| **New Testament** | | 1:21—2:12 | 59 |
| | | 1:22 | 59 |
| **Matthew** | | 1:40–45 | 60 |
| | | 3:14 | 115 |
| 1:18 | 171 | 3:29 | 76, 80, 173 |
| 1:20 | 171 | 4:41 | 53, 102 |
| 1:23 | 129 | 6:7 | 115 |

## Mark (*continued*)

| | |
|---|---|
| 11:27 | 53 |
| 13:5–25 | 9 |
| 13:11 | 76, 173 |
| 14:22–24 | 77 |

## Luke

| | |
|---|---|
| 1:15 | 94, 171 |
| 1:35 | 56, 122, 123, 172 |
| 1:41 | 94, 172 |
| 1:67 | 94, 172 |
| 2:11 | 48 |
| 2:25 | 172 |
| 2:26–27 | 172 |
| 2:26 | 48 |
| 2:40 | 146 |
| 3:3 | 56 |
| 3:8 | 57 |
| 3:10–14 | 57 |
| 3:16 | 49, 61, 66, 80, 87, 94, 172 |
| 3:21–22 | 57, 88 |
| 3:22 | 49, 80, 172 |
| 4:1–2 | 24 |
| 4:1 | 58, 172 |
| 4:14 | 58, 59, 172 |
| 4:18–19 | 48, 59, 199 |
| 4:18 | 26 |
| 4:31–41 | 58, 59 |
| 4:36 | 60 |
| 5:12–16 | 60 |
| 5:17–26 | 59 |
| 5:17 | 60, 94 |
| 6:14 | 115 |
| 7:28 | 56 |
| 9:1 | 115 |
| 9:49–50 | 40 |
| 10:1–12 | 115 |
| 10:21 | 172 |
| 11:13 | 172 |
| 11:19 | 60 |
| 12:10 | 76, 173 |
| 12:12 | 76, 173 |
| 12:45 | 9 |
| 13:34–35 | 10 |
| 14:12–14 | 17 |
| 14:26 | 160 |
| 18:1–8 | 70 |
| 18:8 | 9 |
| 21:10–12 | 9 |
| 21:15 | 104 |
| 21:24 | 19, 24 |
| 22:17–20 | 77 |
| 22:25 | 47 |
| 23:42–43 | |
| 24:46 | 199 |
| 24:49 | 65 |

## John

| | |
|---|---|
| 1:1–4 | 42 |
| 1:9 | 199 |
| 1:12–13 | 64, 131 |
| 1:12 | 64, 134, 202 |
| 1:13 | 64, 167 |
| 1:14 | 53, 127, 138, 199, 200 |
| 1:18 | 138 |
| 1:29–34 | 61 |
| 1:29 | 61, 63 |
| 1:32–34 | 49, 166 |
| 1:32 | 49, 172 |
| 1:33 | 49, 59, 61, 62, 63, 172 |
| 1:34 | 61 |
| 1:35–42 | 56 |
| 3:1–8 | 66 |
| 3:3–8 | 131, 201 |
| 3:3 | 64, 65 |
| 3:5–8 | 65, 122, 125, 167 |
| 3:5 | 64, 172 |
| 3:6 | 65, 172 |
| 3:8 | 64, 165, 169, 172 |
| 3:15–16 | 131, 201–2 |
| 3:16 | 64, 87, 104, 124, 138 |
| 3:18 | 138 |
| 3:34–35 | 49 |
| 3:34 | 172 |
| 6:39–40 | 199 |
| 6:44 | 199 |
| 6:54 | 131, 199 |
| 6:56 | 158 |

## INDEX OF BIBLICAL REFERENCES

| | | | |
|---|---|---|---|
| 7:37–39 | 49 | **Acts** | |
| 7:37 | 70 | | |
| 7:38 | 23 | 1:4–5 | 87, 87 |
| 7:39 | 73, 80, 172 | 1:5 | 173 |
| 10:28 | 131 | 1:8 | 25, 62, 65, 94, 173, 180 |
| 12:16 | 198 | | |
| 12:23 | 198 | 1:16 | 76, 173 |
| 13:31–32 | 198 | 1:23–26 | 117 |
| 14—16 | 71 | 2 | 6 |
| 14:6 | 160 | 2:1–13 | 68 |
| 14:12 | 54, 63, 74 | 2:1–4 | 88, 89 |
| 14:13 | 123 | 2:2 | 78 |
| 14:16–19 | 72 | 2:3 | 80, 127 |
| 14:16–17 | 123 | 2:4 | 80, 87, 89, 90, 94, 173 |
| 14:16 | 72, 73, 76, 146, 200 | 2:16 | 14 |
| 14:17 | 74, 76, 129, 166 | 2:17–18 | 94, 165 |
| 14:18 | 72 | 2:17 | 2, 88 |
| 14:20 | 74, 158, 166 | 2:20 | 165 |
| 14:23 | 74 | 2:21 | 88 |
| 14:26 | 73, 75, 76, 77, 123, 125, 138, 144, 173, 200 | 2:33 | 74, 94, 123, 125, 173 |
| | | 2:38–39 | 87 |
| | | 2:38 | 173 |
| 15:1–8 | 63 | 2:42 | xvi, 129 |
| 15:4–5 | 82 | 3:19–21 | 116 |
| 15:4 | 158 | 3:21 | 199, 201 |
| 15:5 | 62, 130 | 4:8 | 94, 173 |
| 15:26–27 | 72, 75 | 4:12 | 160 |
| 15:26 | 76, 77, 123, 138, 141, 144, 149, 169, 173, 200 | 4:20 | xx |
| | | 4:31 | 94, 173 |
| | | 5:3 | 76, 116, 173 |
| 16:7 | 72, 73, 77, 200 | 5:9 | 76, 173 |
| 16:8–15 | 75 | 5:32 | 76, 174 |
| 16:8–9 | 75 | 6:5–6 | 117 |
| 16:8 | 75, 76 | 7:51 | 9, 76, 174 |
| 16:11 | 75 | 7:55 | 174 |
| 16:13–15 | 23, 125 | 8:14–17 | 68 |
| 16:13 | 75, 76, 80, 123, 169, 170, 173 | 8:14 | 115 |
| | | 8:15 | 174 |
| 16:14–15 | 72, 75, 169 | 8:16 | 94 |
| 16:14 | 76, 123 | 8:17–19 | 90 |
| 16:15 | 123, 140, 144 | 8:17 | 174 |
| 16:22 | 75 | 8:18 | 174 |
| 16:24 | 75 | 8:21–23 | 116 |
| 17:1 | 198 | 8:29 | 76, 174 |
| 17:2–3 | 131 | 9:1–2 | 115 |
| 17:5 | 198 | 9:17 | 90, 94, 174 |
| 20:22–23 | 77 | 9:31 | 174 |
| 20:22 | ix, 80, 173 | 10:19 | 76, 174 |

## Acts (continued)

| | |
|---|---|
| 10:38 | 44, 48, 61, 166, 174 |
| 10:44–45 | 80, 174 |
| 10:44 | 94 |
| 10:45–46 | 89 |
| 10:45 | 94 |
| 10:47 | 174 |
| 11:12 | 76, 174 |
| 11:15 | 80, 89, 174 |
| 11:16 | 94, 174 |
| 11:24 | 175 |
| 11:27–28 | 116 |
| 11:28 | 174 |
| 13:1 | 116 |
| 13:2–3 | 116 |
| 13:2 | 76, 175 |
| 13:4 | 76, 175 |
| 13:9 | 94, 175 |
| 14:4 | 116 |
| 14:14 | 116 |
| 14:23 | 117 |
| 15:8 | 175 |
| 15:28 | 76, 161, 175 |
| 15:32 | 116 |
| 16:6–7 | 76 |
| 16:6 | 175 |
| 16:7 | 175 |
| 19 | 90 |
| 19:1–7 | 68, 85, 90, 91 |
| 19:2 | 80, 175 |
| 19:6 | 90, 94, 175 |
| 19:11–12 | 106 |
| 20:22–23 | 175 |
| 20:23 | 76 |
| 20:28 | 76, 175 |
| 21:4 | 175 |
| 21:9 | 116 |
| 21:10 | 116 |
| 21:11 | 175 |
| 28:25 | 76, 175 |

## Romans

| | |
|---|---|
| 1:3–4 | 125 |
| 1:4 | 169 |
| 1:17 | 104 |
| 5:5 | 25, 131, 175 |
| 5:20 | 9 |
| 6:12–13 | 133 |
| 6:23 | 131 |
| 7:18 | 3 |
| 7:25 | 3 |
| 8:1–14 | 202 |
| 8:1–13 | 133 |
| 8:1 | 158 |
| 8:2 | 175 |
| 8:3 | 3, 133 |
| 8:4–13 | 125 |
| 8:4–9 | 3 |
| 8:5–6 | 133 |
| 8:5 | 176 |
| 8:6 | 176 |
| 8:9 | 130, 176 |
| 8:10 | 158 |
| 8:11 | 125, 176 |
| 8:12–13 | 3 |
| 8:13 | 156, 176 |
| 8:14–17 | 134 |
| 8:14 | 176 |
| 8:15–17 | 131, 202 |
| 8:15 | 126, 176 |
| 8:16–27 | 125 |
| 8:16 | 67, 76, 176 |
| 8:18–23 | 169 |
| 8:21–23 | 122, 151, 156 |
| 8:21 | 134, 156 |
| 8:23 | 134, 176, 198 |
| 8:26–27 | 112, 176 |
| 8:26 | 76 |
| 8:30 | 198 |
| 11:25–26 | 20 |
| 12 | 67, 99 |
| 12:1–8 | 100 |
| 12:1–2 | 118, 202 |
| 12:1 | 133 |
| 12:2 | 119 |
| 12:3–8 | 99 |
| 12:4–8 | 101, 113 |
| 12:6–8 | 118, 119 |
| 12:6 | 97, 196 |
| 12:11 | 176 |
| 14:17 | 169, 176 |
| 15:13 | 176 |
| 15:18–19 | 102 |

| | | | |
|---|---|---|---|
| 15:19 | 176 | 12:29–30 | 102 |
| 15:30 | 176 | 12:29 | 106 |
| | | 12:30 | 105, 196 |
| | | 12:31 | 103, 196 |
| | | 13:1–3 | 97, 98, 103 |

## 1 Corinthians

| | | | |
|---|---|---|---|
| | | 13:1–2 | 83 |
| 1:27–28 | vxiii, 8 | 13:2 | 104 |
| 2:9–10 | 88, 92 | 13:8 | 111 |
| 2:9 | 22 | 13:12 | 153 |
| 2:10 | 33 | 14 | 99 |
| 2:11 | 76, 77, 80, 154, 177 | 14:1–5 | 83 |
| 2:12 | 33 | 14:1 | 85 |
| 2:13 | 177 | 14:2 | 110, 111 |
| 3:9 | 79 | 14:4 | 112 |
| 6:17 | 129 | 14:5 | 109, 110, 199 |
| 6:18–20 | 132 | 14:6–17 | 110 |
| 6:19 | 177 | 14:13 | 109 |
| 7:1 | 98 | 14:15 | 111 |
| 7:7 | 83, 102 | 14:18–19 | 108 |
| 7:25 | 98 | 14:19 | 109 |
| 8:1 | 98 | 14:24–25 | 107 |
| 9:1–2 | 115 | 14:26–33 | 83 |
| 12 | xi, 67, 99 | 14:26–32 | 110 |
| 12:1–8 | 100 | 14:27–28 | 199 |
| 12:1 | 97, 98 | 14:27 | 110 |
| 12:2–3 | 98 | 14:32 | 98 |
| 12:3 | 161, 177 | 14:37–40 | 83 |
| 12:4–11 | 83 | 15:8–10 | 115 |
| 12:4–8 | 101, 113 | 15:20–28 | 135 |
| 12:4–6 | 99, 100, 168 | 15:20–23 | 133 |
| 12:4 | 97, 196 | 15:24–28 | 125 |
| 12:5 | 114 | 15:27 | 51 |
| 12:6 | 118 | 15:28 | 100, 136 |
| 12:7–11 | 24, 101, 102, 113 | 15:42–57 | 135 |
| 12:7 | 103 | 15:42–49 | 156 |
| 12:8 | 104 | 15:42–43 | 198 |
| 12:9 | 104, 105, 196, 197, 198 | 15:45–49 | 126 |
| | | 15:52–53 | 198 |
| 12:10 | 106, 196 | 16:1 | 98 |
| 12:11–13 | 162 | | |
| 12:11 | 76, 130 | | |
| 12:12 | 129 | ## 2 Corinthians | |
| 12:13 | 25 | | |
| 15:24–28 | 125 | 1:22 | 177, 195 |
| 12:28–30 | 113 | 3:6 | 76, 177 |
| 12:28 | 105, 106, 111, 113, 196, 198 | 3:16–18 | 161 |
| | | 3:17–18 | 136, 169 |

## 2 Corinthians (*continued*)

| | |
|---|---|
| 3:17 | 40, 98, 148, 161, 177 |
| 3:18 | 125, 134, 151, 177, 202 |
| 5:5 | 177, 195 |
| 5:17 | 158 |
| 5:21 | 57 |
| 6:1 | 79 |
| 6:6 | 177 |
| 12:12 | 115, 116, 200 |
| 13:5 | 158 |
| 13:14 | 177 |

## Galatians

| | |
|---|---|
| 1:15–16 | 116 |
| 2:9 | 116 |
| 2:20 | 158 |
| 3:2 | 177 |
| 3:3 | 177 |
| 3:5 | 177 |
| 3:14 | 177 |
| 4:6 | 76, 177 |
| 5:5 | 177 |
| 5:16–26 | 125, 133, 202 |
| 5:16–24 | 3 |
| 5:16 | 133, 156, 177 |
| 5:17 | 132, 177 |
| 5:22–23 | 82 |
| 5:22 | 104, 177 |
| 5:25 | 177 |

## Ephesians

| | |
|---|---|
| 1:10 | 196 |
| 1:13–14 | 177 |
| 1:14 | 133, 195 |
| 1:19–23 | 74 |
| 1:20 | 125 |
| 1:22 | 51 |
| 2:10 | 95, 119, 133, 168 |
| 2:20 | 130 |
| 2:22 | 130, 178 |
| 3:5 | 178 |
| 3:9 | 196 |
| 4 | 99 |
| 4:1–3 | 132 |
| 4:3 | 130, 178 |
| 4:4 | 130 |
| 4:6 | 122 |
| 4:7–13 | 100 |
| 4:8–10 | 74 |
| 4:10–13 | 99 |
| 4:11 | 113, 114 |
| 4:12 | 117 |
| 4:22–24 | 63 |
| 4:30–32 | 132 |
| 4:30 | 9, 76, 80, 178 |
| 5:18—6:9 | 132, 202 |
| 5:18 | 80, 94, 178 |
| 6:17 | 178 |
| 6:18 | 178 |

## Philippians

| | |
|---|---|
| 2:1 | 129 |
| 2:6–7 | 50, 52 |
| 2:7 | 128 |
| 3:21 | 51 |

## Colossians

| | |
|---|---|
| 1:15–20 | 151 |
| 1:18 | 129 |
| 1:19 | 49 |
| 1:27 | 158 |
| 2:9 | 49, 88 |
| 3:1–4 | 133 |
| 3:11 | 74 |

## 1 Thessalonians

| | |
|---|---|
| 1:5–6 | 178 |
| 4:3–8 | 132 |
| 5:19 | 9 |
| 5:21 | 11 |

## 2 Thessalonians

| | |
|---|---|
| 2:3-4 | 9 |

## 1 Timothy

| | |
|---|---|
| 3:15 | 130, 148 |
| 4:1 | 9, 178, 199 |
| 4:14 | 117 |

## 2 Timothy

| | |
|---|---|
| 1:14 | 178 |
| 3:1-5 | 9 |

## Titus

| | |
|---|---|
| 1:5 | 117 |
| 3:5 | 64, 178, 201 |

## Hebrews

| | |
|---|---|
| 1:3 | 153 |
| 2:4 | 178 |
| 3:7-8 | 178 |
| 4:15 | 51, 52 |
| 6:4-6 | 178 |
| 6:4-5 | 169 |
| 9:14 | 51 |
| 9:22 | 62 |
| 11:6 | 104 |
| 13:15 | 38 |

## 1 Peter

| | |
|---|---|
| 1:3 | 131, 201 |
| 1:10-11 | 178 |
| 1:12 | 178 |
| 4:10 | 102 |

## 2 Peter

| | |
|---|---|
| 1:3-4 | 203 |
| 1:4 | 131, 132, 134, 202 |
| 1:19 | 116 |
| 1:21 | 178 |
| 3:3 | 9 |

## 1 John

| | |
|---|---|
| 1:1-3 | 127 |
| 1:1 | 127 |
| 2:25 | 131 |
| 3:1-2 | 64, 131, 134, 202 |
| 3:2 | 134, 198 |
| 3:24 | 158 |
| 4:2 | 179 |
| 4:6 | 179 |
| 4:9 | 138 |
| 4:13 | 158 |
| 4:16 | 158 |
| 5:6 | 179 |
| 5:11 | 131 |

## Jude

| | |
|---|---|
| 18 | 9 |
| 20 | 179 |

## Revelation

| | |
|---|---|
| 1:4 | 46 |
| 1:10 | 179 |
| 2:17 | 159 |
| 3:1 | 46 |
| 4:5 | 46 |
| 5:6 | 46 |
| 20:1-6 | 199 |
| 22:17 | 122 |

www.ingramcontent.com/pod-product-compliance
Lightning Source LLC
Chambersburg PA
CBHW050845230426
43667CB00012B/2152